The practice of group analysis

A unique picture of a successful psychotherapy practice, *The Practice of Group Analysis* gives a lively account of the Group-Analytic Practice in London. This Practice is based on group-analytic principles as pioneered by Dr S.H. Foulkes. Approximately 350 people a week are treated in groups that meet on a once- or twice-weekly basis.

The Members and Associates of the Practice have accumulated valuable clinical experience over the years and have developed efficient methods for the assessment and selection of patients for groups. The Practice has a well-run administrative structure, supported by carefully monitored financial arrangements. The contributors describe how the Practice was set up, and how individual therapists work with different kinds of patients, illustrating the group-analytic approach to group psychotherapy from many different points of view.

Written by people who are successfully treating patients and who took part in building the Practice, *The Practice of Group Analysis* is full of valuable and encouraging advice for therapists thinking of setting up a similar enterprise. It will also be of interest to psychotherapists from all fields, especially social work, psychology, medicine and occupational therapy.

Dr Jeff Roberts is Consultant Psychotherapist at the Royal London Hospital. **Dr Malcolm Pines** was, until his recent retirement, Consultant Psychiatrist at the Tavistock Clinic, London. They are both members of the Group-Analytic Practice.

The International Library of Group Psychotherapy and Group Process

General Editor

Dr Malcolm Pines
Institute of Group-Analysis, London, and formerly of the Tavistock
Clinic, London.

The International Library of Group Psychotherapy and Group Process
is published in association with the Institute of Group-Analysis
(London) and is devoted to the systematic study and exploration of
group psychotherapy.

The practice of group analysis

Edited by
Jeff Roberts
and
Malcolm Pines

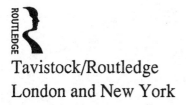

Tavistock/Routledge
London and New York

First published 1991
by Routledge
11 New Fetter Lane, London EC4P 4EE

Simultaneously published in the USA and Canada
by Routledge
a division of Routledge, Chapman and Hall, Inc.
29 West 35th Street, New York, NY 10001

Typeset by
Michael Mepham, Frome, Somerset
Printed and bound in Great Britain by
Biddles Ltd, Guildford and King's Lynn

British Library Cataloguing in Publication Data
The practice of group analysis.
  1. Medicine. Psychoanalysis. Group therapy
  I. Roberts, Jeff II. Pines, Malcolm III. Series
  616.8917

Library of Congress Cataloging in Publication Data
The practice of group analysis / edited by Jeff Roberts and
  Malcolm Pines
  p.   cm. — (InternationaL Library of Group Psychotherapy
  and Group Process)
  Includes bibliographical references and index
  1. Group psychotherapy. I. Roberts, Jeff, 1944– II. Pines,
  Malcolm. III. Series.
  [DNLM: 1. Psychotherapy, Group. WM 430 P895]
  RC488.P72   1991
  616.89'152—dc20   90-11326
  for Library of Congress   CIP

ISBN 0-415-05219-X
ISBN 0-415-04484-7 (pbk)

Contents

Contents

Figures

Contributors

Dr Dennis B. Brown
MD, FRCP (Edin.), FRC Psych, DPM,
Member Institute Group Analysis,
Associate Member British Psycho-Analytical Society,
Lately, Consultant Psychotherapist, St Mary's Hospital, London,
Lately, President Group-Analytic Society (London).

Mrs Elizabeth Foulkes
Widow of Dr S.H. Foulkes,
Founder and Honorary Member of The Group-Analytic Society
(London).

Dr S.H. Foulkes
MD,
Founder of group-analysis,
Founder Member Institute Group Analysis,
Training Analyst, British Psycho-Analytical Society.

Mrs Lisbeth E. Hearst
Dip. Soc. Sci. (applied), MA, PSW,
Member Institute Group Analysis,
Honorary Member Institute Group Analysis, Heidelberg.

Dr Roger Hobdell
MB, BS, DPM,
Member Group Analytic Society,
Training Analyst and Professional Member: Society Analytical
    Psychology.

Dr Colin James
MPhil, MB, Ch.B., FRCP Ed, FRC Psych,
Member Institute Group Analysis,
Member British Psycho-Analytical Society,
Consultant Psychotherapist, Addenbrooke's Hospital, Cambridge,

Former Consultant Psychotherapist, Tavistock Clinic, Maudsley and
London Hospitals.

Dr Lionel C. Kreeger
MB, BS, MRCP, FRC Psych, DPM,
Associate Member British Psycho-Analytical Society,
Founder Member Institute Group Analysis,
Lately, Consultant Psychotherapist Tavistock Clinic.

Dr Jason Maratos
Ptychion. Iatrikis (Athens), M.Phil., DPM,
Member Institute Group Analysis,
Member Group Analytic Society,
Affiliate Royal College Psychiatrists,
Member Association for Child Psychology, Psychiatry and Associated,
Disciplines.

Ms Adele Mittwoch
M.Sc.,
Member Institute Group Analysis,
Member British Association Psychotherapists,
Member Group Analytic Society,
Member London Centre for Psychotherapy.

Dr Malcolm Pines
FRCP, FRC Psych, DPM,
Founder Member Institute Group Analysis,
Full Member British Psycho-Analytical Society,
Past President International Association Group Psychotherapists,
Former Consultant Psychotherapist Tavistock Clinic, Maudsley,
St George's and Cassel Hospitals.

Dr Jeff P. Roberts
MA Oxon, BM, B.Ch., DPM, FRC Psych,
Member Institute Group Analysis,
Member Group Analytic Society,
Consultant Psychotherapist, The Royal London Hospital.

Mrs Meg Sharpe
BA Hons,
Member Institute Group Analysis,
Training Group Analyst Institute Group Analysis,
Associate Professional Member Society Analytical Psychology,
Member Group Analytic Society,
Member American Group Psychotherapy Association.

Dr A.C. Robin Skynner
MB, FRC Psych, DPM,
Founder Member Institute Group Analysis,
Founder Member Institute Family Therapy,
Member American Family Therapy Association,
Distinguished Affiliate Member American Association of Marital and
    Family Therapy,
Member of Council, Tavistock Institute of Medical Psychology.

Acknowledgements

We would like to thank all Members and Associates of the Practice for their contributions and time they have given to reading and commenting on the text at various stages in its development.

Special thanks are also due to Elizabeth Foulkes for spending time with me (JR) to talk about her view of the Practice and also for allowing us to print the chapters from *Therapeutic Group-Analysis*.

June Ansell and Jackie Ashmenall have also contributed immensely in attempting to assemble the book on our obsolete word-processing machine. In addition, June has offered helpful comments and criticism on the work she was typing, as well as contributing her great skill in the accurate transcribing of long and often inaudible dialogues.

Introduction

The Group-Analytic Practice in London is a unique small organisation which provides a context for the application of the clinical method of group analysis, developed by S.H. Foulkes and colleagues in the years following the World War II.

This method is described by Foulkes (1948, 1964 and 1975), in a number of books, as well as by Foulkes and Anthony (1965), and has become a subject of international interest and study. The reader will find that the various authors have written their chapters in such a way that the group-analytic approach to group psychotherapy is well illustrated and illuminated from many different points of view. We did not consider it necessary to clutter the text, therefore, with a redundant description of group-analytic principles and method.

The Group-Analytic Society, which, as will become apparent to the reader, grew out of regular informal meetings between Foulkes and colleagues, continues to provide a forum for all those who profess an interest in both the narrow and wider facets of group analysis. The Institute of Group-Analysis provides a rigorous training in Foulkes' method. *Group-Analysis* is the journal shared by the two bodies.

The Practice itself houses a concentration of once-and twice-weekly groups, which offer the treatment pioneered by Foulkes to approximately 350 people mostly from within Greater London, but surprisingly often from much further afield. The various members and Associates of the Practice have accumulated invaluable clinical experience over the years and have also developed efficient methods for the assessment and selection of patients for groups. The Practice also has an efficient administrative structure, which provides a context for its work, supported by carefully monitored financial arrangements which, by curtailing costs, enable the therapy provided to be within the reach of the majority of well-motivated clients.

The intention of this book is to make available a distillation of our experience, which it is hoped will enable colleagues in the United

1

Kingdom and further afield to become more courageous in the development of similar enterprises.

Chapter 1

A view of the current state of the Practice

Jeff Roberts

The next two chapters will give a picture of the processes which have led to the development of the Group-Analytic Practice up to the present day. In this chapter I will draw a detailed picture of the organisation in its current form. It is our belief that the Practice has achieved a considerable success in two ways. Firstly, it provides a context within which a wide range of people have been and continue to be offered an affordable psychotherapy. As a group-analytic practice we inevitably tend to offer this therapy in groups. None the less the availability of 16 group analysts from diverse backgrounds also allows a comprehensive assessment service, followed by the allocation of patients not suitable for groups, at least at the time of assessment, to the treatment most suitable for them. Referral of some of those not ready for or currently not willing to enter a group may be to a colleague within the Practice, but can be to a member of the large network of psychotherapists and psychiatrists of which we are a member. The breadth and depth of skill available to us, together with the robustness of the group-analytic group means that we are able to offer some form of useful psychotherapeutic help to a wider range of clients than the average psychotherapeutic practice. This diversity of patients can be observed and is further amplified in Chapter 7. The other success of the Practice has been in providing a relatively happy working context for a group of colleagues who have remained together for a substantial period of time. This has not been without conflict, but, none the less, serious, persistent and damaging disagreement has been rare.

Group-analytic psychotherapy, as developed by S.H. Foulkes (1948, 1964, 1975) (Foulkes and Anthony, 1957), has become firmly established in the United Kingdom as a rewarding and effective form of group psychotherapy. It is also beginning to be quite widely practised in Europe, with outposts in various parts of the world including Australia and the Caribbean. As a result of the popular introductory courses run annually in various centres and a steady output of graduates from the qualifying course of the Institute of Group-Analysis, group-analytic ideas inform many of the psychotherapy groups available through the National Health Service in the United Kingdom.

In the private sector to date, however (apart from those groups conducted in London by the Group-Analytic Practice and also the North London Centre for Psychotherapy), there are relatively few once-weekly group-analytic groups. An important factor influencing this development is that many private psychotherapists practise independently, which makes the assembly of a well-selected therapy group a difficult task. The reason for this is as follows. Psychotherapy, as well as being rewarding, is also a painful and arduous experience for its clients. This leads to the occurrence of a sieving process with the purpose of arriving at those patients/clients who will make an authentic commitment. Subsequently the selection of patients who will benefit from group psychotherapy requires a further pass through the sieve. In other words, a significant number of psychotherapy referrals will need to be assessed in order to arrive at one person who will make a commitment to and benefit from group psychotherapy. Furthermore, a therapy group is best composed of people whose personalities, age, sexual orientation and personal difficulties allow the development of an optimally cohesive and therapeutically provocative environment (Chapter 4). Such a group can only rarely be achieved by taking the first eight patients off the waiting list. The independent practitioner starting a new practice, perhaps unsure of his abilities, will not have the number of referrals necessary to start a group quickly. He or she may establish a waiting list, but patients can accumulate slowly and waiting lists tend to decay because patients resolve their own problems or seek alternative therapy.

The Group-Analytic Practice is able to overcome these problems in two ways. Firstly, it provides a base for a comparatively large number of practitioners. Secondly, it has developed a reputation for providing groups throughout a steadily growing referral network. Thus the Group-Analytic Practice has become one of very few small organisations providing private group-analytic psychotherapy for a substantial catchment area, including London and the Home Counties and also as far away as Exeter, Bath, Birmingham, Manchester and Leeds (journeys taking up to four hours by train).

The setting of the Practice

The Practice is housed in a large ground floor flat: 88 Montagu Mansions in the West End of London. It would be hard to find a more convenient location. Baker Street Station is an important interchange on London's underground railway system, which makes possible rapid interconnections with all of the city's main railway stations. The area is a mixture of residential and office provision together with a number of major tourist attractions (Madame Tussaud's, the London Planetarium, Regent's Park and the London Zoo), making it at times quite lively and colourful. Much of the residential part of the area consists of elegant mansion blocks built early in the twentieth century. The majority of these flats are expensive, and a few like 88 Montagu Mansions are given over to medical, dental and related practices. This might be seen as a satellite development of nearby Harley Street and Wimpole Street, which have become dedicated almost exclusively to the provision of consulting rooms for a wide range of medical practitioners, including psychiatrists and a few psychotherapists. Notwithstanding the wealth of this area the economies of Westminster Council, fostered by the free market policies of the Conservative Government of the 1980s, have resulted in the streets around the Practice being less clean and more litter strewn than they might be. One's walk from Baker Street Station (in 1990) therefore is through a bizarre mixture of wealth and filth and is often interrupted by the importuning of tramps and drunks, whose physical and mental state is distressingly poor. Many of our patients will travel a similar path and also incidentally pass by the place where Sherlock Holmes's flat (22b Baker Street) would be, had it existed. They may even see Sherlock Holmes, masquerading as the doorman of the local branch of Hilton Hotels.

The entrance to 88 Montagu Mansions is from a ground-floor hall, itself guarded by a closed door and entry phone. The password for access is the name of the therapist one wishes to see, but clients of Adolf Hitler have on occasions been known to gain entry. From the common hall one goes into a long hall with a right-angle turn by the room which serves as office and reception. Group rooms are entered from the hall throughout its length, each being guarded by a heavy, sound-proofed door. There are seven group rooms in all, each one belonging to, and having been personally furnished by a member of the management committee of the Practice. There are two waiting rooms, one of which doubles as a group room. It is possible for eight groups to be conducted simultaneously, and on certain mornings and evenings there is 100 per cent utilisation of available rooms. The group rooms, which also serve for consultations with individuals, couples and families, vary in size, although all can contain a nine-person group plus therapist without feeling excessively crowded. Most of the rooms fulfil very well the requirements of the physical environment of psychotherapy, being comfortable, quiet and free of internal and external distractions. Recently, however, the block of flats has been the subject of major building works and we and our patients have at times had to endure an intolerable cacophony of intrusive noises. This has made concentration very difficult and wearing for some of our therapists and also at times has intruded on potentially difficult and moving moments in groups.

The flat has no facility for viewing or recording groups and also has no staff room, where we might relax and talk comfortably together. The sole staff area is a small kitchenette in which three *is* actually a crowd. In the areas of teaching, research and staff care I think we demonstrate an overemphasis on practical business orientation, as opposed to having a more rounded enterprise with added commitments to staff support, research and teaching. On the other hand nothing can ever be absolutely right and on the whole the flat serves its purpose very well.

The staff of the Practice

There are 16 therapists at the Practice, all bar two of whom are members of the Institute of Group-Analysis, London. Of these, seven have Full Membership of the Practice and nine are Associate Members. Among the members there are six members of the British Institute of Psycho-Analysis and four members of the British Society of Analytical Psychology. Ten are medically qualified.

The remainder of the staff consists of two full time secretaries and a part-time cleaner. One of the secretaries has a senior position and plays an important administrative role, which will be discussed further in the context of other issues of administration and finance in Chapter 14.

Short autobiographies of current Members and Associates

The clinical members of the staff are quite a diverse group with a range of backgrounds and professional achievements behind them. The state of the Practice in 1989 is substantially a product of the contribution of its members. I have therefore asked each to pen a brief professional, and where he or she wishes personal biography. These are printed below in alphabetical order.[1]

Bryan Boswood, MA, Vet.MB, MRCVS, is a veterinary surgeon who became interested in marriage counselling in the mid-1960s and trained as a counsellor with the National Marriage Guidance Council. He was invited to work as a student counsellor in the Central Institutions Health Service of the University of London and while in that role trained at the Institute of Group-Analysis, becoming a member in 1976. He joined the Group-Analytic Practice in 1978.

Dennis G. Brown, MD, FRCP (Edin), FRCPsych, DPM; Member, Institute of Group-Analysis; Associate Member, British Psycho-Analytical Society Qualified in medicine 1951. Came into psychiatry after research on psychosomatic aspects of skin disorders at Cornell University. Lecturer in Psychiatry in Leeds before coming to London in 1963 to embark on own analysis and psychoanalytic training. Qualified in 1970 after completing research on psychiatric treatment of eczema at Middlesex Hospital, and spending three years at the Cassel Hospital where took first group. Second started after appointment as consultant psychotherapist at St George's Hospital in 1969. Moved to St Mary's Hospital in 1974 till retirement from the National Health Service in 1987. Joined Group-Analytic Practice in 1972 as Associate, becoming Member of Management Committee 1975. Sat in with S.H. Foulkes at his theoretical seminars for Institute of Group-Analysis in 1975–76, and, following his death that year, took this over. Elected Member of Institute of Group-Analysis, becoming Training Group-Analyst. President, Group-Analytic Society 1983–88. Married to an educational therapist (ex-TV, ex-teacher); they have one son.

Caroline Garland, MA (Cantab), began her career as a psychotherapist by taking a degree in English Literature at Cambridge. She qualified as a group analyst in 1980, and then went on to train as a psychoanalyst. She now works in the adult department at the Tavistock Clinic, where as well as teaching and supervising, she heads the Unit for the Study of Trauma and its Aftermath; and in the Psychotherapy Unit at the Maudsley Hospital, where she is a Senior Clinical Tutor. She is married and has two children.

Liza Glenn DA (Edin), BSc (Hons), MBPS; Member; Institute of Group-Analysis joined the Practice in January 1989. Born in the North of Scotland in 1943 and trained in art and design at Edinburgh College of Art. Came to London in 1966 to take up job as interior designer. Became more aware and interested in the 'psychic interior' and began training at first as a Marriage Guidance Counsellor in 1972. Qualified as a group analyst in 1979. Has worked in market research and with the Social Services before going into private practice as a therapist. Attached to a general practice since 1980 and involved in training at the Westminster Pastoral Foundation, Relate and Institute of Group-Analysis. Married, with four children.

Lisbeth E. Hearst qualified as a member of the Institute of Group-Analysis in 1974, from a background of psychiatric social work. She first worked in the then National Association for Mental Health and, after an interval in which she reared her two children, in a child and family psychiatric clinic. While there, she trained in individual psychotherapy and family therapy, and worked with the parents of the referred child patients and their families. After qualifying as a group analyst, she set up and conducted therapy groups for the parents of referred children, for adoptive parents, and for social workers in the area and in residential children's homes. She joined the Group-Analytic Practice in 1978. She is a Training Analyst of the Institute of Group-Analysis, where she is engaged in supervision and the teaching of theory on the Qualifying Course. She conducts overseas training courses in group analysis, and is the Chairman of the Overseas Training Sub-committee.

Roger Hobdell, MB, BS, DPM   After qualifying medically, he went directly into psychiatric hospital work for the National Health Service in 1963. A part-time course in psychotherapy at the Tavistock Clinic alienated him from the Bion-derived style of group work and he came, therefore, to the Group-Analytic Practice for his own group analysis, in 1965. Shortly after, he trained in group analysis before the formation of the Institute of Group-Analysis with S.H. Foulkes, Malcolm Pines, Robin Skynner, Jim Home, Lionel Kreeger and Harold Kaye, among others.

Personal analysis followed with training at the Society of Analytical Psychology, London, and he qualified in 1974 and became a Training Analyst in 1988. He became an associate of the Group-Analytic Practice in 1973. He worked in various therapeutic communities from 1966 to 1979 and was a group conductor and lecturer on the General Course of the Institute of Group-Analysis for many years. In 1986 he produced for the Society of Analytical Psychology a filmed interview with Dr Michael Fordham. He now works in group and individual analytic practice combined with teaching.

Lionel C. Kreeger, MB, BS, MRCP, FRCPsych, DPM; Founder Member of the Institute of Group-Analysis, Associate Member British Psycho-Analytical Society   Qualified in medicine at Guy's Hospital in 1949. House jobs and registrarships in general medicine and neurology. National Service, Royal Army Medical Corps, for two years. Entered psychiatry in 1957, worked at Shenley, Netherne and Westminster Hospitals, becoming Consultant Psychiatrist and Psychotherapist at Halliwick Hospital in 1965, working closely with Pat de Maré to help establish a therapeutic community culture employing small and large groups. Moved to Paddington Centre for Psychotherapy in 1973 and in 1978 to Tavistock Clinic. A serious illness necessitated early retirement from the National Health Service in 1980.

He joined the Group-Analytic Practice as Associate in 1967, becoming a Member of Management in 1972. Qualified as Freudian psychoanalyst in 1969, of the Independent School. Had two analyses, the first Kleinian for five years, the second Independent for four years; also two years in a once-weekly group with S.H. Foulkes. Has written on group psychotherapy, with a particular interest in large groups. Married to a painter and art therapist, they have three daughters.

Jason Maratos, DPM, M.Phil, was born in Athens in 1943. He qualified in medicine in Athens in 1969 and came to England in 1969. He became a member of the Institute of Group-Analysis in 1980 and joined the Practice as an Associate in 1987. He is currently Consultant Psychiatrist to the Department of Child Mental Health in High Wycombe. He is a member of the editorial board of the journal *Group-Analysis* and a member of the Council of the Institute of Group-Analysis. He lectures in Group Analysis in London, Oxford and Athens and has a special interest in borderline disorders.

Don Montgomery, MB, ChB, MRCPsych, FRANZCPsych; Member, Institute of Group-Analysis Born in New Zealand and qualified at Otago Medical School in 1966. Early psychiatric training in Auckland instilled an interest in group and family dynamics and therapeutic communities. Completed general psychiatric training in Sydney and worked as Consultant Psychiatrist at the Royal Prince Alfred Hospital before taking up the post of Commonwealth Senior Registrar in Psychotherapy at the Cassel Hospital. There he trained in psychoanalytic psychotherapy, had an individual analysis and qualified from the Institute of Group-Analysis in 1980. He has served on the Group-Analytic Society committee from 1981, as Hon. Scientific Secretary, Hon. Secretary and member of the Symposium Sub-committee. He has been involved in teaching group analysis in the diploma courses in Norway and Zagreb.

From 1980 he has been Consultant Psychotherapist at St George's Hospital, Kingston, and Long Grove Hospital, and Clinical Tutor in Psychiatry at Long Grove Hospital from 1988 to 1992. In 1987 he became Consultant Psychiatrist in charge of the Gender Identity Clinic at Charing Cross Hospital and has convened a number of group-analytic workshops exploring the social determinants of gender-specific behaviour. He joined the Group-Analytic Practice as an Associate in 1990.

Adele Mittwoch has a background in the natural sciences and mathematics, with long experience of research in industry and with the Medical Research Council. She values this experience and feels that it has given her a sense of proportion and that it taught her the need to look for evidence.

She trained with the British Association of Psychotherapists for individual work and with the Institute of Group-Analysis. She is a Training Therapist for both organisations and is Treasurer of the Institute of Group-Analysis. She is also a member of the editorial board of the journal *Group-Analysis.*

Malcolm Pines, MA (Cantab), FRCP, FRCPsych, DPM I studied medicine with the intention of practising psychiatry and psychoanalysis and was accepted as a trainee by the Institute of Psycho-Analysis at a very tender age. I started psychoanalytical training while still a medical student, but this was disrupted by the death of my first analyst. After qualification in medicine and taking a higher degree in medicine I went to the Maudsley Hospital for my basic training in psychiatry. There I resumed my psychoanalytical training, my training analyst being S.H. Foulkes. It was through this that I entered the group-analytic circle. From the Maudsley I went to the Cassel Hospital, a psychoanalytically staffed, small therapeutic community under the inspiring leadership of Dr Tom Main. After several years at the Cassel Hospital which included promotion to consultant status, I moved to St George's Hospital as Senior Lecturer in Psychotherapy, where part of my responsibility was the transformation of a traditional, organically oriented inpatient unit into one that practised a modified form of dynamic administration and therapy. This was the time when we were trying out large group techniques. Following this I had consultant posts both at the Maudsley Hospital and the Tavistock Clinic.

Through the International Association of Group Psychotherapy I have had the opportunity to study the work of colleagues in many countries, and it was through this that I became aware that the Group-Analytic Practice represents an unique facility.

Throughout my career I have practised as an individual psychoanalyst as well as a group analyst, and have found that 'binocular vision' afforded by this Practice stimulating and challenging both theoretically and practically, and many of my writings have been devoted to this subject.

Together with Earl Hopper I founded the International Library of Group Psychotherapy and Group Process, of which I am now sole editor, and for some years have been the editor of the journal *Group-Analysis*.

Jeffrey Roberts, MA (Oxon), FRCPsych, DPM, first heard of psychoanalysis at Magdalen College School, Oxford, where he was taught by a liberal chaplain, A.S.T. Fisher. He went on to Lincoln College, Oxford. Here he was forced to learn to think and write. He was fascinated by the sciences of mind and brain and was particularly attracted by the work of Sir Charles Sherrington, Kurt Goldstein and the Gestalt psychologists.

From Lincoln College he went on to study clinical medicine at King's College Hospital, London. Here he found thinking discouraged and rote learning promoted, until his encounter with the Department of Psychological Medicine led by Donald Liddell. Here began a fascination with groups after he joined in one conducted for medical students by the middle-group psychoanalyst Irving Kreeger. He qualified in Medicine 1969. Then on to psychiatry training at King's College Hospital, inspired not only in small but also large group work again by Irving Kreeger. MRCPsych, 1974.

In 1977, he became Consultant Psychiatrist at the Ingrebourne Centre, a therapeutic community pioneered by Richard Crocket. From here in 1983 he moved to become Consultant Psychotherapist at the London Hospital.

In 1979 he qualified as a group analyst and was invited to join the practice as an Associate in 1985. His access to Full Membership followed Patrick de Maré's departure in 1987. He believes that one of the contributions that group analysis has made to his life has been to improve his ability to think freely and creatively.

Meg Sharpe, BA (Hons), was invited to join the Practice as an Associate in 1974, and became Member in 1977. Her (unconscious) journey to the Practice began in drama school; she then graduated in sociology at the London School of Economics and Political Science. She worked initially in academic and advertising research.

This was followed by many years in the Middle East and elsewhere before she returned to England when she became involved in research projects in a regional psychotherapy centre, and eventually worked there as the music therapist. This stimulated her interest in group analysis, and she was one of the first eight graduates of the newly created Institute of Group-Analysis. She later retrained as a Jungian analyst with the Society of Analytical Psychology.

She has extensive experience of therapeutic and teaching work in the National Health Service and alongside private practice she has been involved for many years in international teaching programmes for the Institute of Group-Analysis, as well as various assignments involving staff and supervision groups in hospital settings. She has also participated in an assignment as a group analyst to a high-technology company, and is particularly interested in extending the group-analytic approach beyond the clinical setting.

She is married and has two children, three half-French grandsons and one half-American grandson.

A.C. Robin Skynner, MB, FRCPsych, DPM Following war service as a pilot in the Royal Air Force, Robin Skynner undertook medical training at University College Hospital and training in Adult and Child Psychiatry at the Institute of Psychiatry and the Maudsley Hospital. He has subsequently worked with adults and children of an unusually wide range of socio-economic status, from private practice to the poorest districts of the East End of London. His chief interest has been the practice and teaching of psychotherapy, with individuals, groups, families, couples and institutions. He is the author of *One Flesh: Separate Persons, Principles of Family and Marital Psychotherapy* (Skynner, 1976); *Families and How to Survive Them* (Skynner and Cleese, 1983); *Explorations with Families: Group-analysis and Family Therapy* (Skynner, edited Schlapobersky,

1987); and *Institutes and How to Survive Them: Mental Health Training and Consultation* (Skynner, edited Schlapobersky, 1989).

He was formerly Director of the Woodberry Down Child Guidance Unit, Physician-in-Charge of the Queen Elizabeth Hospital for Children, Senior Tutor in Psychotherapy at the Institute of Psychiatry and Honorary Associate Consultant at the Maudsley Hospital. He was a founder of the Group-Analytic Practice and of the Institute of Group-Analysis, and a founder and first Chairman of the Institute of Family Therapy, London.

E.G. Wooster received his psychiatric training at the Maudsley Hospital and after 18 months of working in Bermuda and Boston, USA, he entered psychoanalytic training in London in 1966 and was supervised in groups by Dr Heinz Wolff. He eventually succeeded Patrick de Maré as Consultant Psychotherapist at St George's Hospital, London in a post which for some 15 years included the overall clinical responsibility for approximately 15 outpatient groups.

He has maintained a consistent interest in university student health, having contributed to the London University Extra-Mural Student Counselling Course for 16 years, as well as being a Consultant to the University Student Health practice.

He has contributed to several Group-Analytic Society London Winter Workshops, and in January 1989 jointly convened a workshop on envy and jealousy in groups. He has been interested in the application of psychoanalysis to group dynamics in many fields. He is particularly excited by the work of Matte Blanco on the one hand, and drama on the other, and is currently writing on Shakespeare.

He is married and has three children.

L. Zinkin, MRCS, LRCP, FRCPsych, DPM Having from an early age wanted to work with people in trouble and find some way of understanding and helping them, I have tried in my career to learn these things (and of course understand and help myself in the process).

First having qualified as a doctor, then as a psychiatrist, then at long last as a Jungian analyst, finally much later in life I qualified as a group analyst. I have used these trainings alongside a part-time psychiatric post in the National Health Service. Having also trained in Child Psychiatry, I spent some ten years as child psychiatrist at the Middlesex Hospital, with a special interest in adolescence, combining this with my work as an analyst. This was followed by a further ten years as a Consultant Psychotherapist and Senior Lecturer at St George's Hospital. Now having retired from the National Health Service I continue to work in private practice, doing also a good deal of teaching and writing and still learning.

Working as an Associate of the Group-Analytic Practice continues to be a rich and rewarding experience and I never cease to marvel at the therapeutic power of the group process. For some years now I have been involved in marital therapy, working together with my wife, who is also a psychotherapist. For the last seven years we have been conducting couples' groups, which we are convinced have better long term results than any other form of marital therapy.

The patients of the Practice

The other main contributors to the character of the Practice are its patients. These come from a variety of sources, including a significant number of self-referrals, these often resulting from a recommendation by a current or past patient. Referrals may be made by general practitioners, psychiatrists and psychotherapists, including group analysts currently without suitable vacancies, a variety of medical specialists, social workers, psychologists and other professionals who have identified a need for psychotherapy in their client. A substantial proportion of these referrals have the intention of placing a client in group psychotherapy. Some referrals however are looking for a psychotherapy assessment and recommendation of the most appropriate form of psychotherapeutic help for the patient. Patients/clients thus arrive with a range of expectations and hopes.

One of our members, Robin Skynner, is a family therapist as well as a group analyst, so that families and couples are also referred to the Practice and will be almost always assessed by him. In a similar way a proportion of referrals are made to a specific member of the Practice while others are made to the Practice, often through a letter addressed to the Clinical Secretary (see Chapter 13 for an outline of the division of labour among members).

The Group-Analytic Practice has currently 23 twice-weekly groups. Membership of a twice-weekly group is a requirement of the Institute of Group-Analysis in its training of group analysts. All applicants to the Institute will have a minimum of three-and-a-half years of group analysis as a condition of their joining and as an essential element of their Qualifying Course. Thus each year there are a number of referrals from the Institute of Group-Analysis or self-referrals of those hoping to join this course. Members of the Practice are also asked to conduct the 'psychiatric interview' which forms part of the evaluation of intending group analysts before they are accepted on the Qualifying Course. Currently each twice-weekly group at the Practice has three to four members who are either on the Qualifying Course or intending to join it. Ideally we would like to see no more than three and perhaps even only two trainees in each group, but at present the demand for such places is greater than their availability. Chapter 10 gives detailed consideration to the relationship between the Practice and the Institute of Group-Analysis and the

13

issue of having 'trainees' in therapy groups. Therapists in training can make their own rather special constructive and destructive contributions to the groups which contain them, depending (among other matters) upon the relationship they have with the 'patient' or 'unwell' and more disturbed aspects of themselves. The trainee in the group, however, is primarily there as a patient and has his or her own special additional problems resulting from traineeship and a requirement that he or she will be reported on by his therapist for the Training Committee of the Institute of Group-Analysis (see Chapter 10).

Finally there is a substantial cohort of people who contact the Practice directly as self-referrals. These may have been recommended to contact us by other therapists, but they may also have been directed (for instance) by friends who have been or are currently attending a group. Latterly we have had significant numbers of self-referrals who have read about the Practice. Two books in particular have accounted for a significant number of referrals. Firstly, there is *Talking to a Stranger* (Knight, 1986), which is basically an introduction to different sorts of psychotherapy and where to find it. Secondly, there is *Families and How to Survive Them*, written by Robin Skynner and John Cleese (1983). This last book has had a powerful effect on many people, who more readily recognise themselves and their own lives within it, than in any other popular psychology book that I am aware of. This has on occasions caused problems for those conducting groups, since some of these clients come expecting instant help and a similar experience to the one they had in reading the book. Some readers of *Families* do not recognise in their group what they found in the book and may leave the group prematurely in a disappointed state. This has happened twice in groups conducted by the author of this chapter.

The referral network of the Practice

As group analysts we have an interest in patterns and pathways of communication. We know from the work of Foulkes (1973) that the developing network of communication in a group forms a 'matrix', which provides a supportive psychological background for the group members. In a similar way a Practice such as ours is part of a larger network of communication, which, if looked at from the point of view of one-way traffic, one would term a 'referral network'. The referral network of the Practice does indeed provide a major supportive function for the Practice, in that it feeds in the life blood of the organisation: patients. The network actually consists of a large number of two-way relationships, which have been built up over many years. Each member of the Practice contributes his or her own network of professional contacts. The Practice is also perceived as an entity by referrers who write about patients direct to the Group-Analytic Practice or make telephone contact with the office. This helpful and fruitful network is constantly in flux, but on the whole tends to grow. It is partly and most importantly nurtured by feeding back to each referrer the outcome of assessments and also, as often as is practicable, the process and outcome of therapy. In this way the referrers can feel like participants rather than merely suppliers of patients.

Apart from corresponding and speaking by telephone with our referrers, we like also to take the opportunity of meeting everybody annually at a Christmas party. This counters anonymity and we hope cements relationships for a further year's work.

Assessment and the waiting list

Assessments for psychotherapy and suitability for group psychotherapy are carried out by the Full Members of the Practice. Those who are medically qualified will then provide medical cover for any treatment carried out at the Practice by non-medically qualified Members or Associates. The form of the assessment is left to the discretion of the assessor and involves at least one interview of at least one hour's duration. The content of the interview is then recorded on a form which was proposed as a prototype by Robin Skynner and developed in consultation with other Members during the the first 18 months of the life of the practice in 66 Montagu Mansions. This gives scope for recording important facets of the individual's presenting state in short-hand form, and provides a useful baseline for research purposes (see Chapter 4).

The outcome of an assessment will be an agreement with the patient that a particular course of action is most appropriate for him or her. The choices available are wide, but a common outcome is for the patient to be considered suitable for a once- or twice-weekly group. Sometimes the Member who is assessing has a suitable vacancy and will offer the patient an immediately available place. If this is not possible the patient is discussed at the next clinical/administrative meeting of the Practice (a weekly event), and with the help of the Clinical Secretary either offered to a group conductor with a suitable vacancy or placed on the waiting list. The Clinical Secretary plays an important role in the Practice; namely, holding the responsibility for maintaining an accurate waiting list and an up-to-date record of the requirements for patients of all of the 16 members of the Practice. Whilst it is important to place the new patient in a group which will best fit his or her requirements and accommodate his or her personality type, we find even with the large numbers of groups and patients available that one of the major constraints on the placement of any individual is his or her availability to attend at particular times. This is one of the important items of information sought in the initial interview and recorded on the assessment form.

Meetings of the Members

The Full Members (Committee of Management) meet weekly in order to carry out two tasks. The first of these is to discuss all the patients who will be joining groups. The second is to keep on top of management and administrative issues (see Chapter 13 for further details). The whole membership of the Practice, Full Members and Associates meet termly in order to maintain social and business relationships between the two sub-groups working in the Practice and also probably more importantly to discuss theoretical and practical aspects of the clinical work which the Members are engaged in. In some ways this book is a product of these meetings and has contributions from the majority of the Members of the Practice.

Members of the Practice

As is now clear, there are two categories of membership of the Practice. There are seven Full Members and nine Associate Members. Both groups feel that the other has desirable privileges. Both groups are probably right. The Practice belongs to the Full Members, who are thus directly administratively and financially bound to the Practice and on the whole devote at least half of their working week to clinical work at 88 Montagu Mansions. The Full Members have the privilege of close involvement, and contribute by having greater responsibility and devoting more of their professional time to the Practice. The Full Members have each paid capital in order to purchase a share in the Practice, thereby having an opportunity, not given to the Associates, of making either a long-term capital gain or capital loss.

The Associates on the other hand have the great advantage of being able to use the machinery of the Practice, to assemble groups with an ease which would in no other way be possible for them in the private sector. They are disadvantaged in that they have no direct involvement in the administration and management of the Practice.

The Group-Analytic Practice as a successful small organisation

We are inclined to feel that the Group-Analytic Practice has been a successful small organisation. This does not mean that all the contacts we have with patients and fellow professionals are equally happy and with good outcome. On the whole, however, although there are relatively few research data available, there is little doubt that in terms of providing the setting for a large number of therapeutic groups, which benefit significant numbers of patients, the Practice is successful. It is probably one of very few similar organisations functioning in the private sector.

Colleagues from various parts of the country and indeed the world have asked how this has been achieved and how they might establish something similar. At this point I do not think that it is possible to answer such questions. What I do hope, however, is that this book will provide material of all kinds which will enable both its authors and readers to formulate more clearly ideas about the Practice and to make use of our experience to develop and improve their work.

One important factor in the development and continuing fruitful life of the Practice may be that its Members are all group analysts, who have to a greater or lesser extent spent many years learning to work together with others in groups, with a considerable amount of that work being directed towards the resolution of group conflict. Who could be better equipped to work together in a small organisation than a group of enthusiastic group analysts, with their common allegiance to the Group-Analytic Society and the Institute of Group-Analysis?

Within the larger network of the Practice, the Associate Members, while benefiting from the organisation developed by the Members, only have limited opportunity to influence decision making, which lies almost entirely with the Full Members. There is a chance here for the development of a certain amount of creative tension, which to date is possibly not fully utilised. None the less it is important to point out that the majority of decisions of the Management Committee are those directed at maintaining the successful physical and emotional therapeutic environment which was achieved some years ago through the inspiration of S.H. Foulkes. I believe that a major contributor the success of the Practice is also that in those areas where it matters we are fundamentally a network of equals.

Readers should consider this chapter as central to the structure of the book. It could be seen as a hall led into from the historical chapters. Branching from it are all the other more detailed explorations of clinical, administrative and management issues which are to follow.

Note

1 The current full members of the Practice are: Dr D.G. Brown, Mrs L. Glenn, Dr L.C. Kreeger, Dr M. Pines, Dr J.P. Roberts, Mrs M. Sharpe and Dr A.C.R. Skynner.

Chapter 2

Group analysis and psychotherapy services

Two papers by S.H. Foulkes[1]

A. Group analysis in private practice and outpatient clinics

When group analysis is used as a method of psychotherapy it is called group-analytic psychotherapy (GAP). Whereas in the foregoing we have been concerned with inpatients, we are now turning to outpatient conditions; that is to say, people who pursue their usual lives uninterruptedly while undergoing treatment. This is the chief domain of this type of treatment. When no external restrictions limit its course – for example, in private practice – it has proved to be, in now nearly twenty-five years of experience, an intensive and deep-going form of psychotherapy. Its effects can only be compared to prolonged individual psychoanalytic treatment and in many cases it seems superior to this in its therapeutic effect. It must be said, however, that under these circumstances it tends to be a prolonged form of treatment, to be thought of in terms of several years rather than months. In terms of economy the difference is still considerable; assuming GAP to be on a once-a-week and psychoanalysis five-times-a-week basis the ratio for time spent is one to five. GAP can be stepped up to two or more sessions per week and can be combined with any number of regular individual interviews. It seems likely that the optimum interval between meetings would be less than a week. It is certain that meeting should not be less than once weekly. Some workers advocate 'alternate' meetings, that is without the therapist present, between ordinary meetings. I have as yet no systematic experience with this procedure. It has certainly some advantages but raises a number of serious objections especially from the point of view of the transference situation. My own experience has been predominantly with weekly groups without individual appointments unless these were indicated by particular circumstances. These with increasing experience arise only very rarely.

There is no doubt that an intensive form of psychotherapy results from a combination with individual interviews. In this case every member of the group should have such individual interviews and as far as possible conditions should be equal for all members. During the first years of experimenting with GAP I practised this type of combination. Gradually I have come to the conclusion that individual treatment where necessary should proceed, or better still, follow GAP, but that the aim should be to make concurrent individual treatment unnecessary. Within recent years I have reintroduced a form of combination in the following way: each participant has one personal interview with me in weekly turns, that is to say, meets me once in two months. This modification resulted from the fact that intensity became so great that it was not always possible to deal with individual implications sufficiently within the time available. This procedure has so far worked out very well. If an increase in the number of group sessions to two a week is possible this might well be preferable.

The number of patients might drop by one, two or three below eight, but it should not exceed that number. The group takes the form of 'slow-open' groups, individuals being introduced as vacancies occur from time to time.

These groups contain psychiatrists and other doctors who joined for training purposes. Some of them had undergone intensive psychoanalytic treatment and training. For obvious reasons I tended for a number of years to reserve membership in such training groups to this category. However, deep seated character defences tended to be shared and organised in professional channels. Mutual analysis tended to become predominant, taking the place of frank personal exposure and could easily be rationalised. Now they share groups with other professional or otherwise compatible patients who come entirely for therapeutic reasons and this works much better. The therapists expose frankly their personal problems and it is an object lesson for all when these conflicts involve them in their own relations with their own patients in turn. Not surprisingly perhaps the 'patients' in the group tend to project some categorical differences between themselves and the 'psychiatrists'. This complication lends itself to analytical solution. Under the conditions of a hospital outpatient clinic considerable pressure of numbers and a relative shortage of staff call for many adaptations and concessions. The particular problems which arise under conditions such as these can briefly be put thus: too many patients, among them a high proportion of difficult ones, to be treated in too short a time by doctors relatively inexperienced in psychotherapy.

We will now illustrate the problems of outpatient psychotherapy and an attempt at their solution by a concrete example, namely, the O-P Psychotherapy Unit at the Maudsley as it operated under my direction for a period of twelve years. This will be described in this chapter in the first place in order to present orientation and principles. My own experience has been first at St Bartholomew's Hospital (this has been reported in *Introduction to Group-Analytic Psychotherapy*) and for the last twelve years at the Maudsley Hospital in London.

This latter will be the basis of the present account. As the unit in

19

question, in accordance with the functions of a teaching hospital, served not only the treatment of patients but also the training and teaching of postgraduates, it has been built up with the idea of a close integration between these two functions.

Type of patient. Patients were referred by the general psychiatric consultants of the hospital from their outpatient clinics, mostly when prospects of spontaneous improvement were not good and the case had been unresponsive to treatment. They were mainly psychoneurotic patients who could in principle be expected to benefit from psychotherapy. There was also a sprinkling of psychotic and potentially psychotic patients. Some of these responded well to psychotherapy, others had sometimes to be admitted as inpatients before their treatment could begin. Only in a minority of referrals was there what one might call positive selection, in the sense that patients were referred with a good prognosis and good motivation for psychotherapy. In addition a goodly number of patients were referred whose condition had been serious enough for them to require a shorter or more prolonged stay in the hospital and who were about to be or had recently been discharged.

The psychotherapists available were postgraduate doctors with more or less psychiatric experience, but often little if any experience in psychotherapy. Most of them had expressed a degree of interest and a positive inclination toward psychotherapy and some were training to become psychoanalysts and were undergoing their own analysis. These latter were not necessarily better in the practice of psychotherapy of a shorter variety as they were inclined to consider such treatment as a frustrated form of psychoanalysis. On the other hand they had a much better appreciation of unconscious implications and the dynamics of the transference/countertransference situation. Experience and skill are of particular importance when difficult cases have to be treated in freer style and in shorter time.

Limitations. Our physicians served at this unit for a term of six months or exceptionally one year. Thus no sooner had they acquired some experience than they had to leave. Patients had to envisage the end of their treatment very soon or else be transferred to another doctor with all the problems this raises. For individual treatment the average time available was approximately one weekly session for, say, three to four months. Groups were also held usually at the rate of one session per week, but fortunately it was often possible to carry on for a longer time because the therapists were ready to continue with their groups from personal interest after they had left the department. Thus groups had a lifetime of from one to two years or more. It was also easier for groups to carry on for another term with a new conductor than for patients in individual treatment. This particularly applied to the open type of group.

Supervision. There again less time was available than would be ideally required. It was possible to reserve one to two weekly hours for each registrar but this would include dealing with the practical administrative points and current matters of some urgency. Not more than two or three cases could be supervised regularly in any detail, but in surveying the whole material there was occasion to discuss some specific points in treatment, the handling of particular situations and so on.

Supervision of group treatment. This was done by way of a weekly seminar in which all the groups were reviewed in turn and the points discussed concerning the various groups were of interest and instructional value to all. Of this more later.

Orientation. My orientation to all this has been to accept these difficulties not as accidental complications but simply as a reflection of the situation in which psychotherapy finds itself at the present time. In this way the task was accepted in a positive spirit. This attitude found expression in the organisation of the unit. Without such positive orientation the registrars themselves could not have been expected to approach their task in a positive frame of mind in turn. This, however, is necessary in my opinion if psychotherapy is to be successful. If the psychotherapist – confronted with such difficult conditions – cannot find a positive solution he had better not accept them; alternatively he would have two choices: either to be content with an attempt at piecemeal and symptomatic amelioration or else he must proceed cynically without any conviction that he could do any good. My idea was that it is not much good teaching and preaching therapeutic tenets, however sound they may be, unless the practice upon which they are taught sets a good example. It is not satisfactory to proclaim principles but continuously have to point out that they cannot be practised here and now because of practical difficulties.

Therapeutic aims and the means by which one hoped to achieve them had to be formulated in view of the actual reality of the situation (time, experience, availability, and so on). All individual component factors of the therapeutic situation which condition the dynamics of treatment have to be compatible with one another. For instance, it would not make much sense to put the patient on a couch or to base his treatment on free association or to analyse his dreams if his next interview took place a week later and the total duration of treatment was no more than twelve or twenty hours. Nor would it make sense to embark on intensive interpretations and analysis of transference. In this connection an interesting observation was made which could lend itself to more systematic enquiry and that is that transference reactions seemed to become clearly discernible around the sixth treatment session – in our case mostly coinciding with the sixth week of treatment. In some cases transference had to be taken up or even had to be in the centre of attention from the beginning. In others the therapist was well advised to observe it but leave it alone unless it forced itself into prominence particularly as a resistance. Variations in regularity, dosage of interview in the light of the stage of treatment, particularly its ending were important items in the dynamic handling of the case. The importance of the therapist's attitude and how it was conveyed to the patient in the beginning of treatment were stressed. The termination of treatment was well prepared and ample notice given. In a sense the end was envisaged from the beginning. It cannot be overemphasised how much the result is influenced by the expectation cultivated in the patient in words or by implication or, to put it another way, how much harm can be done by lack of awareness and skill in this respect.

Patients under psychotherapy make infinite claims and it is to some extent true that the more of these are fulfilled the more arise for quite legitimate reasons or from dependency and transference needs. If it is to be kept within reasonable dimensions in time it is important that psychotherapy is never allowed to become an institution. It is my impression in longer and even very long psychotherapy that from time to time an optimal point for ending treatment is reached. When this is missed it takes an increasingly longer time before a similar position is again reached which is favourable for the termination of treatment. It is a kind of spiral phenomenon; for instance a case may have reached a good point after six hours (weeks), again after six months; the next time may be after eighteen months or two years, after which it may be a matter of years. On the whole the tendency is for the therapist to hesitate too long with the termination of treatment and to underrate the patient's ability to manage without him.

As I have sometimes formulated, in many cases we have done a good deal if we helped the patient to translate his symptoms into his problems or, if he had presented us with problems, have analysed with him what had prevented their solution by himself or that and why he looked for answers which we could not give him. This may sound modest, but we have preferred to aim at more modest goals but such as we could reasonably hope to reach under the given circumstances. Furthermore we thought it important that whatever change had been achieved should hold good after the relationship with the therapist had been given up and the patient been required to stand on his own feet again. On average we devoted the last third of the treatment to the working through of this separation from the therapist. Thus it may be stated that in spite of our limitations we aimed at treating the person rather than the symptom and we tended to focus more on central problems and attitudes than on the modification of symptoms.

It has been found useful to plan treatment with the help of a specially devised card. On this was entered firstly a dynamic formulation of the case in co-operation with the registrar who was to treat the patient and who, whenever possible, had seen him together with the consultant in a diagnostic interview. Then followed a formulation of the changes we felt could be achieved and the means by which we hoped to achieve them. After termination of treatment changes claimed were in terms of dynamic changes in the patient and factors operating in the treatment situation, and these were compared with the original assessment.

The problems and principles just outlined are of course the same for individual and group treatment. Indeed, our dynamic formulations influenced our choice for one or the other. Group treatment, however, offers special advantages. First of all, in the diagnostic introductory group the trainee can share the observations and participate in decisions based upon these afterwards. Secondly, group treatment itself as an experience brings the learning therapist into a more natural contact with his patients and influences him to be more concrete and to express himself simply. The supervision in a group situation has all the advantages of group teaching [which are alluded to by SHF in Chapter 20 *Therapeutic Group Analysis*, Ed.].

Apart from this, group psychotherapy enables the therapist to get to know more and a greater variety of patients than he would otherwise do and has the merits of a comparative psychopathology which is displayed in living interaction for him.

B. Outline of a psychotherapeutic unit

In this chapter an account will be given of a model unit as developed at the Maudsley Hospital Out-patient Psychotherapy Department under my direction. It is a model in the sense that it shows a way in which justice can be done to the claims of psychotherapy at an outpatient clinic if it is at the same time to create the best conditions for teaching and learning, clinical study and research. It is not a model in the sense that it should or could be transferred wholesale to other settings. Indeed, it is an intrinsic part of a group-analytic approach that rigid organisation and institutionalisation are avoided so as to allow maximum flexibility to ever-changing conditions. Arrangements should, as it were, be hand-made and in the closest possible contact with the realities of conditions. For this same reason this unit has been continuously changing in detail, and what is given here is a schematic cross-section of its working structure.

During the period under discussion the unit staff consisted of one physician (consultant psychotherapist, half-time) and two full-time registrars. In the year under review 225 patients were referred to the unit. Of these approximately 25 per cent failed to keep appointments or were rejected as unsuitable or transferred for other treatment. In 10 per cent of the total the result was very good, in 40 per cent good or moderately good, and the remaining 25 per cent showed no definite evidence of improvement. Of those treated therefore 13.3 per cent were recovered, 53.3 per cent much improved or improved, 33.3 per cent showed no significant result. These patients were usually sent to the hospital by their general practitioners. Each patient was examined by one of the psychiatric consultants in charge of outpatient clinics who had referred them to us to be considered for psychotherapy. A number had previously been treated as inpatients of the hospital and were considered ready for discharge provided that they could have further outpatient treatment.

The following diagram (see Figure 2.1) indicates the modes and stages of psychotherapy in the unit which was on an analytic basis. It will be seen that treatment was broadly divided into two categories: individual and group. These are shown as two streams, and linking up with the group stream teaching and supervising activities of the unit are represented in the column on the right. Supervision of individual psychotherapy is not shown in this diagram. Patients had either individual psychotherapy or group psychotherapy but some may have had first one and then the other. Patients who had group treatment were given additional individual attention when the need arose. In a preliminary selection from the case notes approximately seven out of ten were found suitable for attending the

Figure 2.1 Modes and stages of psychotherapy in a model unit, Maudsley Hospital Out-patient Psychotherapy Department

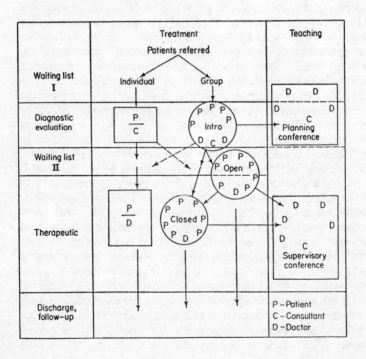

introductory group; the others were seen individually by the consultant in the usual way. The period of waiting for this initial interview was from one to six weeks (Waiting List I).

In order to facilitate comparison, the progress of patients through the unit will now be followed separately according to the two streams.

Individual psychotherapy

At the initial interview the consultant formed an opinion of the psycho-pathological structure and dynamics of the patient, of his capacity and motivation for change, and formulated a provisional plan for treatment, its prospective intensity, mode of operation and target. The patient may then have had to wait from three to six months before a vacancy occurred (Waiting List II).

A treatment session took the best part of an hour. As a rule interviews took place once a week for three to six months (about ten to thirty hours). Physician and patient sat face to face. The degree of control of verbal communication, interpretation of content and relationship ('transference') were modified to suit the needs of the individual patient. The planning of such modifications took into account the way in which these various factors interact and influence one another.

The recognition of unconscious mental processes and their role in the production of the neurosis were considered important. The material for this was provided by the patients' verbal communication, behaviour and attitude towards the therapist.

It was considered important that the atmosphere was one in which judging, censoring, preaching and moralising had no place. Much attention was given to the problem of the patient's dependence on the doctor.

Group psychotherapy

Only three groups are shown schematically on the diagram: an introductory group, an open and closed group. The open group, in one of its incarnations, was used as a preliminary (holding) group. This is indicated schematically by its extension into the space of Waiting List II. It will be understood that these 'groups' represent a number of parallel groups and variation of them. The diagram shows some of the advantages of group psychotherapy: the elimination or reduction of waiting lists, the continuity or gradual transition from one stage to the next, the greater number of patients treated by a single doctor and the looseness of teaching and training opportunities. In addition, group treatment has other intrinsic advantages for certain categories of psychiatric patients.

Now we will consider each section in turn, both regarding therapy and teaching.

Introductory group. This group served many purposes but two of its functions were outstanding: firstly, the diagnostic evaluation in the light of the patients' reactions to the perturbing token therapeutic approach and of the characteristics revealed in their reactions to each other; secondly, this group presented the best possible practical introduction for those selected for group psychotherapy. From a teaching point of view it must be seen in close connection with the 'planning conference' which followed immediately afterwards and which was built up on observations made by the doctors in the introductory group. The number of patients in this group was confined to four or five. These patients had not met one another, nor any of us, before as they took their seats in a semicircle facing the consultant and the other doctors of the unit. Such a situation is understandably tense. After some introductory remarks, however, there was considerable relaxation and the consultant began his investigations as a rule by addressing each patient in turn. He asked them not only about the complaints which brought them to the hospital but sought to throw light on their own expectations and attitudes regarding treatment. The first analytic steps in the shape of clarification, confrontation of contradictory attitudes, rectification, and so on, were taken already on the occasion of the first contact. Their importance must be rated high. Spontaneity and interaction on the part of the patients was encouraged and they soon understood that they were expected to take an active part. They began to compare problems and exchange views. A patient might say with a wistful nod of his head, 'Yes, that is just the way I feel.'

Considerable resistances and objections might be raised. Two experiences were made: that these objections can be voiced without fear and that they were taken up in an analytic spirit. The introductory group meeting brought to light many of the difficulties which each patient experienced in his relations to other people which so often form the hard core of his illness. It was remarkable to observe how these quite unselected patients could be made to interact at this one and only meeting they had with one another and how meaningful this encounter could be. The doctors shared this experience and could observe the consultant's handling of the situation. We thus saw dynamically and often dramatically displayed just those features which affect the doctor and patient decisively when assessing therapeutic possibilities. Thus much could be accomplished in the short space of an hour at this introductory meeting. It was usually possible to recommend to each patient at the end of this hour the mode of subsequent treatment. Individual psychotherapy was recommended to about one in five of these patients while the remainder qualified for group psychotherapy.

Planning conference. Following the introductory group meeting, the doctors met and discussed their observations and formulated more detailed plans for each of the patients seen at the introductory group.

Observations were exchanged, the psychopathology as it had been observed in action was compared with that reported by the referring consultant on the basis of a more conventional examination. Observations were pooled, various interpretations discussed and prognoses considered. Each doctor shared in the decisions of the psychotherapeutic team. On the basis of shared experience we could thus discuss the patients' suitability for treatment, their differential selection for group or individual therapy, our expectations and predictions of therapeutic results. A tentative plan of treatment was formulated as well as the means whereby desirable changes might be achieved. Apart from the patients whom they treated, these doctors thus got to know the other patients as well on whom they would later hear their colleagues report at the supervisory seminar. The introductory group meeting as a whole with its particular dynamics, the physician's actions and interpretations and points of technique were considered.

The latter part of this conference was devoted to a preliminary examination of the case notes of the patients who would be invited to next week's introductory group meetings. In this way each doctor got acquainted with the details of patients whom he would see the following week and their problems and he could thus make his own formulations and check his expectations at the following week's planning conference in the light of the introductory group.

Therapeutic groups

These are represented in the scheme by one open and one closed group, which are, of course, prototypes. An open group would admit and discharge members from time to time. It served a great variety of purposes, not always compatible in one and the same actual group. For some patients it is important to provide treatment as soon as possible. In this case treatment in the open group was preparatory only until a suitable vacancy could be found for them in a closed group. For others it provided a valuable opportunity for further diagnostic observation. It served, however, as the sole treatment group for a good proportion of its membership. It was particularly suitable for two types of patient belonging to two rather opposite ends of a scale:

1 Patients who are less severely disturbed, though perhaps more acutely upset, can benefit from the greater variety of social adjustment demanded in such a group and can soon be discharged.
2 The chronic patient who needs prolonged treatment, partly of a supportive kind but who can nevertheless benefit from an analytic approach. These may attend for prolonged periods. Not much emphasis was placed on regularity of attendance and patients might

be tentatively discharged but return to the group later if they felt any need for this.

Such a group could therefore carry a greater number of people, say fifteen, while the actual attendance might be between five and ten. Such groups could carry on indefinitely, at least in theory, with changing therapists. In practice it must be said that they came to an end from time to time. What usually happened was that a nucleus of 'regulars' developed who sooner or later became refractory towards new members. This might probably be avoided if a sufficient number of parallel groups could be run so the selection could be more careful and turnover be controlled at a convenient rate. What happened in our unit under the circumstances when the refractory stage was reached was that we refrained from adding new members and allowed the nucleus to finish their treatment as a closed group.

The closed group

The closed group ideally begins and ends with the same membership; as a rule, however, one or two patients have to be replaced in the beginning. This kind of natural sorting out could probably be avoided where careful selection is possible. The group also loses one or two members in its course, when this is at all prolonged, for more or less external reasons. At the clinic the life of such a group was between one and two-and-a-half years and it met at weekly intervals. My impression is that a period of nine months is a good yardstick by which to determine a group's duration – or say ten months being a minimum and three such periods perhaps the most desirable. These groups demand regular attendance from each member and they provide an intensive therapeutic experience. Individual interviews were rarely necessary during treatment. The group indicated in our diagram stands for a variety, some of which will be discussed separately later.

The selection of the individuals has been discussed in its various aspects in different places in this volume. The principles of selection are not yet known with any accuracy. The main reasons for this are: (1) that there are such a great number of significant variables, and (2) that in order to carry out such selection far greater numbers of patients and staff would be required than are as yet assembled anywhere to my knowledge. As a rough estimate I think that 200 to 300 currently available and otherwise suitable patients of about equal number in sex would be necessary and up to a dozen trained group psychotherapists. The scientific testing of merits and demerits of various selective factors would, even under such circumstances, be a task of many years.

Our groups are as a rule now of mixed sex, in equal proportion. Care is taken to match such factors as personality, age, religion, social status, education level and so on. Minority conditions where they cannot be avoided should at least not be confined to any one individual in isolation. As to diagnosis, we preferred heterogeneous groups with an admixture of psychotic or borderline cases but preferably not severely depressed patients.

A general principle observed was this: if the range of some of the factors mentioned was great this was compensated by more rigid insistence on uniformity in other respects. For instance, let us assume that social status and age varied considerably, then intelligence should be uniformly high; or if a group was to contain a mixture of single and married women their social status and educational level would be kept steady especially when age ranged widely.

Closed groups can also be selected according to particular problems. If the group was composed in this way, or was otherwise concerned with a shared issue through a common situation in which the members found themselves, greater laxity was possible in other variables. Patients in some such conditions as marked sexual deviation, addiction or delinquency can benefit greatly by inclusion in such special groups when as a rule they would not fit into the usual outpatient group.

This form of group then was our usual therapeutic group. The patients are strangers to one another and are not connected in ordinary life. They were instructed not to meet outside the treatment situation, though preferably this code of behaviour would be based on an understanding of the reasons for it. This is best achieved by taking this point (as well as similar ones) up early, as soon as it arises in the group.

Quite by contrast to this we have from time to time treated small networks of closely related patients in small groups. Such a 'network' is, as it were, a cluster of psychopathological mutual mental involvement of which the patient is part. Frequently, this may correspond to family relationships.

The supervisory conference

Here all groups were discussed. It took place weekly and took two and a half hours. All the doctors engaged in treatment assembled to report on their groups. Over the years there was a constant flow of distinguished visitors, both from this country and abroad, although their number had to be confined to a few at any one time. Special points of urgency which had arisen were discussed, but in the main three groups on average were reported extensively on each occasion. Here again the practical work was made the occasion of instruction. Points of technique and handling were in the foreground, but psychopathological and theoretical problems were fully discussed. In this way all could share in the experiences of each individual group and could in addition compare and contrast their different approaches and above all could exchange their views in lively discussion. It was thus real group teaching in which the consultant joined. The group discussion and group analysis of the doctor–patient interaction is particularly valuable, including observations concerning behaviour in this group itself.

The unit in operation

It may be useful to end this short account by considering what were the standard situations in this unit as experienced, (1) by a patient, and (2) by a registrar

(1) The patient referred by his GP would be examined by a registrar in consultation with a physician, who might then send him to the outpatient psychotherapeutic unit. Here, if he were pre-selected for the 'individual stream', he would have an interview with the senior psychotherapist after an average waiting time of two to three weeks. If accepted for individual psychotherapy, he would have to wait up to six months before notification of a vacancy. Finally he would meet the doctor who was to treat him. Arrangements here varied greatly, but the average was one interview a week of forty-five minutes' duration. If his treatment could not be terminated successfully within six months, he would have to be passed on to a new doctor or complete his treatment in a suitable group.

If a patient were pre-selected for the 'group stream', he would find himself, two or three weeks after referral, in the introductory group. If, after assessment here he was found suitable for group psychotherapy, he might continue a a a member of an open group, whence he passed sometimes with, but often without, a break to the most suitable closed group available for him, or he might have to wait for a suitable vacancy.

(2) The training experiences of the registrar were varied and intense. During his six to nine months on the unit he would undertake the treatment of about 20 individual patients. In this work he would receive weekly supervision by the consultant, in an hour set aside for him. He would conduct one or two groups, having an average number of seven patients each. He would receive guidance at a weekly supervisory conference, where he would also exchange experiences with colleagues. He would have regular opportunity for first-hand observation on the management of the introductory group by the consultant, and a chance to discuss these observations in full at the planning conference afterwards. In addition, he would have access to the total material and sample opportunity for closely observing the large majority of patients passing through this unit during his stay, an opportunity particularly difficult to realise in psychotherapy. He would have continuous opportunities for discussion, for learning from the experiences of his colleagues, and having the benefit of their criticism

on his own handling of cases, and in turn, of actively participating in the critical assessment of their work. The main emphasis in treatment throughout was on interpersonal relationship.

Note

1 These papers are published in the exact form in which they were published in *Therapeutic Group Analysis* (Foulkes, 1964), apart from an editing out of references to other chapters in the original book.

Chapter 3

A history of the Group-Analytic Practice

Edited by Jeff Roberts

The intention of this chapter is to give a historical view of the development of the Practice as seen through the eyes of those who contributed to it. In order to do so, meetings were arranged at which this history could be reviewed. These meetings were recorded, transcribed and edited. The result is a picture of events and personalities which surpasses in depth and vitality that which could be achieved by a purely unidimensional narrative. Some effort on the part of the reader may be required in reconstructing events, which may include even a little reading between lines. This we believe will be amply repaid by the resulting image which is evoked of the Practice's history.

This chapter is made up of the following sections.

A. A dialogue between Jeff Roberts and Elizabeth Foulkes, the widow of S.H. Foulkes, in which we talked of the earliest history of the Practice and its development from work started by S.H. Foulkes in Exeter in 1940.[1]

   The dialogues cover the majority of the developmental history of the Practice, although there is less detail about developments involving the sharing of a flat in Bickenhall Mansions with the Institute of Group-Analysis and the successful purchase of its own premises by the Institute. These developments, which are really more part of the history of the Institute, are alluded to in this conversation.

B. A dialogue between Jeff Roberts, Malcolm Pines, Robin Skynner and Patrick de Maré (recently retired from the Practice).

C. Short biographical notes on all former members of the Committee of Management of the Practice, including S.H. Foulkes.

D. A chronological outline of the development of the Practice, including the dates of important events affecting other related people and organisations.

A. A dialogue between Elizabeth Foulkes and Jeff Roberts, 29 March 1990

JR: Malcolm, Robin, Pat and I met in October and we tried to outline their experience of how the Practice was formed. Many interesting things came up, one of which was Pat talking about how he first met Michael[2] poring over some Rorschach cards and how the light shining on the Rorschach produced a rainbow of colours and he got very excited by that.

EF: That must have been at Northfield, during the war.

JR: It was, and I think what Pat told us was that Michael very quickly after the war set up in private practice and that he was one of the first to join him in a group therapy practice.

EF: Yes, well, it was really first a circle of people who met for discussion about group analysis rather than practice. Then Michael set up his first group which was not ideally selected but he was keen to get going and it was only when he moved into Upper Wimpole Street, which was in 1951, that he tried to expand a bit, it took some time and then Pat was the next to start a group. He found it difficult to get that one together and for a whole year he had two or three regular patients and a lot of people coming in and out. He will have told you that...

JR: He said he had half a group.

EF: Yes, for a whole year, but he hung on and finally it became a proper group, and the next one in was James Anthony. We moved into Upper Wimpole Street in 1951, Michael had to give up his consulting room in Great Portland Street because the house was being sold and so we looked around for suitable premises; for what we called then a group centre. Now this is something that hasn't quite worked out the way people had originally hoped, in which everything was centralised – practice, training, research, everything under one roof – and the idea was originally that the Practice might actually subsidise things like research and training. Now of course with the Institute taking over the training and the Practice being unwilling to move in with the Institute, this has not happened.

JR: Can I just take you back to Michael's first group? Do you know when he actually set that group going in London? I know he was working in Exeter early in the war.

EF: Well it was at number 1 Park Crescent, that I know. I think it was in '46. He came out of the army early in '46 and after organising groups on a vast scale at Northfield, he was very keen to get together a private group. He also met regularly with a number of colleagues interested in furthering their understanding of group therapy.

JR: When do your personal memories actually start?

EF: In May '51 when we moved into Upper Wimpole Street; well, a bit before then, because I had been looking round for premises before we finally moved there. Michael took the plunge and took a consulting flat at Upper Wimpole Street with a view to having accommodation there to run groups. The lease was rather restrictive, it was in only his name.

JR: And that became Michael and Pat and James Anthony.

EF: I'm sorry I can't give any exact details. They had originally hoped to set up something within the National Health Service, soon after its inauguration in 1948. Michael made an application to the Maudsley Hospital (with James Anthony and Kraupl-Taylor, both already at the Maudsley) to run a group psychotherapy unit there, but that was turned down. He was however appointed to the Maudsley himself as Consultant Psychotherapist, but there was then no chance of setting up a special unit for group psychotherapy, let alone group analysis. Having been unsuccessful in this, as well as in another application to one of the London Hospital Boards made by Patrick de Maré, they decided they would try to do it privately. The idea was first of all to set up a centre where everything would be together: practice, training and research. People were very reluctant to take on groups because they didn't feel they had had sufficient training, and in order to get sufficient training you had to have groups. Some colleagues none the less worked in hospitals where they could conduct groups.

During 1950 and '51 we looked for suitable premises and in May '51 Foulkes moved into 22 Upper Wimpole Street, starting what he called a 'pilot centre for group-analysis', where both the Group-Analytic Society and the Practice had their beginnings.

Michael was always determined to have everything under one roof. As you can see, in 1950 he wrote:

> Efforts were made to establish a group-analytic centre. The Hon. W.H.R. Iliffe [who incidentally was a patient of Michael's in the last stages of his analysis] and Miss E.T. Marx [that's me] looked at many houses and investigated different problems in connection with establishing such a centre. Difficulties at the time included the small number of colleagues who could make time to give work to such a centre where the financial outlook was somewhat uncertain, especially at a time when the effects of the newly established National Health Service on private practice were hard to estimate.

EF (continues): Here is something about the group centre....

> The need is for a common working place where a number of qualified specialists and auxiliary workers could combine in the conducting of groups, where they could pool and compare their experiences. Such a centre would comprise two or more treatment

rooms and an administrative office and secretary. The technique of this method is described more fully in other publications etc.

EF (continues) Then it goes into treatment, selection, prognosis, diagnosis, training, research, therapists. It was proposed that therapists would be paid on a sessional basis.

Then there was the move to 66 Montagu Mansions. There was a principle of parity of status among members. All groups conducted by members in private practice should be considered as part of the Group-Analytic Practice and levies should be paid by all members equally on the groups they conduct into a central fund. So this was already worked out. At the time we had dual premises at 66 Montagu Mansions and 22 Upper Wimpole Street, subsequently 66 and 22 became 88: very neat.[3]

JR: Can I ask you about the transition from 22 to 66, do you recall the process whereby that happened?

EF: Yes, Michael had been in the States as visiting professor and his then wife died while he was there. When he came back he was faced with what he called a palace revolution.

JR: Robin Skynner called it precisely the same thing.

EF: I can't quite remember what it was really all about, but he felt these were his premises at Upper Wimpole Street and his lease was restricted and there was trouble about that. I wouldn't like to be specific on what actually happened, but Michael was rather hurt about the pressure he felt on him. They wanted a quick decision about things when he wasn't really in the right frame of mind to make decisions. He wasn't even sure where he was going to live after his wife's death. So he said 'Well, you had better find yourself other premises.' Exactly what it was about I just cannot remember.

JR: It wasn't the desire for growth?

EF: That may have come into it, quite likely that was part of it, but there must have been something else and I also can't even remember who was the spokesman, so to speak, for the palace revolution. It might be Robin Skynner had something to do with it because he used to be quite forthright and outspoken – I don't know what he said about that.

JR: He claimed that, I think.

EF: Yes, I think it's quite likely that he had something to do with it. However, it was all done in the end on very friendly terms, they came to an agreement – there are some letters in here that set out the financial arrangements they made. Bill Stauble, a Canadian who was here then, who had also been a clinical assistant at the Maudsley while he was doing his analytic training, was particularly active looking around because he had more time than the others. He found 66 Montagu Mansions which then later became too small when they found 88 across the road.

Michael wasn't the one to be paranoid, he had a wonderful way of avoiding being paranoid, he was sometimes put into situations where he might well have become paranoid, like at the Tavistock Clinic.

JR: How did he avoid it?

EF: I don't know, he just avoided it. He was quite pleased with himself about his ability to do that. Ferguson Rodger asked him why he took no part in the discussions they had at the Tavistock Clinic at the time. He said, 'Well, I haven't been asked.' He was then invited to attend these weekly meetings with Wilfred Bion and others, but Michael felt that they treated him as a sort of intruder and tried to make him feel paranoid – that was his feeling. He couldn't see much point in that particular collaboration, it also took time out of his private practice while they were all sitting there being paid for their time. He really didn't see why he should go there when he was so clearly not welcome. And of course when the Tavistock was reconstituted after the war, they were all Kleinians, that was part of the policy. Michael remained a strictly Freudian analyst and that was one of the things where there was a clash.

JR: Which way did the clash come? Was Michael disturbed by the Kleinians or were they disturbed by him as one of the Freudians?

EF: Probably a bit of both, I couldn't say really.

JR: I think the three-way split in the Institute of Psycho-Analysis is a tragic one in that there seems to be little creative dialogue between the three groups.

EF: I remember when Michael was teaching there; he took the third-year seminars which were intended to be attended by students from all three groups. He found it very frustrating because it just didn't seem possible to have a good seminar where all these various factions came together.

JR: Yes, once differing schools of thought have taken their various directions they seem unable to meet. I'm wondering really whether our Institute will fragment in a similar way.

EF: I don't know. Michael felt that group analysis could be above these various schools and could incorporate them, as we have Jungian members, for instance, without any need for disagreement. That was his opinion.

JR: The method brings people together and holds them rather than...

EF: The split that has happened is between the Practice and the training and the scientific side, which I think is a pity.

JR: I'm wondering whether this is so much a splitting as a kind of specialisation, a branching off, that was necessary.

EF: Possibly, but we might have all been in one building nevertheless.

JR: Indeed, one of the regrets that I voice in Chapter 1, which is a view of the Practice, is that we don't have a library, we don't have a common room, and we don't have any facilities for viewing groups... in some ways it's too businesslike.

EF: There you see, at Daleham Gardens we have the facilities for viewing, we have a library.

JR: It would require a very large building.

EF: It would. We did at one time make a major application to fund a building. It has always been one of our regrets that our research applications just weren't successful, although we had been encouraged to make them. According to Michael, group analysis was too revolutionary – too dangerous. The Ford Foundation announced a really big sum of money to be given towards research in psychotherapy. It went to the Anna Freud Clinic; that was nice and safe.

EF: You're the youngest member of the Practice and yet they make you write the history.

JR: Well they didn't make me. What happened was when the idea of the book came about Malcolm and I seemed the most interested and the most likely to get on with it. I can see the paradox in this.

EF: Well, historians have to look back at documents and make interviews and things like that, they don't generally write from their own experience. You're probably more detached in a way.

JR: Obviously I come to it with some *naïveté*.

EF: You're not finding it easy to keep the Practice separate from the other parts of group analysis.

JR: They intertwine...separate threads in the same piece of yarn.

EF: And the same people, you see.

JR: I wonder if there's anything else you think I ought to know about any of the personal ties. Let us talk about Jim Home, and obviously Pat has been a pillar of the whole development.

EF: As you say, he's had wonderful staying power. Pat was on the Committee of the Society longer I think even than I. James Anthony was in at the beginning, he went to the States and never came back. Wilfred Abse was in on the early discussions about having a group centre, then he went off to the States as well, so we've lost a few people like that.

JR: I think what one ends up with, which is why I hope to publish the original dialogue suitably edited, and this dialogue with yourself, plus some bracketing or framing material by myself, is a multidimensional picture. I believe that to a certain extent the interpretation of history has to be partly done by the reader.

EF: Yes, but I'm afraid our conversation seems to have been a bit fragmented, we've been dashing around a bit here and there.

JR: You can blame me for that, maybe.

EF: No I'm sure it's just the way things develop. If I think of the sequence, it's really going back to what I said before, the idea of a group centre, then Michael looking for new premises and taking the plunge and taking a consulting flat which had the space to expand a bit....

JR: That was a big leap....

EF: That was quite a big leap and he started having meetings there, the Society had regular meetings, every Monday evening there was something on, various kinds of seminars. Some of the people who came then went into psychoanalysis and therefore were lost to group analysis for a while. Some came back, some didn't come back. Michael didn't like people to be in group analysis and psychoanalysis at the same time, certainly not if they were in a training analysis. We had lively meetings always, from the beginning, with 20 to 30-plus people at our meetings.

JR: I get a sense that you're still a bit cross with us really!

EF: I? Why should I be cross?

JR: With the Practice... I don't know, because of the split between the Practice and...

EF: No. 'Sad' perhaps would be the word, but not cross. I think it's a pity because if it were all in one big building with a library for everybody and a common room I think it...

JR: it would provide the very academic and stimulating environment that I miss at the moment.

EF: Yes, sometimes the most important conversations take place in the little kitchen at 88....

JR: I know, isn't it a horrible venue for meetings? [4]

EF: Or at Daleham Gardens in the office, with three people trying to work and the telephone and God knows what, people start having these quite important little conversations. There really should be a proper space for that.

JR: Well, maybe just between you and me and maybe it will sneak into the book, I would actually quite like to see us housed in a bigger, perhaps less worrying building than Montagu Mansions. We are going through enormous increases in service charges... but there's one other question – Michael's curtains.

EF: You mean his Persian ones. We went to Liberty's to buy some curtains. Michael didn't have his glasses on and he didn't really look at the detail of the design, he just liked the colours and general effect. He had no idea that it contained these rather ghoulish scenes. I was quite surprised that Robin took them over later, when he bought some of Michael's consulting-room furniture. I think he was first in what had been Michael's room which is now Malcolm's, and later Robin went into the large room which was originally just a group room and waiting room.

Detail of S.H. Foulkes' curtains

B. A dialogue between Jeff Roberts, Malcolm Pines, Robin Skynner and Patrick de Maré, 15 October 1989

JR: I'm interested in the crucial transitions, like when Foulkes first sowed the seed of the Practice.

MP: Well he started in private practice straight after the war. [See dialogue with E.T. Foulkes.]

JR: So Foulkes came out of the army and straight into premises in London?

RS: Well he went to the Maudsley, didn't he?

MP: No, Barts – he was chief assistant at Barts first, and went to the Maudsley later. He was under E.B. Strauss at Barts. When he wrote his first book he was still at Barts [Foulkes, 1948]....I remember his being at Upper Wimpole Street, where I used to go for analysis.

JR: That was your training analysis?

MP: Yes.

JR: Did he become a Training Analyst with the London Institute of Psychoanalysis before or after the war?

MP: After. He came to England in 1933. Before the war he worked only in London, while also studying for a British medical qualification, and gaining the membership of the British Psycho-Analytical society. I know he said he sat in a lot with Ernest Jones, and said he and Jones

39

got on very well. He gave his paper on introjection to the Psycho-Analytical Society in about 1936, 1937, which was a good paper (Foulkes, 1937), then in 1939 he went to Exeter and was employed by a general psychiatrist in a big psychiatric practice. That's when he first started working with groups: he was down in Exeter away from London, and could do what he wanted to. He worked with Eve Lewis, a psychologist with whom he wrote his first paper on group analysis [Foulkes and Lewis, 1944].

RS: We were talking earlier about the Members who were working with Foulkes – were we all working with him at that time.

MP: I can't remember actually doing groups at Upper Wimpole Street.... [He did – E.T. Foulkes]

RS: I don't remember you doing them....

MP: No, I think you got in early because I was in analysis with him, so naturally it took time before I could begin to collaborate.

RS: I had my main group analysis with him after I started in the practice. He invited me to join him when James Anthony left to take a professorship in St Louis. I went to Foulkes at the Maudsley, plucking up my courage, thinking I would ask him if he would consider me if ever he had a vacancy at his practice. I thought this was the most outrageous thing to ask, but I thought if you don't ask you can't receive. I got there and he said, 'Oh just the chap I wanted to see, Skynner, I wanted to ask you if you would join me in my Practice.' So I joined him ... when I was still a senior registrar at Brixton Child Guidance Clinic, that would be 1958. Who else was there as well? I don't know because we never met each other....

MP: So you were the first one to join the Practice after James and Pat.... And do you think it was you who took the initiative to get us together to make a wider practice and get separate premises?

RS: Well I think it was, it was in my mind for at least a year before. Other people may have had the idea and been planning at the same time, but certainly I was thinking about it long in advance of actually doing it and wanted to do it in a way which was beneficial to all of us, including Foulkes, of course, and myself. We were in our separate premises in 66 Montagu Mansions by the autumn of 1960. We were very much a band of brothers, through our connection with the Maudsley.

MP: What would be interesting to remember is how we got the financial structure, the idea for levies. I remember Foulkes telling us about making the monthly payments, dividing the annual fee..., that's what he said he had eventually decided to do, so he didn't have to argue with people about missed sessions, it was a flat fee. I remember that, that was a big release for us as to how to set up the fee arrangement. But how we got the idea of running the Practice with a levy system to support the administration and share charges....

RS: It worked so well.

JR: You had moved to 66 Montagu Mansions by October 1960 and presumably had many meetings to plan this new arrangement.

RS: We met over about a year, with occasional meetings which were mostly held at the flat I had in Belsize Park Gardens.

JR: Foulkes wasn't entirely on board with this?

MP: No he didn't come to those meetings. This was to enlarge the Practice and I don't think there was any question at that time that he would move from Upper Wimpole Street.

RS: The young lions, as it were, wanting to have an organisation in which we could all have more say and could all be more equal, which could develop freely, where we wouldn't feel under the rule of Foulkes.... So it was a kind of benign palace revolution. Pat [de Maré] always appeared terribly unhappy about the whole thing. He was worried that we were going to do something against Foulkes or that he was going to be seen as someone who was plotting against him, as in a sense we were doing. We were plotting, but in a way which was certainly not hostile to him, we wanted to include him, but include him as a senior respected member, rather than as ruler, and master.

MP: He took this in a benign way too, didn't he. He grumbled slightly, but never stood in our way. He might point out objections but was never obstructive.

JR: He would have been about 60 at the time? [5]

RS: He died in 1976 and I think he was 77. He must have been born at the turn of the century – he must have been 60.

JR: And you were calling yourself the Group-Analytic Practice at this point?

RS: I think we did have long discussions over that, should we have a hyphen in it? He had the Group-Analytic Society and talked about the Practice, his Practice, whereas the change of name was important and something that we all owned, as it were, Foulkes included, but we all owned it as well.

JR: From 1960? Who was there in 66 Montagu Mansions?

RS: Malcolm and myself....

MP: Jim Home, Pat de Maré, Ronald Casson.

RS: I think that was it.

MP: We were all part-time with our rooms and I always remember that Ronnie Laing used to use my room in the evenings at one time, when he started in private practice, he and Esterson came along and used my room in the evenings.

RS: I met him in the early sixties on a Saturday morning – those were days when we all used to wear suits and ties... and here was this chap with an open-necked shirt looking rather scruffy and I thought he was a...

MP: A Glaswegian toughie.... I'm trying to remember if anybody else used our rooms part-time. We used to hire the rooms out. And we all put up that bit of capital, £100, I suppose we had to buy the lease, didn't we?

RS: That was how much we needed. We didn't pay more – I know – it seemed an enormous outlay and a great risk to raise this £100 which I borrowed from the bank....

MP: It would be the equivalent of over £1,000 now.

JR: Was it the same pattern of once-weekly and twice-weekly groups going on at that time?

RS: No, I started the first twice-weekly group – Foulkes hadn't done one. But in about '62 I decided to join one of Foulkes' therapy groups and stayed four years. During my time in this group I began doing a twice-weekly group. So I was in this group with Foulkes and had the unpleasant experience that the group I was conducting was moving me along faster than could be processed in Foulkes' therapy group. Up to that point he had combined, combined seeing people in a once-weekly group with seeing them in rotation, one each week individually, which was a very helpful thing.... I said to him I couldn't cope unless I got more therapy than I was having, and if the group didn't become twice-weekly I would have to leave. So in effect I forced him to make it twice-weekly. It was a measure of Foulkes' flexibility and openness that it was possible then to have therapy with him after our revolution and also all the struggles over money – none of that mattered to him.

MP: It was an open system with lots of feedbacks, the experiences feeding back into changing methods of practice.

RS: You went into a group, didn't you, much later?

MP: Yes, much later, I'd never been in a group for group analysis myself; later on we had this group in which he died.

RS: So that's how the twice-weekly groups started, and we all quickly appreciated their advantages and we moved towards running more of them.

JR: It's clear to me that the twice-weekly group is qualitatively as well as quantitatively different – in the last chapter I point out that it is anomalous that few if any of us could actually have had supervision in the conducting of a twice-weekly group. The Institute still trains people to conduct once-weekly groups, whereas the real analytic experience I think is in the twice-weekly groups. I think the Institute may have to give some attention to that because I don't think one should really become a Training Analyst without having had supervision and learning....

MP: Although I have great attachment to the once-weekly groups, I think they do enormously well....

JR: I agree.

RS: Also I feel that if you learn to do a once-weekly group, it's like going to a public school; if you can cope with that you can cope with anything.

JR: I suspect that there might be a need for some supervisory experience and actually clearer evaluation of the differences between the two by the Institute....

MP: Let's talk about Pat; what initiatives did Pat introduce, what was his goal in the Practice, what was special about Pat in the Practice?

RS: Well, what was special about him was that he took on extremely difficult character disorders, borderline psychotics, that no one wanted to deal with or had the patience to deal with in the same way. He worked with them over very long periods of time, say ten, fifteen years, and he did extraordinarily well with them.

MP: It's important to remember that he was the consultant psychotherapist at St George's, where he was very attached to the Friday evening social club, that went on for years and many people got their first experience of being in a therapeutic system by going to this. He had a belief in the very long-term effect of a group climate and he brought that atmosphere to the group Practice. Pat's groups were in a way almost an extension of the club, whereas others of us were used to a disciplined framework, you [RS] with family work, me [MP] with analysis, and we didn't have that sense of the emerging social framework, in the way that he did.

RS: I think he had a very important effect on us all. We were often arguing and quarrelling with him and he used to make me furious. None the less, he had a very good effect in showing us that you could work with very loose boundaries in a way that made it possible to include people whose boundaries were very shaky and to hold them while their boundaries were gradually forming. I remember one woman, I used to watch her coming down the street I didn't know anything about her except that she looked extraordinary; but I watched this woman over about ten years and she began to dress colourfully and enjoy herself. I think he taught us all that people we often felt were hopeless were not hopeless and that time was very important.

MP: He gave us an alternative framework to the psychoanalytic one because he always emphasised something different, he was gradually evolving his ideas towards the large group, citizenship and things of that sort.

RS: His other big contribution didn't apply to the Practice so much. He is the champion of the Large Group....

MP: The Large Group on the Introductory Course was important for us all, wasn't it?

JR: To learn politics?

RS: Not only to learn politics. We actually became very close and able to work together in a way that I think few other people I've seen can, in that even if we were all disagreeing about certain things, we could immediately get together to collaborate on some common object.... Indeed, one thing which brought us closer together and made us very much a band of brothers was working together in the large group on the General Course. In fact I planned this in 1963 and it started in 1964. It began as a course for the Association of Psychiatric Social Workers – a group which unsuccessfully approached all kinds of organisations including the Group-Analytic Society, to arrange a course in group therapy for their members. The second time they came I was on the committee of the Society. I wanted to start a course to train my own social workers in group work, so I planned a course with them, initially for eight social workers – the kind of course I wanted to see running for mental health professionals generally. The committee of the Society was all for it.

MP: I was going to say two things. One is, of course, this increased the Practice because we began to get referrals through this and people came in at the end of the course wanting therapy.

JR: What we're coming towards now is the development of the Institute and presumably the Qualifying Course?

MP: That took a number of years. The Introductory Course became a great success with the number of applicants increasing dramatically over a five-year period. It was only a one year course and we had people coming back and asking for more. We then ran what we called an Advanced Course, which was selected topics with supervision. Then after at least another five years, we decided that we would take the next step and develop a proper training.

RS: Jim Home was very strongly wanting this. We all wanted it, but nevertheless Jim stepped forward. He'd been in the background before, but he'd developed a lot and took a leading part in developing the Qualifying Course.

JR: Jim Home? He seemed at times to be the most thoughtful of us all, the most academic.

MP: Jim had been a colonial civil servant, he was in the Sudan, wasn't he? That was his background.

JR: Prior to going into analysis, with the middle group.

MP: Yes.

JR: How did he come to group analysis? He was a psychologist as well, wasn't he?

MP: No, he was very interested in philosophy and I think his original degree was probably in Classics, or English. He was religious, and had a very deep interest in theology. How did he come to group analysis? I think he was interested in the ideas of group analysis because his opposition to psychoanalytic theory of the older type was very strong. He wrote a paper called 'The Concept of Mind', which is really a turning point in a lot of psychoanalytic theory, in which he questioned the psychoanalytic approach to the mind. Do you know that paper? You find it referred to time and time again; it was written in 1966 I think [Home, 1966], it's quite a famous paper.

Pat de Maré enters.

MP: We can go back to the early days now, Pat.

PdM: Michael: well of course the first time I met him was when he was at Northfield, with Martin James.... It's all a bit hazy now I'm afraid. I was there on three occasions. I think once was with Rickman and Bion, that's all been written up [Bion, 1958]. There's no point really in writing books because people never read them. There's no question a few diagrams are better.

MP: But I think the really interesting thing for us would be when you started in the Practice; it wasn't called the Group-Analytic Practice to start with, was it?

PdM: No: my situation was I first started with Foulkes and he had one group and I had half a group.... It was after the war. The interesting time for me was Northfield and I'll tell you what Foulkes did. He inspired – rushing around Northfield connecting the different groups of all kinds.

JR: That was his inter-group activity rather than...

PdM: He was very much inter-group, he was the Large Group really – no wonder he felt excited, I don't suppose he ever subsequently had the same excitement and that was generated throughout. I didn't like the look of him at all when I first saw him at Northfield. I thought, 'God, what's this?' Then I met him personally a week later or something up in his big consulting room and he said he was interested in the 'Rorschach test' and there were all sorts of colours on the desk, bright colours and it was a wonderful sunny day and it was kind of brilliant, you could sense an excitement and brilliance and that's really when I felt suddenly very drawn to him.

MP: But you stayed in contact.... How did you stay in contact and what did that lead to?

PdM: Well, we had a personal liking for each other and so we kept in touch. I don't know quite when it was I saw him again but we arranged to meet, I think it was probably at the Royal Medical Psychological Association. Then there were the Monday meetings, with people like Jane Abercrombie, she was often there, Elizabeth Foulkes was there.

JR: This was the embryo Group-Analytic Society?

PdM: It must have been. He clearly had a vision of what it was going to be, but even he was surprised by the strength with which it took off, so then he had the Monday meetings and that was at 22 Upper Wimpole Street and I suppose that must have been the first time I met Jim and then anyone who was into groups at that time.

JR: In fact these Monday meetings are the ones that have continued to happen under the name of the Society, as the Monday scientific meeting...

MP: The analysts had Wednesday...

PdM: That's where I first saw you at a Monday meeting and I thought, 'Ah, there's trouble for me.' You were one of these people who always smiles and I'd get frightened of that. You were very confident.

MP: We were trying to remember how we got the idea of enlarging the Practice, Pat.

PdM: Well I didn't know much about what was going on really because you and Robin, I thought you were Maudsley people who thought it was a good idea to start a private practice.

MP: But you were already in a private practice.

PdM: Ah yes, but that was quite separate, it was my own private practice and then a half-group with Foulkes.

MP: What do you mean a half-group?

PdM: Well, we couldn't get people. He had a full group, about seven at the most and I had a group that fluctuated between three and four.... Well, we went on with it, both of us, it took courage.

MP: Pat, what about Harold Kaye, when did Harold come, what's the story of his coming to England and working with Michael?

PdM: He was a businessman in America and was very wealthy, and he had heart attack and his wife died, so he wanted to change his life. Then he got interested in psychotherapy for some reason... and he came to England and approached Foulkes.

MP: Did he come to England because of that?

PdM: Yes, he deliberately came to meet Foulkes and I remember early on he was quite friendly with me to begin with but not subsequently.

MP: He was a co-therapist with Foulkes, wasn't he, they ran a group together? He may have been an observer to begin with, then a co-therapist, that's where he got his background from, then I suppose we invited him to join the Practice; he may even have proposed himself.

RS: I can't remember where the proposal came from or who proposed him. It didn't come from one of us, did it?

MP: No, from Foulkes I think.

RS: Then we met him and we agreed, I think.

MP: In fact he was very useful, he was vigorous.

RS: We thought he'd bring all this money into the Practice, or at least some financial expertise. This side of it didn't work out.

MP: He always had his calculator with him and he was always wrong.

RS: He could make money for himself but with us his financial ideas never worked.

PdM: He would be writing in all the meetings.... He said conducting groups was easy as falling off a wall, being an entrepreneur.

MP: Pat, Jim had been a colonial civil servant, hadn't he?

JR: He always came across as a gentleman.

RS: He was. And he brought something of those attitudes.

JR: So that's Ronald and Jim and Harold. Lionel must be on the horizon somewhere by now?

MP: Well, you introduced Lionel, didn't you [PdM]? Working together at Halliwick, that's the way Lionel came in. Wasn't it through you?

PdM: Yes, of course it was.

MP: The other thing I can't remember Pat, is how did we begin to have Associates, and can you remember who were our first Associates, why we didn't do it all ourselves?

PdM: I know Ken Nuttall – he had done private work as a GP and he didn't realise that we weren't just in this for the scientific interest – you had to be fairly active in keeping your group going, nurturing it, cultivating it, feeding it, making sure it wanted to go on. This was clearly good for the group but it carried financial benefits for the conductor as well.

MP: And in the same way we had Sandy Bourne for a little while. And then Roger's been with us a long time. Was he with you at George's?

PdM: No...

MP: Because everybody else we've got has come through the Institute, I think.

JR: As people who have qualified....

MP: Yes, except Gerald Wooster, that was a different way. And then Dennis, I knew Dennis from the Cassel so that's comparatively later.

JR: And Colin later still?

MP: Yes....

RS: Meg came from the Institute didn't she?

MP: We knew Meg through the Institute, she had been Co-ordinator of Training, that's why we knew her so well.

RS: And we wanted a woman in the Practice.

MP: Joe Swift was one of our Associates for a long time.

RS: I'm not sure if he wasn't the first, or one of the first.... I was the Clinical Secretary for the first five years. We wouldn't accept a fixed Chairman for the first five years. We rotated monthly. Having escaped from a what at times had felt like a dictatorship we were very sensitive about anyone being the boss, or in charge. We had a Treasurer: Ronald Casson. And as I say, I did the Clinical Secretary job for five years and then after that I was Chairman.

JR: In our final chapter, Malcolm, in which we write how to set up a similar practice, I consider the significance of the twice-weekly group. I was also thinking of various permutations of groups. For instance, why don't we reconsider having twice-weekly groups combined with a large group, things like that? If we had had large enough premises I think we could have made more use of larger or median groups.

MP: Well, we often talked about having large groups and Pat of course would always have liked that. The other thing that I once tried to get us to do was to establish a therapeutic day hospital. I'd visited one in New York and Iannis Tsegos does it now in Athens, but we were just daunted by the task.

PdM: Well, what I would like, of course, would be if the Practice took the large group seriously and had it as therapeutic option, that I would love, then I think it would take off. I would think very much that people who are terminating their therapy in small groups could be offered the large group as a kind of progression.

JR: I would like to hear a little more about Foulkes. I have heard a great deal about his inspirational quality, and would like to hear some more about his character. I've become aware this afternoon that he was not so directly involved in setting up the Institute, setting up the Qualifying Course or setting up the Practice, as I had believed, though I have heard from you of the way in which he allowed it to happen.

RS: Yes, that's the point. All these things happened to some extent independently, rather as a result of the way he led. He appeared to say little in groups. When you got in therapy with him he hardly said anything. But of course tremendous things happened in the group and he was a kind of enabler who brought the best out of all the people who gathered round him, so to say these things happened independently of him isn't quite true; they happened very much as a result of our all being inspired by him.

MP: I think the person who best described his style is James Anthony in a paper in *The Evolution of Group Analysis* [Anthony, 1983], who said talking with Foulkes is 'like watching a fish swimming under the water, you'd catch a glimpse of it every now and then it would disappear and come back again', there's always some sense of depth and elusiveness and you couldn't quite catch what it was all about, and then suddenly you'd see it and then you'd lose it again, and he was very much a monologuist, wasn't he? If you sat with him it was a monologue while he went through his own ideas.

PdM: 13 hours.

MP: You once sat for 13 hours while he...

PdM: No I'm joking, but it was many hours.

MP: Yes, same with me. He'd ring me up occasionally and say are you doing anything today I'd like to talk to you, or let's have a talk. I'd go there and have no idea what it was about or what for and I only wish that I could remember those conversations, but they go through your mind, you can't hold them.

RS: They were stimulating, they left you thinking, didn't they? It was always a pleasure to talk to him on his own or in a very small group.

JR: There's a paradox here in that we're talking about somebody who seemed to be thinking rather on his own and yet who pointed out that mind and thought was a group phenomenon.

RS: It makes sense doesn't it? That's what you expect of people who can't do something. I'm sure we take these things up because we can't do them, because we're not very good at them, we want to learn more.

JR: But out of his way of doing groups comes this notion of ego training in action, whereby people are encouraged to be active and not passive. He obviously had a special talent for it because I must say my groups need more from me than Foulkes would give to his groups. I wish I knew how to be facilitatory in the way that he was.

RS: But I think his groups needed more from him also, I think our frustration was justified because part of his limited involvement with the group was his reluctance to take any kind of position and to confront someone when they should be confronted. There are times when someone holds the whole group up... and I thing confrontation is then necessary.

MP: I saw him do that in the group that I was in....

RS: Well, he did it with me, come to think of it, quite a lot! He certainly confronted me in no uncertain terms and that was almost the most valuable thing I got from it, I didn't get away with it.

MP: I think that he often got lost in his own thoughts, you know, he was spinning away....

PdM: He used you in order to think... like a spindle, and I think that it was nice to see him thinking. Sometimes he would lean forward and you would think, what's he looking at? But it was a thought inside his head, he wasn't looking at you....

MP: And you could never get away in less than two or three hours, it was never a question of dropping in for a quick chat.

RS: Also I didn't want to get away, I was very captivated and interested. He used to enjoy my side of the conversation. Although he did most of the talking, nevertheless I talked as well and I felt I was engaged with him and he was enjoying talking to me. There are two other things: I thought he was very confused, his thought was really confused. Partly that was why he was original. The two things went together because he wasn't a clear thinker and couldn't put things very clearly. The second thing was that he was an extraordinarily nice person in the sense that he was a good man, he was warm and very positive in the sense we've described, even though he would resist your moving away from his ideas or struggling with him; when you did so he would always come half way to meet you or accommodate to some degree.

JR: Did he have any real children?

RS: Oh yes, three. One, a daughter lives in Mexico. She trained with the Mexico City Institute of Family Therapy. I asked her once why he had this extraordinary effect on so many people, whether she'd ever noticed anything that would explain it because we couldn't, and she said, 'Well, no, the only thing I can say is that when I was with him I laughed a lot.' And I thought that was absolutely fundamental because you got an enjoyable chuckly feeling from conversations with him, he was in a good humour most of the time. He was happy and I think in many ways a very normal and healthy person, and he had a very healthy kind of family life as far as one could see, in a conventional sort of way. I felt vastly the better for knowing and being influenced by him. You should read my 'Foulkes Lecture' (Skynner, 1984) – there's a lot in there about him, it's all about him. One other thing about Foulkes, come and look at his curtains.

JR: In your room?

RS: The colour's beautiful, but look at the detail! [See Plates I and II]. When I was in Foulkes' group he used to say, 'I don't understand why you've got to be so violent, Skynner, I don't think it's necessary to be violent, I'm not the slightest bit violent, I can't see why people are violent.' But have a look at those curtains!

PdM: The other thing he said that we've all read is a good chairman leads from behind his group.

MP: I came across a profile of Kurt Goldstein and I think there's so much of Foulkes that he took from Goldstein. When Goldstein was examining a patient, the patient was the expert whom he was learning from and the atmosphere of the head injury clinic in Frankfurt was like a therapeutic community. [Foulkes, 1936]

C. Short biographical notes on former Members of the Practice[6]

James Anthony, Foulkes' co-author of the Penguin *Introduction to Group-Analytic Psychotherapy*, is a psychoanalyst, trained in London, where he began an eminent career as a child analyst and child psychiatrist. He studied child development under Piaget, and after leaving the Maudsley Hospital, occupied a chair in Child Psychiatry at St Louis, Missouri. He is the author of many papers on group analysis, psychoanalysis and child psychiatry. His collaboration with S.H. Foulkes, who became his training analyst, began at Northfield Military Hospital. At present he is Director of Psychotherapy at Chestnut Lodge, where he is developing a programme of group psychotherapy for adolescent inpatients.

F.R.C. (Ronald) Casson joined the Group-Analytic Practice through his connection with P. B. de Maré, with whom he worked at Northfield

Military Hospital. This was where he first encountered Foulkes and the group-analytic approach. After the war he joined one of S.H. Foulkes' groups and subsequently became a Full Member of the Practice. He had a particular interest in addictive behaviour, and was a consultant to Gamblers Anonymous. He died in 1974.

Sigmund Heinrich Fuchs was born in 1898 in Karlsruhe. He qualified in medicine in Frankfurt in 1923, which he continued to use as a base until emigrating to England in 1933. Here he spent two years studying with Kurt Goldstein, before taking his wife and two children to Vienna where he undertook a psychoanalytic training. His analyst was Helen Deutsch.

With his wife Erna[7] and by now three children, he came to England in 1933. He then set about obtaining a British medical qualification and membership of the British Psycho-Analytical Society.

In 1939 Foulkes moved to Exeter, where he became a psychotherapist in a large psychiatric practice. It was here that he conducted his first group-analytic group (Foulkes and Lewis, 1944). He was called-up to the army and posted to the Military Neurosis Centre at Northfield near Birmingham in 1942 and here took part in developing a whole range of innovative treatments, many of them group based and, in fact, pioneering both group-analytic and therapeutic community methods.

After the war he quickly started to conduct group-analytic groups in private practice and obtained an appointment at St Bartholomew's Hospital, where he worked until his retirement in 1963. From this time he continued to work in private practice and right up to his death he was a great inspiration to colleagues. He died suddenly from a coronary thrombosis in 1976, aged 77, while conducting a seminar.

Henry James Hamilton Home, MA (Oxon); Member International Psychoanalytic Association; Member British Psycho-Analytical Society; Member Institute of Group-Analysis He was born in 1913 and was educated at Cheltenham and Balliol, where he read PPE. He served throughout the war in the Lothian and Border Horse. He spent several years teaching in the Sudan. On his return to the United Kingdom he started psychoanalytic training in Edinburgh, transferring from there to London for a Freudian training with the Institute of Psycho-Analysis.

While practising privately, he also joined with Dr S.H. Foulkes and others in the exploration and application of the then novel idea of group analysis, to which he increasingly devoted his time and interest.

In the mid-sixties he ruffled the feathers of many orthodox Freudian psychoanalysts with the presentation of what became a classic paper, 'The Concept of Mind' (Home, 1963). He was an early member of the Group-Analytic Society and a founder member later of the Institute of Group-Analysis, becoming Training Secretary when the Institute inaugurated a Qualifying Course for group analysts. He also organised the first of the annual London January Workshops. In response to the needs for training in group work elsewhere in Europe he travelled abroad frequently, and he developed a particular interest in working in Yugoslavia.

Elected President of the Group-Analytic Society in 1978, in 1979 he suffered a stroke which eventually led to his semi-retirement. He died in 1986.

D. Colin James, M. Phil, MB, ChB, FRCPEd, FRCPsych., Member of the British Psycho-Analytical Association, Member of the Institute of Group-Analysis. Having qualified in Medicine at Birmingham, I studied postgraduate Medicine and Neurology in the Midlands, gaining my membership of the Royal College of Physicians of Edinburgh in Neurology, subsequently gaining my fellowship. I started to train in Psychiatry at the Maudsley Hospital in 1966, and continued research work in Electroencephalography and Evoked Potentials. While at the Maudsley I became interested in psychotherapy under the influence of Henri Rey, Heinz Wolff and Willie McIntyre. I commenced my training at the Institute of Psycho-Analysis in 1967 and qualified in 1971. In that same year I was appointed Consultant Psychotherapist at the London Hospital. Soon after that I was invited to join the Group-Analytic Practice as an Associate Member. I subsequently moved to the Maudsley Hospital as a Consultant Psychotherapist in 1977 and soon after that became a Full Member of the Group-Analytic Practice and was subsequently elected to membership of the Institute of Group-Analysis.

I have been a long-standing member of the Group-Analytic Society Committee and its Secretary for five years as well as Co-chairman of the European Working Party, which became the European Sub-committee.

In 1983 I was appointed Consultant Psychotherapist to the Tavistock Clinic and worked in the Adult Department until 1988. I helped here to re-establish a group therapy service.

In 1988 I was appointed Consultant Psychotherapist at Addenbrooke's Hospital, Cambridge, in the Department of Psychotherapy. Since moving I have re-established my psychoanalytic practice and hope shortly to re-start a practice in group analysis.

Latterly I have become interested in integrating the concepts gained from experiences under the auspices of the Tavistock Institute of Human Relations at the Leicester Conferences, and my group experience has made me interested in the manner in which organisations function. I agree with Elliot Jaques that we do not know how to organise nor function in institutions, yet many of us spend our working lives in them.

Harold Kaye was born in the United States and pursued a successful commercial career before embarking on a second career as psychologist and psychotherapist. He came to England to train as an analytical psychologist and, at the same time, as a group analyst with S.H. Foulkes. An energetic and enthusiastic man, his sudden death at the age of 60 was a grievous loss, as he had contributed considerably during a period of rapid expansion of the Practice. He was a notable connoisseur of modern sculpture and painting.

Patrick de Maré, who is of Swedish origin, was born in 1916 and educated at Wellington School, Cambridge and St George's Hospital, London. He graduated in medicine in 1941 and joined the RAMC in 1942. He trained as an army psychiatrist under Rickman and Bion at Northfield Hospital. He worked as head of a recuperation centre during the European campaign and later returned to Northfield to join S.H. Foulkes and Tom Main in the second 'Northfield Experiment'.

After the war he was to become a Consultant Psychotherapist at St George's Hospital and in 1952, together with S.H. Foulkes, he founded the Group-Analytic Society. He was one of Foulkes' earliest clinical collaborators and worked in the Group-Analytic Practice until 1987. He also worked with Lionel Kreeger and Silvio Benaim in Halliwick Hospital's ephemeral therapeutic community.

In 1975 he started a large group under the auspices of the Institute of Group-Analysis, in which Robin Piper joined him in 1976. This large group, which was established with initially some 20 members, still operates a median group. In 1984 he launched a weekly seminar on large groups, which in 1986, became part of a recognised large group section of the Group-Analytic Society.

D. Chronological table of important events in the history of the Practice

1933 S.H. Foulkes arrives in London.
1940 Foulkes starts his first group in Exeter (Foulkes, 1948: 39).
1942–46. Foulkes at Northfield, meets James Anthony, Patrick de Maré, Martin James and others.
1946 Foulkes in private practice at 58 Portland Place.
1950 Foulkes appointed to staff of Maudsley Hospital.
1951 Foulkes moves to 22 Upper Wimpole Street. This he saw as a 'pilot group centre'.
1952 3 June. Inaugural meeting of the Group-Analytic Society.
1958 Robin Skynner joins with S.H. Foulkes in his practice.
1960 Aug.–Sept. The 'Young Lions' move to 66 Montagu Mansions, with a formal adoption of the epithet 'Group-Analytic Practice'.
1964 First year of the 'General Course in Group Work'.

1964 First 2xw group, started by Robin Skynner.
1966 Move to 88 Montagu Mansions.
1971 Inception of the Institute of Group-Analysis.
1971 First batch of Qualifying Course students start course.
1974 First batch of Q.C. students qualify.
1973–83. Period of overlap of premises, with Institute of Group-Analysis at 1 Bickenhall Mansions.
1976 S.H. Foulkes dies.
1983 Institute of Group-Analysis and Group-Analytic Society move to 1 Daleham Gardens.

Notes

1 In a recently published book of the selected papers of S.H. Foulkes, Elizabeth Foulkes (Foulkes, E. T., 1990) has produced a short but scholarly biography of S.H. Foulkes, which can be profitably read as a background to the contents of this chapter. The same book also contains the paper by Foulkes on introjection referred to in this chapter and not previously readily available. Furthermore, there is a chapter in which Foulkes (1936) describes his work with Goldstein, to which Malcolm Pines alludes in the final passage of the second dialogue.
2 S.H. Foulkes was known by those who were close to him as Michael.
3 This simple statement appears to me to sum up a remarkable and perhaps healing coincidence (Ed.).
4 The dimensions of the kitchen at the Practice are approximately 5 ft 6 ins by 4 ft.
5 He was born in 1898 (Ed.).
6 Not including former Associate Members.
7 Foulkes was married three times. His first marriage to Erna Stavenhagen ended in divorce in 1937. His second marriage was to Kilmeny Graham who died in New York in 1959. His third wife was Elizabeth Marx to whom he was married for the last 16 years of his life. All his three children came of his first marriage.

Chapter 4

Assessment and selection for groups

Dennis Brown

The initial consultation is a crucial meeting. It usually decides a person's suitability for group-analytic psychotherapy. Both patient and consultant assess the nature and significance of the presenting problems and their background. Both need to agree on the appropriateness of group analysis in the Practice as a way through them. This is a complex process and I shall therefore describe it in eight more or less consecutive stages:

1 Preparation for the consultation;
2 The nature of the assessment;
3 Selection of the most appropriate form of therapy;
4 Preparing the patient for a group;
5 The procedure for matching new members and the groups they join;
6 Management of the waiting list;
7 The limits of group analysis; and
8 Several important issues, such as contact with referrers, cover over holiday breaks, private health insurance, claims and illness of the conductor.

1 Preparation for the consultation

All medically qualified members of the Management Committee, currently six out of seven, see an average of one to three new referrals each week for consultation.[1] Patients are referred to these consultants personally or to the Group-Analytic Practice as a whole through the Clinical Secretary or Administrator. Probably because the Practice is seen to function as a team, personal requests are often made to 'you or a colleague'.

Patients are usually seen within two to three weeks of the referral, sometimes sooner if spaces become available – for example, through cancellation. We regard anything longer than this as unsatisfactory, and if too much of a waiting period develops, we make arrangements for more consultation spaces. When the appointments are sent to the patients they are requested to confirm that they will keep the appointment and a letter is sent to the referrers informing them. This enables the referrer to arrange to see the patient again before the appointment, should this be necessary, and to know when to expect to hear the outcome of the assessment.

Patients rarely fail to keep their appointments if, as requested, they confirm them. Such a failure is less likely if the waiting period for the consultation is not so great that they seek alternative help, or feel themselves to have improved spontaneously. Anxiety and misunderstanding about the referral, or poor motivation for self-exploration and radical change, are probably the main factors in failed attendances. It is perhaps not surprising that a failure to keep initial consultation appointments seems to be much rarer among self-referrals, particularly those resulting from the recommendation of an ex-patient or somebody currently in a group.

People referring themselves as well as new professional referrers are informed, when they phone, about the procedure, fees for consultations and therapy and, if appropriate, the nature of the Practice. (Sometimes enquiries are made by people in the belief that we are part of the National Health Service.) All patients are sent notes for guidance (see Figure 4.1) along with their appointment.

Figure 4.1 Notes for the guidance of patients referred for diagnostic assessment or treatment

---

Patients have occasionally attended for an initial consultation under the misapprehension that the diagnostic and treatment services available from the Group Analytic Practice or its members are part of the National Health Service. This note is therefore enclosed to ensure that patients referred are aware that the initial consultation for diagnostic assessment, and any treatment which may subsequently be recommended, are on a private fee-paying basis.

The purpose of the first consultation is to examine and clarify the nature of the problem, to give an opinion whether or not it can be helped by any of the forms of individual, group, marital or family therapy available within the Group-Analytic Practice and, if it does appear treatable, to discuss the various possibilities so that the patient can reach a decision either during the interview or at a later date after further consideration.

The cost of the different forms of treatment is of course fully explained at the initial consultation, but if you do require more information in advance, the Secretary will be pleased to provide it for you if you telephone. However, you may like to know that the normal fee for the initial consultation is £   (or £   in the case of a married couple seen together and £   for a family). This is payable whether or not further treatment is in fact advised or arranged, and it is also chargeable if the interview is cancelled too late for the time to be offered to another patient; PLEASE GIVE US AS MUCH NOTICE AS POSSIBLE IF YOU CANNOT COME.

2 The nature of the assessment

At this point I shall be drawing on my own methods and experience, which I believe are basically the same as those of my colleagues. What happens in the consulting room when an individual assessment is made is inevitably private. Having introduced myself to the patient in the waiting room, greeting him or her with a customary handshake, we go to my consulting room where we sit in identical chairs to emphasise the joint nature of the evaluation. This is the room in which I conduct both individual and group analysis, so it gives the patient an opportunity to assess me in the atmosphere in which I work, while I assess both the patient and his or her problems, and our interaction.

I explain that we have an hour or so in which to talk in order to gain a better understanding of the problems that led the patient to seek help; and that at the end of this time we should be able to decide on the best way of arranging it. Indicating that I would like to hear about the problems and also the patient's background and development, I leave it to them to tell the story in their own way and order. Few of us write any notes during the assessment interview, but we all use the same 'assessment form' (see Figure 4.2) in the writing-up of the assessment afterwards.

This provides an underlying structure to our collection of information in the consultation that facilitates efficient formulation by the consultant, and communication of this to the referrer, to colleagues at our weekly clinical intake meeting and to the therapist who eventually takes the patient on for treatment. It also frees us to attend to the details of the patient's story and also to how they tell it, to what they do not tell us spontaneously, to body signs and language, and to the interplay of communications between us. This includes transference and countertransference as they develop in the interview. It is important to discern whether and how the patient brings his or her problems into the consulting room through their relationship with the consultation procedure and ourselves.

However, direct questioning in some detail may be necessary in assessing the patient's response to any previous therapy, but particularly when there is a possibility that there is an underlying psychotic or organic condition. It might then be helpful to know about genetic loading, suicidal risk and so on. In such instances it is important to make a psychiatric diagnosis to facilitate communication with referrers, sometimes to ensure that the patient has psychiatric treatment in addition to or instead of psychotherapy.

For all types of psychotherapy my experience is that psychiatric diagnosis is less important than the patient's balance of strengths and weaknesses. The former include their motivation for insight and change, and their creativity. Of particular importance is their capacity to engage with another person to begin to understand themselves and their

Figure 4.2 Assessment form

PATIENT NO:

NAME_____GROUP WITH_____DAY_____TIME_____
   (Mr, Mrs, Miss, Ms, Dr)

                                           Home _____

ADDRESS_____Tel:
                                           Work _____

AGE   D.O.B.   OCCUPATION_____

Single/Married/Separated/Divorced/Widowed/Cohabiting
                          RELIGION_____NOM/DEV

INTELLIGENCE: Sup/Above Average/Average/Below Average
                          NATIONALITY _____

SOCIAL BACKGROUND: Upper Mid/Middle/Lower Middle/Working

EDUCATION:
University/Tech College/Public School/Grammar/Secondary/Comp/Primary

CAN ATTEND:
Morning Monday/Tuesday/Wednesday/Tursday/Friday/Saturday Not before _

Lunch   Monday/Tuesday/Wednesday/Tursday/Friday   Between_____

Evening Monday/Tuesday/Wednesday/Tursday/Friday   Not before___

REFERRED BY_____ON_____LETTER_____

INITIAL INTERVIEW WITH_____ON_____LETTER _____

PRESENTING SYMPTOMS

PERSONALITY AND INITIAL CONTACT

DYNAMIC FORMULATION

PREVIOUS TREATMENT

Motivation: Strong/Moderate/Fair/Poor

Capacity for Insight: Strong/Moderate/Fair/Poor

Personality Resources: Strong/Moderate/Fair/Poor

Agreed Fee_____Once/Twice Weekly_____Leaflet Yes/No

Figure 4.2   Assessment form *continued*

FAMILY HISTORY

RELEVANT INFORMATION

Next of Kin _____   G.P. _____

Address_____   Address _____

_____   _____

_____   _____

_____   _____

Began Group Treatment _____

Ended Group Treatment _____

Result: Recovered/Relieved/Not Improved/Deteriorated

Reason for Leaving_____

Letter to Referrer_____

relationships with others at greater depth without the danger of acting out or decompensation. The rule-of-thumb criteria I use for analytic as opposed to supportive or behavioural therapies are: (1) the patient's problems are understandable in psychological terms, (2) he has adequate motivation for insight and change, (3) has sufficient ego-strength and (4) the capacity to form and sustain relationships (Brown and Pedder, 1979). The history of even one good relationship can make a big difference in helping a person towards sufficient trust and toleration of frustration, especially in the short term.

A less tangible factor that can swing the balance towards long-term analytic therapy in doubtful cases is what (as a Yorkshireman) I can best call an element of 'grittiness' in the patient's personality. However chaotic or desperate he or she is, one senses a core of strength and determination in them that is very different from stubbornness. It is similar to what Rayner and Hahn (1964) called 'Positive Persistence', which (along with the capacity for self-appraisal and self-responsibility) they describe as a necessary characteristic for brief analytic psychotherapy. But what I am describing can be more covert, and may require much of the interviewer's intuition and countertransference to pick it up. In cases of doubt I prefer to base the decision on how best to treat someone on the psychodynamic formulation (see below) rather than on impersonal psychiatric classification. However, commonly accepted generalisations are useful as a warning against over-optimistic therapeutic zeal when dealing with particularly vulnerable patients – such as those with a strong personal or family history of psychotic illness, or evidence of a serious personality problem, be it borderline, narcissistic, hysterical or obsessional.

The well-known generalisation that phobic states are best treated by behavioural therapy has probably more to do with the patient's predominant defences in such states (for instance, externalisation) and their generally poor motivation for self-responsibility and insight. There are exceptions to this general rule which lead to some patients doing well with analytical psychotherapy, group or individual. Likewise, the fact that schizophrenics tend to do better with support and family intervention in the acute stages of the condition has, I believe, more to do with their ego-weakness, and if this can be restored with appropriate treatment, including medication and hospital care, some can later benefit from a more analytical and insight-orientated approach, especially in a group, albeit a gentle and supportive one.

The psychodynamic formulation is of greater importance to the patient than a psychiatric diagnosis; it is more meaningful and useful in furthering their self-understanding and less static and stigmatising in its implications. It is also more useful to the therapist who takes the patient on for treatment. It should reflect the developmental and relationship problems that the patient has had in his or her family of origin and/or current networks, taking into account the effect of trauma, developmental deficit and unconscious conflict. It should give us some idea of the degree and developmental level of the psychopathology, and the possible hazards of treatment as well as mitigating factors. These latter will include any good early experiences and relationships, any areas of achievement in which a sense of self-worth could be developed, and satisfying current relationships, creative work and hobbies.

Of special interest when assessing indications for group psychotherapy is an appraisal of the social birth of the person. Did it allow the person to feel safely at home in him- or herself and with others, without excessive reliance on defences that are too primitive or too prominent? Or was it so traumatic and conflict-laden that it led to severe distortions and restrictions of character, and thus failure to achieve and attain life's rewards. This appraisal includes an assessment of difficulties in relation not only to parents but also to siblings, including those who have died or never been conceived. These can often help us to understand problems in establishing peer groups and a sense of belonging that require a therapeutic group to resolve.

In assessing ego-strength and motivation for insight and change, we have to consider both the patient's hold on both external reality and their contact with their own inner selves. How they deal with stress, anxiety, frustration and loss are very important – including their experience in and finishing any previous therapy. How much can they bear without recourse to denial and splitting, dangerous loss of impulse control or self-destructive tendencies? Repeated risk-taking, resorting to addictive behaviour, or serious somatisation into major psychodynamic diseases can indicate the overrunning of their limits. A history of repeated dropping out of relationships and failing to complete ventures can be a bad augury for sticking at therapy.

The degree and extent of childhood amnesia is a valuable indicator of repression and restriction of personality, and soon becomes apparent when one enquires about childhood memories. I usually ask patients to tell me their very earliest memories, as these are often significant, and like recurrent early dreams and nightmares can be used in dynamic interviewing and formulation. The readiness to make contact with unconscious aspects of themselves can also be gauged by asking whether they remember their dreams now. Sometimes a dream the night before consultation can bring to life the patient's concerns and anxieties about meeting the consultant or entering therapy.

The interview should provide a taste of the psychotherapeutic approach, which includes an aliveness and readiness to discuss what goes on between patient and therapist. Patients have a right to learn something about themselves and their relationships from the interview. I always make a point of feeding back to patients the essence of my psychodynamic formulation of their problem, and the way in which psychotherapy might help if group therapy seems specifically indicated, and point out what particular advantages it would have. Their responses can prove crucial.

An important part of the assessment interview is the discussion of treatment options, including what is practicable and the patient's capacities, preferences, wishes and fears. This might well include discussing the patient's feelings about being referred on for treatment by someone other than the consultant.

3 Selection of the most appropriate form of therapy

S.H. Foulkes (1975: 65) held that group psychotherapy is indicated whenever psychotherapy is appropriate and that its range is broader than individual psychotherapy. This statement needs qualifying. If we consider the range of group methods, including activity groups and homogeneous groups, almost anyone can benefit from a group approach. But if we are thinking of group analysis – that is, long-term analytical group psychotherapy – we have to consider for each patient (1) their motivation, (2) the practicality of intense prolonged psychotherapy in a group, and (3) the indications for and against an analytical uncovering approach, as discussed earlier. It is not a cure-all. In acknowledgement of this, Robin Skynner and I wrote a clinical paper (Skynner and Brown 1981) that was designed to guide general practitioners, psychiatrists and other referrers in making a decision about what form of psychotherapy is likely to be helpful, and proposed a framework in which to consider this. We decided to reverse the historical and 'common-sense' order of individual, group and finally family therapy, the sequence in which the modalities of treatment have developed in the course of this century. (Skynner came to group analysis from a background of child psychiatry, working with children and their families, while I came from a background first in adult psychiatry and then in psychoanalysis.) We decided to put the family modality first to emphasise the value of taking a systems approach to emotional disturbance. We suggested that each approach – family, group and individual – had its own advantages.

Family therapy has the broadest spectrum of applicability, and the greatest economy in time. It enables us to influence others in the system than the presenting patient, who might not be either the sickest member of the family or the most treatable. As S.H. Foulkes (1975: 11) put it, we should consider the patient's intimate plexus in which disturbances arise, not just internalised childhood experiences, and treatment of this (family) plexus should, if possible, have priority over individual or group psychotherapy.

Group therapy has also a very broad spectrum and great economy in terms of therapists' time. It has a particular advantage for those with initially low self-understanding and psychological-mindedness, dependent people and those with uncertain identity and social difficulties. Foulkes (1975) also believed it not helpful to select patients in terms of diagnostic labels except in considering contra-indications – for example the very paranoid, acutely psychotic, severely depressed, suicidal or antisocial. Individual therapy has the particular advantage of flexibility. It allows the level and rate of therapy to be 'titrated' for each individual's need – for instance short-term counselling for those in a crisis – and also provides the undivided attention that those people with very severe early deprivation might require even to begin to trust and contact their 'true selves.' It is also useful for those needing prolonged preparation for either individual or group therapy. And of course it is essential for those who wish to work as psychoanalysts, as is group analysis for those who wish to work as group analysts.

Because we provide a special facility and expertise in group methods, most of our referrers will already have done some of the selection by referring to us patients for whom a group approach is particularly appropriate. However, there are a large number of patients who are referred for a general psychodynamic and psychotherapeutic assessment. Dr Skynner in particular gets a large number of referrals of couples and families because of his particular experience and renown. Others of us are more often referred individual patients for whom a series of consultations or individual analytical psychotherapy might be provided within the Practice, but more often through our wide-ranging network of therapists in London and elsewhere.

In the late 1970s Clarkin and Frances reviewed, on the basis of research and clinical consensus, the selection criteria for family evaluation and therapies, group therapies, brief psychotherapies, and finally no treatment. They give a good account of the indications for group psychotherapy gleaned from the research literature (Clarkin and Frances, 1982). As this accords well with our own clinical experience I will summarise these indications here:

1 Problems in interpersonal relationships;
2 Patients willing to share and be open with others;
3 The showing of excessive intellectualisation;
4 A danger of regressive transference, or
5 Intolerance of dyadic intimacy and the likelihood of producing harmful countertransference in individual therapists.

Likewise they give a list of contra-indications that also accords with our clinical sense and experience. These are:

1 Acute psychiatric emergencies;
2 Patients who are likely to respond to brief therapy,

3 Patients who are likely to refuse group therapy, or
4 Patients who would be destructive to the group process or be made worse by it. For example, they are too ill, too demanding, too dishonest, manipulative or explosive; to which I would add, they are too likely to be isolated and unpopular in a group.

It is usually possible to make a reliable judgement in one consultation lasting between an hour and an hour-and-a-half, but in a proportion of cases, particularly when motivation is uncertain and the degree and nature of the disturbance is problematic, a second consultation is called for within the next week or two, and there are even some cases where a decision can be postponed over a period of a few months, during which time the patient might be seen a few times to assess his or her progress and use of the dynamic consultations. Currently, only about one in three consultations lead to patients joining an analytic group – more when the referral was of an individual than of a couple or family. Recently there seems to have been an increase in highly disturbed or doubtfully motivated patients for whom a quick move into a group is not indicated without lengthy assessment, consideration of other options and gathering of information from previous professional carers, psychiatrists or psychotherapists.

To quote from a recent annual report to referrers:

In 1988 there were 437 consultations with individuals and families of whom 157 were taken on for ongoing group-analytic psychotherapy, once- or twice-weekly. Most join as individuals, but a proportion join couples' groups with their partners. Of those who did not join groups, some were taken on for individual analysis or psychotherapy within the Practice or, more frequently, placed with colleagues outside the Practice for this; some only wanted or needed a few further consultations, either individually or as a couple or family. Occasionally we recommended counselling, behavioural psychotherapy, relaxation techniques (e.g. Autogenic Training) or bodywork (e.g. Yoga, Alexander Technique) as an alternative or adjunct to a more exploratory analytic approach.[2]

At present we have 52 groups running, 29 once-weekly (5 are couples groups) and 23 twice-weekly. Most of the once-weekly groups are held in the evening or late afternoon, but we have one on Saturday morning. We recommend that patients join for at least a year, and most stay for two or three years, and aim for a general maturation of personality and improvement in relationships.

Most groups have a fairly wide age range, but we aim always to have at least one group specially catering for young people (usually 18 to mid-twenties), and at least one for older people (usually fifties and sixties). We are hoping to start a group shortly for people with psychosomatic problems and difficulties in expressing their feelings, and we are considering short-term groups (say, for one year) both for men and women who would like a single-sex group perhaps as a prelude to joining a mixed group.

If there are particular types of groups which you feel we could usefully provide, we shall be very interested to hear from you.

Prominent among those for whom group analysis is specially indicated are people who have had long periods of individual analytic treatment in the past. Even those who have gained much from intensive psychoanalysis can remain stuck in their development towards maturity in relation to others. The relationships in a group are closer than the psychoanalytic dyad to those in everyday life. Confrontation with the experiences, reactions and needs of others inevitably throws light on one's own. It develops our altruism and capacity to share, both to give and receive.

Figure 4.3 The nature of group-analytic psychotherapy: notes given to new group patients

Group-analytic psychotherapy

Joining a group for psychotherapy is in many ways a new experience and will involve your making certain arrangements. These notes are offered for your guidance.

Group sessions last one and a half hours. It is important for your own progress and for that of the Group that you attend regularly. Holidays should be arranged with this in mind.

The relationships in a psychotherapeutic group are exceptionally close and confidential and it has been found that meetings between members outside the session tend to retard progress. If you do chance to meet other members outside, it is best not to discuss Group matters and to mention it later in the Group.

Termination of treatment should be by agreement. You are asked to give one month's notice of termination.

If you have to be absent from the Group for any reason, it is helpful if you can inform the therapist in advance. If you have to be absent at short notice, you can telephone the secretary (071-935 3103).

The standard fee of £   per annum is payable at the rate of £
per month in advance. This fee is calculated to cover 40 sessions of treatment in any calendar year. If fewer sessions are provided the fee will be adjusted pro rata. For twice-weekly groups the fee would be £
per annum. (Fees are reviewed and may be adjusted from the start of each calendar year in the light of changes in the economic situation.)

Accounts will not normally be rendered for Group sessions but if you wish to have one you should ask your therapist.

4 Preparing the patient for a group

Preparation for a group can usually be done within the first consultation meeting, though it may require several consultations or even a period of individual therapy. During the initial consultation we give people a brief information sheet about the nature of group analysis (see Figure 4.3). Here the nature of the commitment and issues of confidentiality and fees are described. We also point out at this time that fees need to be adjusted each January in line with increased costs, more or less following the rate of inflation. We point out that at least a year's attendance in a group will be required and that most people will stay for two or three years.

Patients usually leave by agreement when they feel they have got what they want from the group, or progress has come to a 'plateau'. Although this is usually by mutual agreement, patients are free to leave when they wish but are asked to give at least a month's notice. This is very useful in the early stages when some people have difficulty in settling into the group, and might be tempted to make an impulsive and later-regretted withdrawal. It provides the patients and the group with a breathing space in which to question the nature of their anxiety and to rally their motivation.

It is often helpful for patients for whom we expect that entry into a group might be difficult, to discuss with them some of the dynamic issues that can reasonably be anticipated in joining a group. For the group itself there might be feelings about the replacement of a departed member, which might include relief as well as a sincere sense of loss, the resentment of which might be related to the revival of early experiences about new siblings arriving in a family. For the patient there will be inevitable anxieties, particularly for those who have difficulties joining and trusting groups, perhaps related to a disrupted childhood: so that entering the therapy group might stir up feelings originally experienced on starting at a new school: feelings of exclusion and exposure, loss of previous relationships and anxiety about and establishing new ones. We explain that they will be joining an already existing group, from which someone has recently left – a so-called 'slow-open' group. This may stir up feelings about replacing a sibling in early life. If more than one new member is due to join at the same time, it is usual to inform them. They often develop a special twin-like alliance, a mixture of mutual protection and rivalry.

We also bear in mind the danger of newcomers saying too much too quickly with consequent anxiety and withdrawal, though this can usually be left to the conductor in the group once the patient has joined.

5 Matching individuals and groups

Ultimately we are talking about patients' characteristics and their capacity to be contained within and to promote, or at least not to destroy, the therapeutic processes in a group. Therefore, ultimately the most important question is whether this patient is going to fit in to this particular group. This accords with the earlier statement of Foulkes (1964) that contra-indications are few 'and show themselves individually if each case is considered on its own merits'. He noted that while strong paranoid features are unfavourable and psychotics should not be in the majority (except in groups of psychotics) 'individual psychotics inside a group of psychoneurotics did particularly well and influence the group as a whole favourably' (p. 35). We believe the same is true of reasonably contained borderline personalities.

Of course we also need to think about the therapeutic potential of the group as a whole, and therefore to consider the need for a good balance of personalities and problems – for example, not more than one or two borderline personalities, nor a predominance of severely depressed people, or extremely stuck 'alexithymic'[3] personalities. If we have a choice of groups, then we also need to know which groups are dynamic, fast moving, sophisticated, confronting rather than supportive – or the reverse. In the Group-Analytic Practice we have a weekly clinical meeting which reviews all the patients assessed in the previous week. Here we discuss their selection for group analysis, and their suitability for particular groups or for a period on the waiting list until an appropriate vacancy arises. Therapists are able to say what sort of patients they would like to fill a vacancy (see Figure 4.4), and we are able to consider the particular interests and skills of therapists in dealing with particular sorts of patient.

The range of patients who can be helped is very wide, both in age and personality, and quite severely disturbed patients can be contained and helped in well-functioning, well-selected groups, differentiating between, for example, faster-and slower-moving groups (see Figure 4.5). These include borderline personalities, alexithymic personalities, people with past histories of manic-depressive and schizophrenic illness, those recovering from severe eating disorders, and sexual problems and other psychosomatic disorders.

At any one time we have about 50 groups meeting once- or twice-weekly at a wide variety of times, early morning, lunchtime, afternoon and evening during weekdays and on Saturday mornings. During the initial interview patients will have been asked about their availabilities at these various times, and told that the more flexible they can be, the shorter is the time that they are likely to have to wait for a suitable vacancy. As most people leave groups at the Christmas, Easter and summer breaks, newcomers are most often taken in after these breaks.

At present all groups are 'slow-open' (as defined above) with equal numbers of men and women, and with mixed background and psychopathology. One of the difficulties of starting specialised groups is to get eight people who would benefit from it to meet at one time. We can always maintain some groups for late adolescents and for people in later life, but a new group for psychosomatic and alexithymic patients recently failed in that form because of the problem of recruiting enough patients at the available time; it was finally merged into a more heterogeneous group. Whether we can succeed in setting up time-limited, single-sex groups will depend on recruitment. If we cannot, with our large number of referrals and therapists, one wonders whether this could be achieved in a very specialised setting such as the Women's Therapy Centre.

The presence of colleagues in the team with expertise with couples and families enables us to run not only couples' groups, but to have them available for consultations with the spouses or partners of those patients who are having difficulties in an ongoing relationship for which both partners need to take responsibility. Sometimes this results in both of them joining either a couples' group or separate stranger groups. It would seem that any group practice should have at least a close working relationship with a colleague skilled at working with families and couples; ideally, a colleague who combines these skills with being a group analyst.

6 Management of the waiting list

Management of the waiting list is important in order to ensure that patients do not wait unduly long. Each consultation is given a sequential number which enables us to assess how long they have been waiting if they are not taken into a group straight away. It has been very useful having a word processor and computer to reduce the work needed to keep the list constantly updated for the weekly meetings of the Management Committee, and to keep a check on the times that the new patient will be available for a group so this can be matched with the vacancies as they arise.

This facilitates regular supervision of the waiting list and communication with all 16 therapists to ensure that we have accurate information about current and expected vacancies in their groups. It is the principal responsibility of the Clinical Secretary, and on the whole works quite sensitively. Not only has the patient been assessed in depth, but we know a lot about the therapists and the type of group that the patient will be joining. However, before a patient joins a new group, the group conductor arranges what we term a 'preliminary interview'. This is a meeting of variable length, for which no charge is made, in which patient and therapist can get to know each other, make a final commitment and arrange practical details such as when the patient will join. Some conductors like a longer preliminary interview than others, more of a second assessment, feeling that it increases their understanding of the patient and increases the motivation of both of them. Indeed we all feel this need with some new patients. Very occasionally a conductor will choose to see a new patient a few times individually to further this end before the patient actually joins the group, and it might be specifically recommended at the initial consultation.

Occasionally there are problems with a patient settling into a group. Because of the structure of the Practice it is possible for the group conductor to discuss the difficulties with the initial consultant. This might lead to an offer to the patient of an opportunity to discuss the difficulties individually with either, especially if there seems to be a risk that the patient might drop out. Then, very occasionally it may be thought worth considering a change of group and therapist, or the addition of some initial sessions with the same therapist or another.

7 The limits of group analysis

As discussed earlier, despite the existence of clear-cut contra-indications to group analysis as a long-term analytic therapy, it has a very wide spectrum of indications and applicability. Nevertheless there are patients who get to a certain point in their group analysis, but cannot progress without moving into a period of individual therapy, sometimes concurrently, but sometimes leaving a group altogether to continue their 'voyage' in individual therapy. More often than not, in my experience, these are people who have very early damage within the dyadic relationship, sometimes experienced as a tremendous narcissistic vulnerability, for whom mirroring at a very infantile level is necessary for healing and

Figure 4.4   Vacancies in groups: a form for therapists to specify vacancies

Conductors having a vacancy:

Group number (if more than one):

Group time(s):

Ideal new member for optimal balance of group:

sex _____

age-range _____

marital status_____

other characteristics _____

_____

_____

Wish to avoid:

Figure 4.5 Matching patients in groups: a form for therapist's group

as at January 1990
(0-4) – absent to high)

Dear

It would be helpful, in matching potential recruits to your groups, to have a picture of a current composition and characteristics. (We plan to repeat this enquiry every six months).

1. Group time(s)	
2. Approximate age range	
3. Analytic (0–4)	
4. Supportive (0–4)	
5. Regressive potential (0–4)	
6. Inhibited (0–4)	
7. Confrontational (0–4)	
8. Speed (0–4)	
9. Nature of any recent crisis: e.g. drop-outs, problem patients	
10. Special features of group:	

the emergence of a 'true self'. Sometimes the period of time they need in individual therapy seems very short – much shorter than if they had been in individual treatment from the beginning.

Such deep borderline or narcissistic damage cannot always been predicted in the most skilled assessment interview, and the treatment has to be started in order to deepen and complete the assessment. My impression is that these people need a degree of 'benign regression' within a relationship that can be tested over a sufficient period of time, in order to allow a 'new beginning' (Balint, 1968); sometimes a particular group cannot provide this, and a patient may need to move into concurrent individual therapy or, less often, move entirely from group to individual analytic psychotherapy. Thus the fact that groups promote maturity can, for a few very damaged personalities, be a disadvantage. They may finally benefit from a group after they have had experience of themselves in a facilitating dyadic relationship. But as Rutan and Alonso (1982) have said, 'it is possible to overcome resistance, in each modality, by sometimes adding the other concurrently, but in that case, as usual, the group is the central treatment'. In other words, the advisability of adding individual to group psychotherapy for a group member should not be taken by the group and its conductor as indicating any lessening of the value and centrality of their work with that patient.

8 Other important issues

It is very important to keep in touch with referrers. This is done by writing to them, and perhaps phoning, after the initial consultation, and letting them know when patients start in groups and finish, and informing them of the outcome. We also keep in touch with them at a more personal level by inviting them to an annual Christmas party, and sending them an Annual Report about the work of the Practice.

If we are concerned about a patient during the 12 weeks in the year when the groups do not meet, we inform his or her general practitioner or, if they were referred by one, their psychiatrist. Moreover, we let the patient know that there is always medical psychotherapeutic cover available through the Practice office.

When the group conductor is not medically qualified, medical responsibility is carried either by the medically qualified member of the Practice who carried out the initial assessment, or sometimes, when more appropriate, by the patient's general practitioner or psychiatrist. This extends to providing medical backing for private health insurance claims to cover the cost of the initial consultation and therapy itself.

One further advantage of working in a group practice, beyond the advantages of pooling patients, experience and mutual support, is that when a member of the Practice falls ill (or even dies – see Chapter 12) other members can help out. A group can often continue well for a few sessions without a conductor, depending on its stage of development. But should the conductor have a protracted illness, we can make arrangements for a colleague (usually from within the Practice) to take over the group until that conductor returns.

Conclusion

In assessing and selecting someone for group analysis we need to ask whether this patient is likely to benefit from and benefit a group of fellow patients committed to long term exploration of themselves and interpersonal relationships through processes of insight and change. Or is the patient too disturbed or poorly motivated to tolerate exploration and insight, or too deprived and damaged to tolerate sharing in a group, or as yet too unprepared? In that case would psychiatric management or individual therapy – supportive, brief or analytic – be more appropriate? Or, if the family as a whole is clearly involved, would a conjoint approach be more effective?

For a whole range of patients and problems, a long-term analytic group can be an effective therapy and an experience that promotes growth and maturity (Brown, 1987). But we need to evaluate the group; how much support and holding (Winnicott, 1960) can it give, how much containing (Bion, 1962; James, 1984), how much confrontation (Brown, 1988), how much intimacy, how much benign regression, what range of subjects is it equipped to explore; also in what phase of the group; and with which therapist?[4] Only then are we able to complete the assessment of the indications and contra-indications for psychotherapy of this patient in this group and select each appropriately. The procedures we have developed, and described above, from referral to consultation, and finally to the preliminary interview with the would-be therapist, aim to answer most of these questions. We believe that the methods of working together over the last few decades at the Group-Analytic Practice have enabled us to refine these procedures in a way that may provide a useful model to others.

Notes

1 Like other members of the Management Committee, the non-medically qualified person is well known within the referral network and beyond, is a qualified analyst as well as a group analyst, and has worked in the National Health Service as well as conducting training courses overseas. She gets patients referred to her for consultations, and because of the need for medical cover, one of the medically qualified members of the Management Committee will then see the patient in order to assess them for medical cover. We believe this provides an important safeguard, medical and psychiatric as well as legal.

2 Counselling or behaviour therapy are especially indicated where the need and motivation for an analytic approach are absent, or if such an approach is likely to be too disturbing. Relaxation techniques are helpful when tension is a major problem; and bodywork can be indicated when a person is out of touch with or not at home with their body.

3 Alexithymia is a term which has been coined to describe the inability to put feelings into words, found in certain individuals. Its cause is poorly understood. There is a strong association between this disability and a tendency to develop psychosomatic illness (see Chapter 7, section 8).

4 We are currently developing a system of rating groups along some of these dimensions to assist the matching of groups with new members.

Chapter 5

The twice-weekly groups

Lionel Kreeger

It was not until the early 1960s that twice-weekly groups were started at the Group-Analytic Practice. I believe that Robin Skynner was the first member to convene a twice-weekly group, followed soon by S.H. Foulkes and Harold Kaye working together as co-therapists, and Malcolm Pines. I joined the Practice in 1968 as an Associate, but it was not until January 1972 that I began my first twice-weekly group, being supervised by Harold Kaye over the first year of the group's existence. This supervisory requirement was related to the trainees in the group who were starting the Qualifying Course at the Institute of Group-Analysis. It continued as a slow-open group for 17 years, terminating as a whole at Easter 1989, when a natural and spontaneous conclusion seemed appropriate, and it was possible to work through the termination phase over a period of one year by fixing an agreed ending well in advance.

At present there are 17 twice-weekly groups being run at the Group-Analytic Practice, all of them having a conductor recognised as a training analyst for the Institute of Group-Analysis, and therefore able to accept Qualifying Course students who are required to be in twice-weekly groups throughout their training, a minimum period of three-and-a-half-years in all. Ideally two trainees in each group offer the best balance for the group as a whole, but often the demand for vacancies is such that there has to be a greater number in each group. It is not unusual to have three or four trainees, and on rare occasions there have been even more, but this is undoubtedly undesirable, leading to undue emphasis and preoccupation with training and professional matters, at the cost of time available for more general interaction. If there is only one person training in the group, this tends to put him or her into an isolated position, often subject to envious attacks by the other group members, particularly if they would also like to be accepted for the training, but have not so far succeeded in their application, or have been rejected by the Admissions Committee.

It has been my own regret that I have never had the opportunity of participating as a member of a twice-weekly therapy group, my group experience being limited to a once-weekly group over a period of two years. I do experience some envy of twice-weekly group members, particularly when the group is at its most dynamic and creative best. There is always some vicarious gain to be had, but it is limited by the extent of one's objective position and the restriction of negotiation within the transference and counter-transference. I am convinced that it is when I feel moved or excited by developments within the group that the group as a whole is also experiencing significant insights and changes. Equally, I may become aware of changes within myself as group conductor when there is creative movement within the group. This position differs from other group therapists such as the late Henry Ezriel, who is quoted anecdotally by Irvin Yalom (1985) in his book *The Theory and Practice of Group Psychotherapy*. Yalom details Ezriel's rigidity in his projection of the group therapist's role as a blank projection screen to facilitate his sole task of interpretation, and recounts the following:

> In one group in which the majority of members remained in therapy for nine years and three for 11 years, the members at the end of therapy discussed the changes that had occurred in each person; they all agreed that, aside from being a decade older, Dr Ezriel had not changed whatsoever. 'That,' states Dr Ezriel, 'is good technique.'

Yalom expresses his scepticism, and I am in full agreement with him on this issue. In general terms, the twice-weekly groups are more intense and committed than those meeting once-weekly. This is in no way intended to diminish the value of once-weekly groups, and at times the dynamic interaction and movement within some once-weekly groups can be more impressive than that which may occur in a twice-weekly group that is somewhat stuck or going through a negative or destructive phase. When I am asked during a consultation with a new patient why I recommend a twice-weekly group in preference to a week, my usual reply is to compare the twice-weekly group with individual psychoanalysis or three or four-times-a-week analytic psychotherapy, whereas the once-weekly group is more akin to or once-or twice-weekly individual psychotherapy. This assumes a greater commitment to the group, both emotional and financial, and also a preparedness to work at depth and become intensely involved in the dynamics of the group and its transferential network. A common misconception is that the twice-weekly group will produce results more quickly and that therefore it will be of shorter duration. I have to explain that, like psychoanalysis, which needs at least four or five years to complete, twice-weekly groups also require three to four years in order to 'work through' the complicated transference distortions that emerge in the course of treatment, and to arrive at a satisfactory resolution. Sometimes even longer periods of therapy are necessary, and it is not unusual for people to stay in the group for up to seven or eight years.

Group-analytic principles

S.H. Foulkes and his followers have developed a theoretical and practical system to cover the events and developments in small stranger groups. Such concepts as the 'transference group', 'group matrix', 'location', 'translation', 'mirror reaction', 'resonance', and 'polarisation', are vital to the understanding of the dynamics of the group. Briefly these concepts are defined as follows.

Transference group (capital 'T')

This is the classical psychoanalytic situation in which earlier family relationships express themselves within the group context, linked to internalised object relationships. The capital 'T' distinguishes it from small 't' which covers all aspects of relationships in the group, of lesser significance to psychoanalytic work. For example, Patrick de Maré has coined the term 'transposition' to clarify that some group relationships may be exact, reality-based reduplications of earlier experiences, the transposing of experiential contexts, rather than being part of the transference distortions. The standard joke runs as follows. Patient to the dozing group conductor: 'You're just like my father; he also fell asleep when I was talking about something important!'

Group matrix

A hypothetical web of communication and relationships within the group, the common shared ground on which all else rests. Foulkes distinguished the 'foundation matrix', based more on the primary-level biological and cultural elements, from the 'dynamic matrix', which replaces it: 'The artificially created, strange but potentially very intimate group network... the theatre of operation of ongoing change'.

Location

The process and psychological work which places any event in the proup within the context of the configuration, ground or gestalt of the total network or matrix of the group.

Translation

The move from less to more articulate communication, from unconscious to conscious awareness, from symptomatic and symbolic meaning to a clearer understanding of unconscious processes.

Mirror reaction

Aspects of the self reflected by members of the group through image and behaviour, allowing identification and projective mechanisms, enabling the individual to become aware of these hitherto unconscious elements.

Resonance

The phenomenon of intensification or amplification of a particular theme or conflict within the group, resulting from shared, largely unconscious communication between its members.

Polarisation

The splitting of complex reactions into their elements, resulting in divergent attitudes towards issues, the combined reactions producing the emotional spectrum that facilitates insight.

Psychoanalytic application

Psychoanalysis is a scientific discipline in which certain theories are derived from its observational data, with the express aim of ordering and explaining those data. Two fundamental principles of mental functioning underlie the framework of psychoanalytic theory and practice – the predominance of unconscious activity, and psychic determinism – that is to say that events are consequent to previous experience and do not occur just by chance.

Transference

Freud's (1912) first major paper on transference, 'The Dynamics of Transference', stressed that transference was not restricted to the psycho-analytic dyadic relationship, and that it was 'to be attributed not to psychoanalysis, but to neurosis itself'. The manifestations of transference in groups allows for a multiplicity of relationships concurrently, and often results in a rich and deeply experienced re-enactment of the primary family group. The frequently expressed criticism that transference is diluted in groups is unacceptable, and at times the intensity of transferen-tial distortions may be greater than that occurring in individual therapy. It may well be the effect of resonance that takes some people beyond the limitations of the dyadic setting. The capacity to allow the spontaneous feelings of loss and sadness during the termination phase of a group may well be enhanced by the collective experience, the mourning process being greater than its individual parts.

Transference neurosis

Eventually, neurotic conflicts become centred on the analyst in the dyadic relationship, producing 'a new edition of the clinical neurosis', taking on the features of the original illness and providing an artificial illness accessible to analytic intervention. This is the essence, the *sine qua non* of the dynamics of cure that allows 'working through' of the repressed elements to free the patient from the grip of the mechanisms of repetition. Eventually, unconscious neurotic dystonic aspects of the personality become conscious, amenable to confrontation and change, allowing increasingly ego-syntonic development and growth. 'Where Id was, there shall Ego be.' The question as to whether transference neurosis occurs in the group setting to the same extent as in psychoanalysis may be argued. There are many who would question it, particularly among psychoanalytic colleagues, some of whom might state that it is in order to add a little of the wine of psychoanalysis to the water of psychotherapy, but that it is not permissible to add any of the water of psychotherapy to the wine of psychoanalysis. But most group analysts would nowadays agree with Foulkes (1964) when he stated in *Therapeutic Group Analysis*:

> True transference neurosis of the individual can clearly be recognised in the group and therefore also analysed. It is true of course that this transference neurosis does not develop in the same pure style as in individual analysis and that it cannot be analysed and worked through in the same detail. Whether this is due to the group situation or to the fact that I am referring to weekly sessions remains to be seen. It is also true that the transference neurosis develops in a different way in view of its multi-personal distribution.

Later, in Foulkes (1975), he went further, saying:

> Transference neurosis... is a regular occurrence and always contains the key to the very basic and individual side of the patient's neurosis, in an exact parallel to the transference neurosis in a two person situation in psychoanalysis.

Working through

This is the essential process in psychoanalysis and psychoanalytic group psychotherapy that distinguishes them from other non-analytic methods. It can be defined as 'a sort of psychical work which allows the patient to accept certain repressed elements and to free himself from the grip of mechanisms of repetition' (Laplanche and Pontalis, 1973). The resolution of the transference neurosis is negotiated by the work and learning involved in working through, with increasing insight leading to significant and permanent characterological and behavioural changes.

An example is that of Miss D, who reported the following dream early on in her group analysis:

> 'She was hosting a party of important guests, suddenly becoming aware with a feeling of horror that the drink she had to offer them was an inferior British sherry. She was overcome with feelings of humiliation and inadequacy.'

Three years later, while working towards termination in the group, she had this dream:

> 'She was sitting at the head of a long dinner table about to offer after dinner drinks to her guests. She suddenly realised that all she had available was the same inferior sherry as in the first dream. She was about to collapse in despair, when she became aware of a figure standing by her side. She turned to find that it was me (the group conductor), and I was pointing to a box by her chair. She opened it and found many litre bottles of the most excellent liqueurs and brandies.'

It required very little interpretation for her to realise the extent of change in her inner world, from the empty and desolate quality previously to the richer and more promising developments of the past few years.

Levels of transference

The group conductor must remain in touch with the dynamic movement underlying the interactions and associations within the group. What is the developmental stage appropriate to the material presented by the group? Is it at a part-object or whole-object level? Are the themes consistent with oral, anal or genital organisation? Can the transference phenomena be understood primarily in terms of the dyad (patient/conductor or patient/group as mother) or to the group as family (parents as individuals and siblings)? At a primitive and deeper level, the following example comes from a group nearing a long holiday break:

> 'Ms A detailed the conscious fantasy that had preoccupied her for the past few days. She imagined that she was a baby sitting strapped in a high chair being fed by me, the group conductor. I was sitting in front of her pushing spoonfuls of banana custard into her mouth. Other group members resonated to this theme. Mr X spoke of his wife being away and looking after the children by himself. He had prepared a bowlful of banana custard for dessert, something comforting for him from his own childhood. Mr Y told us that he had woken in the early hours and

had gone down to the kitchen for a snack and eaten a banana. Mr Z, a manic-depressive showing marked concreteness of thinking, stated that they had run out of bananas, but he would ensure that he bought some on his way home after the group!'

It was clear that the group as a whole was in a phase of oral dependency in anticipation of the forthcoming break. For Ms A it also reflected her intense envy of the group members in the sense that she had been most helpful recently, offering them interpretations of a very positive and valued quality, but leaving her feeling markedly deprived and empty. She had been ravenously hungry all week, eating double meals three or four times a day, with additional snacks in between, but nothing really satisfied her. Hence the need for the banana custard fantasy, of being fed by another.

At a higher developmental level:

'Mr M arrived for his first group session one week early! He had been seen in consultation shortly before the Christmas break, and it had been agreed that he would join the group at its second meeting after the holiday, to allow the group to meet before the new member appeared so as to do some work on preparing for the new group baby. When, in the corridor outside my room I looked at him in surprise, he gave a sad little smile and said, "Ah – you don't remember me, do you? " I replied that I did indeed remember him, and that we had arranged for him to join the group next week, not this.'

It later transpired that he was always ignored or forgotten by his father, and that his response to me was typical of the father-transference that needed to be worked through. Later in the same group, there was a short but heated exchange between another man and myself in which I was particularly responsive and warm in my reactions to him, but Mr M criticised me for being very cold and uninvolved with the other, and it was possible following this to do the analytic work that revealed his own defensiveness against his jealousy of father's love and warmth to his elder brother.

Therapeutic factors

Irvin Yalom (1985), among others, has identified and described various guided human experiences, which, through their intricate interplay, lead to therapeutic change, and may constitute a rational basis for the therapist's tactics and strategies. He lists 11 therapeutic factors in all, including universality, altruism, group cohesiveness and interpersonal learning. He describes how interpersonal distortions lead to disturbed relationships, and how the group offers the 'corrective emotional experience' that leads to increasing self-esteem and individual autonomy. He tends to prefer the term 'interpersonal distortions' to that of 'transference' and maintains that the working through of transference distortions is but one phase of interpersonal learning. He indicates that 'there are two major approaches to facilitate transference resolution in the therapy group: consensual validation and increased therapist transparency'. Although he does give further stress in the third edition of his book to the concept of transference, indeed a chapter to itself, it is clear that he is more attuned to the resolution of transference distortions through reality testing encouraged by therapist disclosure, rather than through the psychoanalytic process of working through.

Countertransference

Freud (1910) used the term 'countertransference' for the first time in his paper, 'Future Prospects of Psychoanalytic Therapy'. He regarded it as the analyst's transference to his patient, or to his patient's transference, and was 'almost inclined to insist that he shall recognise... and overcome it'. His lack of further exploration of this area is probably related to the limitations of self-analysis. Attitudes towards countertransference were changing radically when Paula Heimann (1950) published her paper 'On Counter-transference', in which she wrote:

> My thesis is that the analyst's emotional response to his patient within the analytic situation represents one of the most important tools for his work. The analyst's countertransference is an instrument of research into the patient's unconscious... his unconscious perception of the patient's unconscious is more acute and in advance of his conscious conception of the situation.

Foulkes (1975) in *Group-Analytic Psychotherapy, Method and Principles* acknowledged the usefulness of openly analysing his countertransference in the group at times, but insisted that it should not be made routine, and that on the whole the conductor should be economic with this type of communication.

> The best hint one can give him as to when such an interpretation on his part may be useful or even necessary is when he becomes aware that some resistance against communication is located in himself, is involving him if not caused by him. Furthermore that he follows the overall rule to interpret only in order to improve and also deepen communication.

One example of countertransference work comes from a group which seemed to be functioning well and constructively, apparently requiring very little participation from me. It was quite easy to let the group get on with it, no special demands were being made on me, and yet I began to feel slightly uneasy, after a few minutes becoming aware of a sense of mild anxiety, with apparently no obvious reason or cause for it. I felt somewhat inhibited, a bit paralysed in my thinking. Quite suddenly, about half-way through the session, I remembered a cartoon sketch from a Monty Python programme on television the evening before:

A baby is in its cot, sucking contentedly on its dummy surrounded by family and friends who admire it, coo to it, all is peaceful and happy. Someone disapproving of an infant having a comforter goes to remove it from its mouth. The mother screams, 'No, don't do it!' But too late. The dummy is removed and immediately the baby sucks in its breath, and the whole of its surroundings, people, objects, furniture, disappear down its throat, leaving the room empty and desolate.

My first reaction in the group was a suppressed internal chuckle. I had laughed helplessly the night before at this piece of comic genius. But then my mirth was replaced by a sense of guilt. What on earth was I doing allowing my attention to stray to thoughts of television programmes rather than sticking with my careful attention to the dynamics of the group? Was I escaping from my own anxious response, or distancing myself from my responsibilities as group conductor? After a few moments, I realised I was probably on the receiving end of a powerful 'projective identification', the group disowning its own greedy and devouring, omnipotent oral needs, and instead pushing them (unconsciously) into me. I had come to contain their overwhelmingly destructive fantasies, albeit expressed humorously, experiencing their fear that their collective greed would desolate me internally. I shared my experience with them, it seemed to make good sense, they accepted back their fears that they could annihilate me, and were able to explore this hitherto avoided area. I felt freed within myself, again more able to function rationally and appropriately within the group.

I have tried to share the flavour of some of the experiences of the dynamics of twice-weekly groups, and to indicate what I feel are the more important aspects of their development and emerging culture. It is difficult to offer a validated consensus of our collective overall approaches, and essential differences exist both in theoretical and technical aspects. However, the Members and Associates of the Practice are linked by certain essential group-analytic convictions, and these override the personal deviations from the group-analytic norm. Our mutual trust, respect and tolerance are vital to the quality of the work that we undertake, and one of the great strengths that supports us through difficult and challenging situations is the easy availability of informal mutual supervision and advice, often undertaken in our tiny kitchen area which can become extremely crowded, somewhat reminiscent of the famous cabin scene in the Marx brothers' *A Night at the Opera*!

A last anecdote to exemplify the good-natured competitive quality of our interactions: I came out of a group in which I had been criticised and castigated for never allowing a discussion of sexual feelings. All that could be talked about in this group was depression and loss. We were told how in Robin Skynner's groups they were always talking about sex, and often having an exciting and stimulating time; why couldn't I be more like him! The person making the complaints felt deeply frustrated and disappointed in the way that the group was going. I left the group feeling a bit upset, thinking that maybe the criticisms were justified and that I needed to look at my difficulty in allowing more light hearted sexy and enjoyable interaction within the group. I went along to the kitchen to make a cup of coffee and Robin was there. I told him my story and he laughed. He said that he had just come out of a group in which he was attacked for being only interested in sex. 'Why can't we be depressed and stay in touch with our feelings of sadness and loss like in other groups? Why can't you be more containing like Lionel Kreeger?'

Chapter 6

The once-weekly groups

Adele Mittwoch

Note: In my clinical illustrations I have named all male patients George, all female patients Anne.

Once-weekly makes sense. According to the Bible something good and unique was created on every weekday. We are used to things happening at specific times regularly each week: fish for dinner on Fridays, games at school, clean lab. coats in the laboratory every Monday morning, board meetings in business, ward rounds in hospitals and so on. People flock to educational activities such as evening classes that take place on the same day and at the same time each week. Weekly sessions of group psychotherapy were offered when this form of treatment was first introduced, and they are still the norm for outpatient treatment in groups. At the Group-Analytic Practice in its early years once-weekly groups were offered exclusively, and we currently have 26 such ongoing groups.

The theory and technique of group analysis employed in the Practice derive from the work of S.H. Foulkes, who expanded the principles of psychoanalysis to the social situation of the group. It may seem paradoxical that psychoanalysis with its traditionally prescribed five weekly sessions could have made the leap to once-weekly group-analytic sessions. Foulkes (1948), moreover, began his group-analytic work in the residential setting of Northfield Military Hospital where the therapeutic endeavour pervaded all activities with none of the time boundaries that govern outpatient treatment. The once-weekly out patient group was established in the first instance as a practicable measure. Foulkes began work with such groups not long after the war at St Bartholomew's Hospital and also in private practice.

Times change, and established patterns fall into disuse. Fish on Fridays may be almost out-dated, shops in this country may soon be free to open on Sundays, the privileged have clean underwear every day rather than once-weekly, cakes and sweets are no longer a weekend treat but freely available to be indulged in right through the week and at any time of the day. Twice-weekly groups were first started in the Practice in the 1960s and 22 such groups are running now.

ting at the Practice

(1948) described the setting of his first private group as follows:

private group meets in the evening after supper in a rather modest room too, hired for the purpose – it is only slightly more reminiscent of the atmosphere of an ordinary living room and scarcely more comfortable.

Things have much improved since then. Jeff Roberts has described in Chapter 1 the main aspects of the accommodation at Montagu Mansions. I want to fill in on some features of the setting, looking at it from a personal angle. I like the structural and ornamental details in the rooms of this old building. The whole flat is well carpeted and kept in an immaculate decorative state. Members of the Management Committee choose the décor for their own rooms and furnishing, such as desk, couch, bookcases, curtains, ornaments and pictures. These not only enhance the environment but also characterise the setting as a place of learning and become absorbed into the group matrix.

Chairs vary from room to room, but ten chairs all alike are provided for each room. All chairs are comfortably padded, and with an eye to durability and healthy posture they are more upright than the style used in the past.

Chairs not needed for sessions can be stacked at the side. The lighting in each room can be adjusted to suit. Heaters are provided, fans for use during heatwaves, ventilators where necessary. Disturbance from outside is relatively rare. Nevertheless no group meets on a desert island and extraneous sounds do at times intrude from other group rooms or the hall, police sirens, drilling works outside, and so on. I for one would not wish it to be otherwise, as long as disturbances are brief.

Associate Members of the Practice seldom have a choice of room, but I am very pleased with the rooms made available to me for my once-weekly groups. In fact the only room that meets with criticism, as far as I know, is the waiting room, which has to do double duty as a group room. As it happens, none of the once-weekly groups meets in this room. Vases filled with fresh flowers are placed in the hall and in each of the rooms. It says a lot for the reliability of the florist who delivers on Mondays and the skill of the secretary who arranges and rearranges them, that the flowers for my Friday evening group are still a joy to look at. Meg Sharpe's Monday morning group, alas, meet before the flowers have arrived, but as the members never come in on other days they do not feel deprived.

A small round table occupies the centre of the group circle in each room. Foulkes (1975) writes about this table:

It symbolises a kind of centre of the group, and is also a neutral point to look at. A small table is also ornamental and helps to establish a setting more pleasing than the relatively stark and artificial appearance when there is no table. A large table might create the atmosphere of a board or a committee meeting and it also hides people; thus no table is better than a large one.

If truth be told, there was a time when the central table met the need of the smokers in groups for easy access to ashtrays. I remember the days when two to three ashtrays might be placed on the central tables. Dr Foulkes, whose seminars I attended in the early 1970s, spoke of his dislike of a polluted atmosphere, and Harold Kaye at the same time saw the lighting up of cigarettes as introducing smoke screens, acting-out and tension-reducing manoeuvres. While I could acknowledge some point in these objections, I never introduced a no-smoking rule as I preferred to see habitual smokers in their natural state without the constraint of an imposed deprivation. With the passing of time the culture we live in has changed. No one now smokes inside the group rooms and ashtrays are no longer needed.

A large box of paper tissues placed on the central table tends to be in the focus of vision at the Group-Analytic Practice. Distressed patients are handed the box to mop up their tears. Ella Freeman Sharpe (1930) writes: 'If a patient wept and had no handkerchief: if a patient had a cold and no handkerchief, I should lend one.'

In my early days as a psychotherapist I followed Ella Sharpe's example. Patients would take these handkerchiefs home and bring them back washed and ironed (sometimes not too well). These days disposable tissues are the answer. I dislike the idea, though, of giving such tissues prominence of place. However regressed patients may become in a therapeutic session, when they begin to recover they may take stock of themselves as adults in the great wide world and reach for their own handkerchiefs. I therefore like to have the Kleenex available if needed but more discreetly placed on the desk. Another reason is that I consider these big boxes of Kleenex for Men – useful as they are – ugly and suggestive. 'Kleenex for Men – now softer than ever', runs a radio advertisement, currently being repeated *ad nauseam*.

The growth of the Practice over the years inevitably has created space problems, and three small lavatories meagrely provide for our patients' considerable needs. At times when several groups start or end simultaneously queues congest the narrow corridor and patients sometimes enter the group room late. I cannot resist telling about George. At the end of a session he took his jacket off, placed it on a chair and made for the door. I looked puzzled. 'It is difficult enough to squeeze into the loo without a jacket,' he explained with a smile.

Jeff Roberts in Chapter 1 has referred to the lack of a one-way mirror with adjoining viewing room and video facility. Therapists who may use our experience to set up their own practices may well consider such equipment not a luxury but essential for current-style teaching and research. I will not here argue this point, but speaking for myself I am happy to work in surroundings that are as yet free of the impact of high tech. We do not even have clocks on the walls, even though we are all pretty good at observing our time boundaries.

In this context I will outline the temporal arrangements for groups at the Practice. All group sessions last for one-and-a-half-hours, and patients can enter the group rooms about a quarter of an hour before the start of the session. Once-weekly groups meet on every weekday and one on Saturdays. One group starts in the early morning before eight, two at lunch-time, two in the late afternoons, 15 groups between 6.00 p.m. and 6.30 p.m. and six groups between 7.00 p.m. and 8.00 p.m. Most patients can be offered groups that suit their choice of day and time.

Age of once-weekly groups

All our groups are slow-open, with perhaps two or three patients terminating each year and new ones taking their places. The 'group' of conductors is also slow-open, though the turnover is much slower than that of patients. Groups whose conductors have retired or died have been taken over by other conductors.

From the information about once-weekly groups given to me by the present staff I have culled the following. Four groups with an average of seven years reached their natural and appropriate ends, with adequate work towards termination. Two groups started in 1972/73 were fused into one in 1980, and this group is still running. Two groups were closed because they were not viable. Four groups changed from once-weekly to twice-weekly. Of 20 currently running groups the youngest was started one year ago, the oldest about 26 years ago; the average is about 11 years.

The long life of the groups gives our patients a unique sense of security. The disadvantage is that once a room is booked it will not become available for anything else in the foreseeable future.

Membership of once-weekly groups

I confine myself here to the members of our heterogeneous groups. They suffer from the full range of neurotic disorders, including psychosomatic symptoms; a few patients with fairly severe character disorders and some borderline patients are successfully absorbed. A light sprinkling of members are students on counselling courses or who are training in psychotherapy and who are studying both individual and group work in their courses. Compared with the twice-weekly groups, however, the number of people with professional interests is very low.

Well over half of our once-weekly patients have had no previous psychotherapy. Some have had occasional sessions with a psychiatrist, some have had counselling, others have undergone analytically orientated psychotherapy or even intensive psychoanalysis over many years. Some patients have had some previous group experience, perhaps in hospital and conducted not necessarily with an analytic orientation.

A once-weekly group makes sense, as I said. Twice-weekly makes equal sense or even better sense but not to our once-a-week patient population. Their sense of commitment just does not stretch that far. In general, I would say, it stretches further than that of patients presenting themselves for groups in the National Health Service or other public institutions that are provided free of charge or at minimal cost.

We need to distinguish between a sense of commitment on the one hand, and motivation on the other. I mean by motivation the resolve to undergo treatment and see it through. Such resolve springs in the first instance from suffering, and is strengthened through preparation for group treatment first by the referrer, then by the psychiatric consultant at the Practice, lastly by the prospective group conductor at the pre-group discussion. In group treatment it is particularly important to gauge the patient's motivation at the last stage before a place is offered, as it is very discouraging for a group when someone drops out prematurely. Sufficient motivation is necessary irrespective of whether a patient is interested in once-or twice-weekly treatment. When I set up my first groups I allowed 20 minutes and saw prospective patients at half-hour intervals; according to what I had been taught. In common with other group conductors I now tend to see prospective patients for a full hour and/or see them two or three times to test their suitability, prepare them, and above all to ascertain that they are sufficiently motivated to make a long term commitment.

Once-weekly patients are obviously less willing to commit time and money to their treatment. A few people simply could not manage more time, the great majority are afraid of becoming too self-absorbed or dependent. Similarly, some once-weekly group members could not afford the cost of twice-weekly treatment, while others are quite affluent. It is interesting to speculate how many of our once-weekly patients would opt for twice-weekly treatment if the fees were halved, and my hunch is not many. Patients getting into financial difficulties often have their fees adjusted by the conductor. I have done this without regret in several instances, leaving the decision of how much someone can afford to the person himself. In other cases a dwindling bank balance is a manifestation of the problem over commitment. Some of our patients have the whole or part of their fees paid by their medical insurances. On the whole there are no adverse effects, but poor motivation may raise its ugly head, as in the following example:

> George's group fees were paid under his employer's insurance scheme. He changed his job to one offering no cover for private medicine and at the same time found a pretext for ending group treatment. The other members were furious about his unwillingness to make more effort and his meanness.

In my experience, members of once-weekly groups are happy with the arrangement and only very rarely yearn for more frequent sessions.

Compared with twice-weekly groups the once-weekly group records probably show a higher rate of absence and late attendance. This is by no means universal, and once-weekly groups may go through long phases of excellent attendance until the group dynamics cause the situation to deteriorate. The better motivation and sense of commitment of Practice patients compared with those in the National Health Service is no doubt largely influenced by their social standing. Of the 15 members currently attending my two once-weekly groups the following data are relevant:

Social background (class): 5 upper middle, 8 middle, 1 lower middle, 1 working.

School: 6 public, 7 grammar, 2 secondary.

Further education: 6 university, 7 technical college, 1 SRN, 1 PSW.
All but one are professionally active.

Our patients' backgrounds and current circumstances in general are conducive to a steadier lifestyle than that of many in the world at large. This is reflected in the attendance records of our groups and in a relatively low drop out rate. Problems in the area of motivation and commitment nevertheless exist, and I shall return to this topic in the next section.

The therapeutic work

Is once-weekly enough?

> George was a member of a therapeutic social club. One day I commented on how well he looked. 'Yes, I feel well', he said, 'and I am making very good progress in my analysis.' What he meant by analysis was a 10-minute appointment every six weeks with a psychiatrist! Dr X not only kept an eye on George's medication and gave a pep talk, he also tended to supply at least one interpretation.

The point of this story is that anything can be 'enough' provided the patient gives his heart to it and keeps up the momentum. I am not suggesting that 10 minutes every six weeks is to be universally recommended. Irvin Yalom (1975: 278) writes:

A once-weekly schedule is the most common format in outpatient work, but in my experience the group often suffers from the long interval between meetings. Often much has occurred in the life of the members that cannot be ignored, and the group veers away from an interactional mode into a crisis resolution format. When the group meets more than once-weekly, it increases in intensity, the meetings have more continuity, the group continues to work through issues raised the previous week, and the entire process takes on the character of a continuous meeting.

Foulkes (1975: 86) expresses the same idea:

once-weekly is a minimum.... However I have found twice-weekly sessions much more satisfactory. (The continuity is much enhanced) and only with twice-weekly groups have I learned fully to appreciate to what extent the individual sessions hang together.... Twice-weekly sessions make the whole procedure much more interesting and valuable.

Yalom and Foulkes write from their extensive experience and I cannot therefore argue with what they say. My own more limited experience does not altogether correspond to theirs. Continuity between meetings is certainly more obvious in the twice-weekly groups, such as when someone opens a session with 'I was furious last time when you said...'. In a once-weekly group, especially when it happens to be in a crisis intervention phase, the continuity is much more hidden. It peeps through when members refer to group material from the past.

Anne felt unhappy in her job largely because her colleagues were much younger than she. She worked with children and said that she was old enough to be their grandmother. 'Children usually like grandmothers,' I murmured, but this simple intervention was not taken up by the group. Months later when Anne was gaining strength she recalled what I had said on that occasion. She had become much more comfortable not only with the children but also with her colleagues in a new mother–daughter relationship.

I do not find once-weekly groups lacking in intensity. All groups can go through dreary phases, but intense feelings and activity are never far from the surface. Lionel Kreeger and Jeff Roberts have given me some notes on their experience of once-weekly compared with twice-weekly groups. Jeff finds that 'conducting a once-weekly group is more frenetic, the pace in some ways being much faster'. Lionel has worked with different kinds of once-weekly groups. He has had

> extremely limited, unexciting, supportive groups, where people cannot use dynamic transference interpretations, and who need to be held or nursed, counselled in very concrete and simplistic terms, the whole experience being sometimes quite tedious and boring for the group conductor.... On the other hand, [he has] been running a once-weekly group with a number of professionals in it, where the quality of interaction is as good and exciting as in the twice-weekly groups.

Group members who have undergone prior analysis and/or are training with analytically orientated organisations do bring a psychological sophistication and can act as pace makers in the group. This applies very much to our twice-weekly groups that contain several students or prospective students of the Institute of Group-Analysis. It often takes time to establish an ethos of psychodynamic awareness in the once-weekly groups, and yet it can be achieved from a baseline of nil.

Anne had entered a once-weekly group because of problems in her marriage and without any psychological wisdom. She had reached her last session after a productive membership of three years. Shortly before the end of the session the group was struggling with George's resistance. Anne became quite vehement: 'George, I have ten more minutes. You can't let me leave before you understand that when you talk in this way about others you are saying something about yourself.'

Twice-weekly groups are sometimes said to work in greater depth than is possible with once-weekly; but what is depth? It is quite possible at least in the heterogeneous once-weekly groups to overcome deeply felt shame or to reach strongly repressed layers such as envy, sadism or suicidal inclination. I would say that 'depth' is a misnomer for 'working through', for which there is naturally less scope in the once-weekly groups. The necessary working through just has to be done by patients outside the group sessions.

Once-weekly groups are particularly suitable for holding the seemingly untreatable patient, who may yet recover. I have described elsewhere (Mittwoch, 1982) the case history of a silent borderline patient who was enabled to exchange his world of fantasy and social isolation for a new life involving realistic relationships. Another patient covered his intense anxiety with obsessional quarrelling in the group. Normal group work almost came to a standstill, and I was put under pressure to remove this patient from the group. Here we had a clear case of transference neurosis, and I could always see bits of progress. This patient stayed in the group for ten years and finally left much improved.

Foulkes, whom I quoted above in this section, refers to the twice-weekly groups as more satisfactory and more valuable compared with once-weekly. At the same time he says, and we would all agree with him, that twice-weekly sessions 'do not shorten appreciably the duration of the total time taken for treatment'. It must be said that twice-weekly sessions are more satisfactory for the conductor. For the same number of patients the initial interviewing and the administrative work is double for once-weekly groups and there is more strain on the memory. Some group conductors help their memory along by means of lengthy notes. I am not one of them. This is partly because I am lazy, but also because I believe that the discovery of things that I forget can lead us to new analytic insights. Similarly I never encourage patients to write down their dreams, as I do not believe that we can chase the unconscious with a pencil. I was spoilt in a once-weekly group over a period of five years by a woman who remembered absolutely everything. It seemed to me to be one of her defences against total disintegration.

I return now to the topic of motivation and commitment. Problems in this area do surface, and can wax and wane in the case of certain patients and sometimes for the whole group. Such problems are much more prevalent in the once-weekly groups.

Anne was a passive patient, but attended regularly for the first six months after which she found reasons for staying away. To start with, she told us, she lived just from one session to the next. Now she did not need the group so much. This patient was acting out in the face of fear of helpless dependence. Paradoxically, when two years later she had established a pattern of regular attendance she could begin to work towards ending. She had also become much more stable and reliable in her social relationships.

My style of leadership has to take account of the frequency of sessions. I am a bit more active in the once-weekly sessions. If someone stays away without notification I might make contact by letter or telephone after the first occasion. Similarly, when someone storms out in anger, not to return before the end of the session, I would get in contact with the patient on the next day. This is not always necessary. George had left half-way through the session, slamming the door on us. In the office Kay, a former phone sitter, greeted me with a smile. George had popped into the office saying, 'See you next week', and I knew that he was having us on.

Sometimes when a once-weekly patient is going through a particularly stressful time I may offer an individual appointment or two, or I might arrange for more regular support sessions to be offered for as long as necessary by a colleague. In once-weekly groups more than in the twice-weekly a patient in difficulty might be inclined to telephone me in between sessions. Groups whose conductors are unavoidably away for an extended period may work alone for a few sessions before a group sitter can be found. The period of working alone is less in once-weekly compared with twice-weekly groups. At times when group numbers have shrunk and morale is low it is absolutely necessary to re-establish solid commitment before I would introduce new patients. Members of the Practice have sometimes referred to the once-weekly groups as their bread-and-butter. The Practice actually derives more income from the twice-weekly patients, even though they are fewer in numbers. I suspect that the bread and butter idea may have arisen out of a mix-up with 'You shall gain your bread by the sweat of your brow' (Genesis 3: 19). Too much sweat and toil on the part of the conductor is ultimately not to the benefit of patients. A more relaxed attitude can only be achieved through the conviction that one has got something good to offer. Robin Skynner has said to me that many a deprived patient has not actually gone short, but has been affected by his mother's neurotic guilt about her insufficiency.

A student on the Institute of Group-Analysis Qualifying Course presented his training group in my supervision seminar. His group members expressed nothing but moans and disgruntlement from the word go. It emerged that my student, who had had a five-times-a-week analysis behind him, felt frustrated in his own twice-weekly therapy group. It took a long time for things to improve. First he came to appreciate the help given to him in his therapy group, then he had to learn that even in a once-weekly regime he could offer a lot.

Before I close this section I will address myself to the way in which the specific setting at Montagu Mansions can feed the group process. For any particular group there are other groups nearby. Some contact is actually made in the waiting room; most remains in the realm of fantasy. Is the grass greener elsewhere or, as in a Chinese folk-song, does the moon shine brightest over my valley? These fantasies provide good stuff for analysis. Pat de Maré, on the other hand, gave two of his once-weekly groups the chance to test out their fantasies by letting them meet altogether on one or two occasions.

Here is another example of the way our setting can feed into the group fantasy:

> A young group of mine were meeting for the first time without me, for which they had been well prepared. Due to an unfortunate administrative muddle the premises were locked before the end of the session at 9.30 p.m. My group members did not panic, and tried a series of telephone numbers which they found in the office, until they reached Dr Kreeger, who sped along to let them out. Next week they proudly talked of their calmness, but also voiced the fantasy that it had been done on purpose to test them. Although on all subsequent occasions I

gave them the key to the flat, the paranoid fantasy re-emerged every now and again for over five years.

Duration of treatment and outcome

Foulkes (1975) writes on duration: 'a minimum for any one individual is one year...and the maximum in my experience was 8 years...the optimal time seems to be 3 years or perhaps 2 years. In my own groups [the average is] about 3 years if one discounts the drop outs.'

I have collected some statistics on duration for my two once-weekly groups at the Practice that have been running for 13 years and 9 years respectively:

All in all 50 patients have left.

Of these six dropped out after three or fewer sessions.

Nine further patients dropped out within one year, average 7½ months.

Of the remaining 35 patients the minimum was one year, the maximum ten years, the average three years five months.

My own experience is thus very similar to that of Foulkes. None of us at the Practice to my knowledge have measured statistics on the outcome of treatment. For my part I would rather not subject my patients to questionnaires at the beginning and end of treatment, and worse still at various stages of follow up. I would always regard the questions, the responses and conclusions as suspect.

I do believe that we can obtain a rough idea of outcome from the way patients end their treatment. My three patients who never integrated at all obviously showed no improvement. The drop-outs within the first year I would classify as no more than slightly improved, although one lady who packed it in after nine months declared herself to be delighted with the result. Of the other 35 patients eight ended by fizzling out or else by giving no more than a month's notice. These probably come under the category of 'improved'. The remaining 27 patients left after satisfactory consultation with the group followed by two to six months' work towards termination. These patients seemed to us much improved. My tally is therefore:

Non-starters   12 per cent

Slightly improved   18 per cent

Improved   16 per cent

Much improved   54 per cent

I end this chapter with the termination of just one patient whom we regarded as much improved. This man, a barrister, handed each of the remaining group members a card, bound with pink tape like a legal brief. The message inside said, 'Best wishes'. I reproduce the outside below.

I would like to juxtapose this card with a diagram of Foulkes (1948) from his early writing (see Figures 6.1 and 6.2).

My patient knew nothing of Foulkes but, like him, he regarded his group treatment as a preparation for life. May he and all the others who have left enjoy long lives.

Figure 6.1 Foulkes' view of the relationship between various therapies and 'Life'

Source: Foulkes 1948

Figure 6.2 George's Testimonial

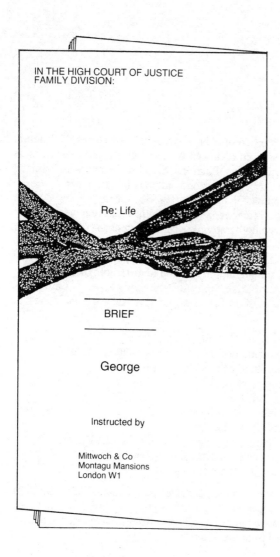

IN THE HIGH COURT OF JUSTICE
FAMILY DIVISION:

Re: Life

BRIEF

George

Instructed by

Mittwoch & Co
Montagu Mansions
London W1

Chapter 7

Special categories of patients in groups

Edited by Jeff Roberts

The patients of the Practice may be viewed from a number of different perspectives. This has been reviewed with sensitivity and thoroughness in Chapter 4 by Dennis Brown. Each individual will come with a unique difficulty and we do our best to respond uniquely to him or her. None the less, people can be characterised and categorised, with varying degrees of precision. There are moreover a range of rather clear-cut categories of people who request psychotherapy. To a certain extent it is found that their needs and responses in psychotherapy correspond to the category in which they are placed. In this chapter therefore we look at how we in the Practice think about and attempt to respond to different types of people.

In the ten sections of this chapter the following types of patient are considered by Members of the Practice who have had a special interest in them:

1 The borderline patient: Malcolm Pines
2 The borderline patient, an alternative viewpoint: Colin James
3 The sexually disordered patient: Jeff Roberts
4 Older patients: Lionel Kreeger
5 Younger patients: Jeff Roberts
6 Interminable patients: Malcolm Pines
7 Couples in groups: Robin Skynner
8 The patient with somatic symptoms and illness: Jeff Roberts
9 The schizoid character in groups: Jeff Roberts
10 The psychotic patient: Lionel Kreeger

Consideration is given to the particular problems and advantages of treating each type of person in groups, and each author has outlined concisely and instructively how he believes different categories of patient may be helped in groups at the Practice.

1 The borderline patient
Malcolm Pines

Psychotherapists have always had to deal with 'difficult patients', but when we began the Practice we scarcely knew of the 'borderline' category. Certainly we had our monopolisers, our actors out, our dramatisers. I recall a patient who frequently left the session in a rage to lock herself in the lavatory and who refused to leave the building at the end of the session; another who constantly threatened suicide during her long train journey to and from London; another who slowly went into a fixed delusional state.

I found how strong and containing groups can be both to the patient and to the therapist during these critical and difficult times and also how the therapist has his unique contribution to make during the extraordinarily powerful episodes that borderline patients can generate. One such was between a roughly built farmer who had a great hatred of his mother and an older woman patient upon whom he vented his rage, seeing her only as self-centred, withholding and castrative. That this woman had such elements in her character and displayed these in her behaviour was undeniable, though she could also be sensitive and sympathetic and had attempted to show this man her concern and understanding, particularly for his early maternal deprivations. However, the rage built up and the critical episode and turning point came when he threatened her with physical violence during a session and she did not back down from her assertions about him. Each attacked the other head on, only seeing in the other what was most feared and hated in themselves and in their introjects.

This state I have termed 'non-dialogical mirroring', which is equivalent to what I have also called 'non-reflective mirroring' (Pines, 1984). My interventions, showing them their mutual projective systems, enabled each eventually to acknowledge in themselves what they saw, feared and hated in the other. This 'mediation', which represents the introduction of the more comprehensive point of view on the situation which can only come from the third person who has managed to integrate and comprehend what is happening, enables the primitive dyad to move into a less primitive triadic relationship through the mirroring which the third person has been able to give them. In legend this is symbolised by the myth of Perseus who was able to slay the Gorgon with the aid of a mirror that Athena, the goddess of wisdom, had given him from her breast-plate. What had previously been a face-to-face, deadly confrontation which could only lead to petrification had through the uses of the mirror opened into a space that allowed both for reflection and subsequently for creativity.

Over the years we have become familiar with the current understanding of borderline patients and have contributed to the literature. We are confident that the maturational capacity of the properly selected and conducted analytic group will, in the majority of cases, enable the borderline patient to remain in such a group for long enough to grow beyond the level of primitive responses. As a rule we try to limit the number of borderline patients in each group to one or two; beyond that the load on the other members and the therapist may be too great. As it is, the borderline patient may consume a large amount of available time and attention and limits may have to be strongly emphasised and monitored. We do not routinely use combined therapy, having found that a twice-weekly group will usually prove adequate to contain the patients' needs and indeed this can sometimes be done in a group that meets only once-weekly. However, our Practice is sufficiently flexible to allow for variations on this ground plan in some cases. Occasionally the patient will be seen alone or in joint marital or family sessions in addition to the regular group. Pharmacotherapy may sometimes be indicated.

Our knowledge of 'borderline patients' prepares us for the type of behaviour the patient may show – the rages, the overwhelming anxieties, the regressive episodes, the massive projections and splitting. But we are greatly impressed by the positive aspects of the other group members' responses, with the patience, the understanding, the ability to emphasise and to share in the primitive levels of needs and conflicts that the borderline patient often shows. Indeed, these more primitive levels of mental life are often welcomed and respected by the more neurotic patients, for this is a way in which they can gain access to shut-off aspects of themselves. The process of change can be partly understood as a 'metabolisation' of the primitive self and object representations or, in Bion's (1962) terms, move from beta to alpha elements. Diagnostically it is important to distinguish between borderline patients and persons with psychotic illnesses. Occasionally we see patients who are at the early stages of the schizophrenic process, and the pros and cons of psychotherapy have to be carefully evaluated. The support and understanding of the group have to be balanced against the psychotic patients' need to maintain distance, which may mean the adoption of psychotic mechanisms of defence. Again we have carefully to discriminate a very schizoid patient from the potentially psychotic. The initial interview is always important, for if the therapist can feel that he has gained access to the patient's inner world, has been experienced as helpful and has had a sense of warmth aroused together with a desire to help, this is usually a positive prognostic sign.

When do we turn a borderline patient down for group analysis? Not because he or she has failed to respond to the previous individual therapy, which very often includes full psychoanalysis. In fact many of our patients have been in such therapies and either have come to an impasse or terminated with the sense of incompleteness or disappointment in the individual therapy. For many such persons, probably for most, the group is experienced as a liberation. The patient can now interact freely with fellow patients and put to positive use the gains made in dyadic therapy where he or she had not had the sense of being able freely to interact with a responding other. They can also review the transference relationship in the light of the new transference to the other members of the group, which of course also includes the group conductor. For the patient who has been on the couch in individual therapy the face-to-face situation is a very significant change, and often the redundant, passive, regressive, dependent relationship that characterises the end of many individual therapies can be discarded. Many of our best patients – by that meaning that they are able to use the potential of the group – have come from prior individual therapies.

Those borderline patients who are referred to individual therapy with others or taken on ourselves as individual patients include: (1) those who are primarily seeking out individual therapy and who are sufficiently well motivated for it and who have the emotional and financial resources available for the lengthy and difficult process of psychoanalysis. (2) Those who seem to need at least a preliminary period of individual therapy during which they gain in confidence in the working alliance with the therapist and are able to begin to explore their inner world. Some very fragile or paranoid patients come into this category. (3) Patients who are in acute emotional crises, which often characterise borderline patients, for which a group will neither be willing nor able to offer help. A new patient inevitably disrupts an ongoing group, and the existing group members will not have sufficient knowledge of our working relationships with the new patient to take these crises on board in the way that they are able to do with a patient who is already a group member. (4) Sometimes we see a patient who seems to have a very destructive potential in whatever therapy they take part. This is shown by the life history of broken relationships, often including other therapies. These patients border on the psychopathic or delinquent categories. (5) Some patients have such unrealistic expectations for therapy and such grandiose claims of themselves that almost any therapy seems inappropriate.

Technical recommendations

1 Proper selection and placement in an appropriate group.
2 Integration into the ongoing group process which often means not allowing the patient to monopolise and enabling the new patient and other patients to recognise what they have in common or what the presence of the new patient may stimulate.
3 Recognising and dealing with the primitive relationship patterns of the borderline patient. The well-known projections and splitting, the ability to provoke either extreme attacks or idealised support from

other patients, the isolation of the therapist from the rest of the group in either an idealised or paranoid pairing relationship with a borderline patient are typical examples.

4 Medication when this is needed.

5 Confrontation and limit setting which, if they are not done by the other group members, need certainly to be done by the therapist.

6 In our Practice we feel free to work quite intensively with individual members of the group. This is done with the confidence that the figure ground *Gestalt* means that the other persons are not simply spectators of the therapeutic interaction but are responding to it in their own characteristic ways. There are times when it is very much the therapist's responsibility to try to reach and to understand the patient's dynamics, and this is usually seen as a safe and containing procedure by other group members though it will inevitably arouse some jealousy or envy.

Conclusion

The group-analytic group is one of the best therapeutic situations for the borderline patient who is not operating at the most primitive level. The maturational capacity of the group brings out the truth of Balint's dictum that after psychoanalysis the patient is often less neurotic but not more mature, whereas after group psychotherapy the patient who may not be much less neurotic is certainly more mature.

2 The borderline patient, an alternative viewpoint
D. Colin James

Some thoughts are outlined below concerning the borderline state and its management in group analysis including the specifics of dealing with the regressed patient. It is commonly thought that, because of the sparsity of psychoanalytic and psychotherapeutic help for 'borderline' patients, group analysis is indicated, if only as a means of beginning the therapeutic process for such patients. Most of the patients will only benefit eventually from individual psychoanalysis. The beginning of intensive treatments of borderline states are fraught with anxieties and conflicts, often with a great deal of resistance and a tendency to act out. Because of the difficulties of procuring such treatments, and because the beginnings are so difficult, a group approach is often the only way to make a start.

I write from my clinical experience at the Group-Analytic Practice, of such an approach, not only to indicate its value, but also to emphasise some of the difficulties, indeed dangers, of this approach; 'dangers', that is, if the whole picture and its implications are not taken into account.

The value of this approach is that the group experience provides some social contact and enables the borderline patient to begin to relate to other people in a setting which allows interaction, yet retains a safe boundary, inhibiting acting-out and encouraging understanding. On the other hand the presence of a borderline patient in a group sensitises others to the most primitive elements of their own personalities. These elements are often rigorously defended against, and yet their exclusion from consciousness inhibits the very interaction which the person might want with others.

The management of severely disturbed patients, or those who regress during treatment, is a current and ongoing theoretical and technical problem in group analysis. This should not be as surprising as it is sometimes felt to be. After all, Foulkes (1964), early in his work, described the regressive components of being in a group, while Bion (1961) stressed the very primitive experiences to which a group subjects even the 'normal' adult. Group settings arouse in us anxieties whose origins are encountered very early in our lives, and unless these anxieties are accepted, the group process can easily be obscured by a sense of conviviality. The aim then becomes to make everything 'comfortable' while not dealing with the source and nature of the anxieties. These anxieties are troublesome to all people in all group situations.

One of the dangers of treating patients with borderline features in a group, is that such a patient often 'takes on' all of the anxiety and becomes a recipient of projections for the other patients who do not manifest such primitive anxieties. The others then behave as if the disturbed patient is the only contributor to the anxiety felt by all. Yet, each person is part of the whole process, and it might be that the more disturbed patient is acting out not only for himself but also for the others. He might have shown himself to be habitually more anxious in the group than the others seem to have been, and have gained the label of 'the difficult' patient.

From an object-relations theory point of view the problems which people starting in a group describe are often neurotic in their presentation. These can also be conceptualised in terms of very primitive defence mechanisms, which have been developed around early conflicts within the relationship with mother. The group process is unquestionably disturbed by the projection of any person's primitive processes, and yet some group processes are very much the result of these projections.

The anxiety generated in the group by the projection from a disturbed patient of these primitive ideas is often intense, and what tends to happen is that the group supports the more disturbed patient at any one time to focus his attention and projections on to the conductor. Whatever the material involved, be it aggressive, seductive or perverse, the tension evoked by projection by a disturbed patient on to (and in fantasy 'into') the conductor necessarily disrupts the group process and often prevents the group from working as a whole.

Sometimes for quite long periods the conductor has to tolerate this state of affairs, seeing it partly as a manifestation of a disturbed person's ideation but also recognising and dealing with the fact that once that process starts everyone else in the group is involved, and the conductor encourages and facilitates the more disturbed person to continue along that path. It is sometimes impossible for the conductor to encourage other members of the group to intervene and look at the experience which they are having. Paradoxically, the more disturbed patient becomes the victim of everyone else's projections entrapped by having opened up a channel, so to speak, through which the more primitive elements in the personalities of all the people involved get projected.

The management of this is perhaps one of the most difficult aspects of group therapy. Unquestionably the conductor's own personality is involved and his or her own countertransference is the main instrument leading towards understanding. He has to be acutely aware of the primitive elements of his own personality that might get caught up in this process and at the same time realise that it is only through those primitive mechanisms and his understanding of them that any light can be shed on the situation.

When there is a recognition of the similarity of these phenomena, there is often a sense of cohesion and of jointly dealing with the more primitive development towards a more mature mode of relating. This step forward paradoxically facilitates further regression when the occasion arises, but with a more rapid understanding of the regression and the possibility of working at an even deeper level.

It is here that the concept of 'holding' and 'containing' come into their own in group analysis. These apparently similar concepts are very different, and are often confused. Briefly, 'holding' is a concept used by Winnicott (1960) to describe the need of the mother to take care of the infant in a devoted manner at least at first, when the infant is utterly dependent and resourceless. Bion (1962a) developed the concept of 'containing' in respect of a hypothesis of a mental process, in which elements of primitive psychic experience which cannot be understood by the infant, are fantasied as being projected into the mother. She, by dint of her maturity, is able to bring her understanding to these experiences, and being attentive to her infant, facilitates the beginnings of understanding of these experiences in her infant. I have elsewhere attempted to describe how these two concepts, while being similar in many respects, have important differences, with major theoretical implications. Nevertheless both theories emphasise the importance of the role of mother in providing an optimal environment in which the earliest rudiments of understanding can develop. Their importance for several aspects of therapeutic situations cannot be overemphasised (James, 1984). The corollary to this in group analysis is that the members in relationship to each other, as a whole, serve as the container. The conductor's holding or containing capacity becomes very important as a model around which the group's containing capacity forms.

What is being described here says something about those people who have difficulty in relating in the real world and who are often the ones who come for group analysis. Difficulties in adult relationships stem essentially from some difficulty in early object relationships which have been accommodated by the development in the personality of certain neurotic characteristics, but which essentially cover over these earlier deficits (a view currently held firmly in psychoanalytic circles).

The patient entering a group, whatever the symptoms, makes some sort of commitment to the process. There is an acknowledgement of dependency and an immediate resistance to this; having striven to deal with the symptom during life, the patient gradually allows him or herself to be involved in the process of the group and gradually submits to an exploration of those processes. For all patients this confronts the need to examine the issue of how they relate in fantasy to other people. The boundary between self and other becomes a crucial issue.

There are complex reasons for ignoring these early mechanisms in group analysis and in group process, and there are differences about the theories of the origins of these states, and some lead to a denial or ignoring of their happening. Personally I have found that the formulations of Winnicott (1953, 1960 and 1969), Fairbairn (1941, 1952 – see also Sutherland 1989), and those of Bion already referred to, clarify these situations.

I have also always been indebted to Henri Rey (1968), who very early in my learning about group process and therapy told of his custom of always having a disturbed patient in his groups. The patient, used to functioning at a more primitive level socially, seemed to undertake the brunt of the pain of these primitive processes. There is a great danger in group analysis that we get caught up in, and yet ignore, group dynamics, and defend against the very primitiveness of our behaviour in groups by splitting, denial and projective identification. We owe it to our patients to help each of them beyond the feeling of comfort and friendship in group situations, towards being more fully aware of the difficulties in accepting and dealing with each of their own primitive aspects, and learning from them rather than defending against them and forever adopting a rather false-self stance to the world.

Hence the importance of the proper management of the disturbed patient, not only for himself, but also for the sake of what other members might learn about themselves, through such an experience. This to me is emphasised by Bion (1962b), as learning from experience (see also Bion 1962c). In my view this is an important element of what happens in group-analytic groups, even though traditionally the underlying experiences tend to be ignored; they might even be rationalised by being explained within some other formulation such as coherence or containing in the sense of supporting, rather than as a rigorous dynamic interaction aimed at understanding and taking responsibility for one's own response to one's own experience.

The acceptance of the inevitability of any.group to encourage at times regression to primitive levels of functioning is a prerequisite to understanding the individual's experience in a group. For the borderline patient this is particularly important. The acceptance leads to working through of the primitive levels. Only then can the individual function more independently and develop further the more mature accomplishments of his or her personality which can then be contributed into the group experience.

3 The patient with gender problems and other sexual difficulties in groups
Jeff Roberts

The sexually disturbed or disordered person is often difficult to treat and can be experienced as extremely conservative and rigid in the area of sexuality. In this area he or she brings to mind the poor hobbit, Gollum,[1] who is progressively reduced to a shadow of his former self by 'his precious', a magic ring to which he clings with pathetic tenacity, despite the fact that its influence is destroying him. All of the apparently untreatable psychological disorders, and those in which an analytic therapy appears to be interminable, appear to have an element of a clinging of this sort which keeps them active.

The range of difficulties for which people have been offered group-analytic psychotherapy is very wide, and although inevitably biased towards the neurotic end of the scale in fact encompasses the whole spectrum of psychological and psychiatric disorder. Not surprisingly therefore we encounter, in assessments and in our groups, a range of sexual disorders and dysfunctions.

A survey of our work in this area over the past two years, using a simple questionnaire, shows that 75 patients in our groups during this time were considered to manifest some form of sexual disorder. The overall findings of this survey may be seen in Tables 7.1 and 7.2.

As shown in the table below, only in four cases was the admission to a group-analytic group considered to have been a poor decision. Indeed the overall record of this group of patients for staying in therapy is extremely good. It is of interest to note, however, that the sexual issue was the presenting problem in only 16 out of the 74 identified sexually troubled patients.

Some form of maturation or change in the sexual disorder was apparent in 34 out of 75 cases (46 per cent). This is, moreover, a group of whom many are still in treatment, and is not any indication of final outcome.

A significant proportion of these patients were not asking for help with their sexual disorder and indeed would wish to repudiate the term 'disorder'. These are the homosexuals, who now rarely come asking for treatment of their homosexuality. Thus, whatever position one takes on the nature of homosexuality, regarding it either as a developmental deviation or perhaps a 'normal variant' of personality expression, few homosexuals approach us at the practice, or me in my own psychotherapy practice, asking for reorientation.

Our survey brought some interesting statements concerning sexual aspects of personality development and expression from members of the practice. These useful and pithy comments are quoted below and each was made by a different Member or Associate. In my own opinion sexuality and sexual expression are located at the very core of the individuals psyche (this is no radical idea) and is likely to be among the most fundamental and conservative components of personality.

1 Sexual difficulties, either in orientation or performance, are probably most resistant to change. Such difficulties have remained in patients who have shown many significant changes in other areas.
2 The sexual disorder is like a fingerprint of the entire personality. Patients do not have to 'reveal' their sexual disorder for you to know

Table 7.1   shows the categories of patients with manifest sexual 'issues' in groups in the Practice, during a two-year period, ending December 1989.

Homosexual female	7
Homosexual male	18
Persistently bi-sexual	4
Transvestite	1
Sexual identity confusion	16
Paedophiliac	5
Heterosexual dysfunction	10
Homosexual dysfunction	1
Late and current virginity	11
Polymorphous perverse	1
	74

Table 7.2   shows the number of these patients who presented with a sexual issue, and gives some indication of outcome to date.

Sex issue presenting	16
Evolution/maturation	34
Poor decision to put in group	4
Early drop outs (<10 sessions)	1
Premature terminators	4

what they are. If they change for the better, the chances are that their sexual functioning will change too.

3 Progress is dependent on general opening up and change in ways of relating, combined with working directly on a 'real' or metaphorical enactment of the problem within the group context.

4 This is difficult. With the 'fixed' position of a deviance there is little chance of a 'cure' or change in orientation. There can, however, be significant gains in terms of relatedness and social functioning.

5 Progress often seems to be achieved by oblique rather than direct exploration, the sexual difficulty turning out to be a symptom of a deeper interpersonal difficulty.

6 In a carefully selected group, two or three patients with sexual dysfunction, especially patients with sexual identity confusion, potency problems and frigidity, have an excellent chance to tackle their problems. Improvement seems to me to be the rule rather than the exception.

7 I have a feeling that sexually disordered patients are very difficult to engage in treatment and even more difficult to get into a group in the first place, this being related to a deep inner sense of shame and fear of exposure. (This seems to me to be very much the case with those who have been sexually abused, Ed.)

8 I view group analysis very positively for these patients, particularly with those who are homosexual or have sexual identity confusion.

Our members seem to me to have wide-ranging but on the whole convergent views on the suitability of group analysis for these patients. One strand emerging from these views is the conservative nature of sexual adjustment. Another is that our experience tends to be positive, both in the contribution these patients make to their groups, but also in gains these patients can make in a group-analytic group. Formal research would be helpful here, particularly focused on outcome, as assessed after termination of therapy. Overall this category of patient adds a valuable extra dimension to our groups, and I particularly like to have an overt homosexual dimension in all of my groups when I can.

4 Older patients
Lionel Kreeger

For practical purposes it is convenient to consider two age ranges for groups for the older patient, 45–60 years and the over sixties. I tend to refer to the former age grouping as a 'mature group' or 'mid-life group'. I have run two groups for this age span, each for about two years. I have tried several times over the past decade to organise a group for the over sixties, but without success. It did not prove possible to collect enough patients at any one time to form a viable nucleus to get it started. Fortunately it has been possible to include people in their sixties or older in existing mixed groups within the Practice, particularly when the structure of the group has been multi-generational from the start. It has not been unusual for people in their seventies to be active and valued members of some groups.

Undoubtedly it is a most important area of our work. With an increasing life span there will be more demand for psychotherapy, even full psychoanalysis, and certainly for group analysis. I saw a man of 83 years recently, deeply troubled by a life-long sexually perverse preoccupation, embarrassed and depressed by its unabated continuance. We met several times and he obtained some relief from sharing his discomfiture and guilt. I thought he could benefit from group therapy, but would have needed to be with others of his age. I told him I would keep him in mind if I did manage to get a suitable group together, but in the meantime he did need continuing help. As he had done some autogenic training in the past, mostly self-taught from books, and found this technique useful in relaxing and clearing his mind, I referred him on to a colleague for a more thorough grounding in the method. He did so well there was no purpose in keeping his name on the waiting list for a group.

I find that a large proportion of our referrals are in their middle years, many in the throes of a mid-life crisis, with acute problems concerning relationships, marriage, family conflicts, work and loss of creativity. Increasing physical defects and illness create anxiety and depression, particularly among the men who tend to somatise their emotional conflicts rather than experience them more directly. Preoccupation with death and dying is commonplace, increasing in intensity in later years. Rosemary Gordon (1977, 1978), a Jungian analyst, has written on 'Dying and Creating' (or 'Death and Creativity', an earlier paper) with the message that it is those people who can prepare to die well who can also be in better touch with their creativity.

Groups with a mature membership

The two groups that I ran for about two years each were remarkably similar to each other, both in composition and process. The age range was roughly from 45 to 60 years, with equal sex distribution. Most were married, divorced or separated, but a few were single and unattached. Most had grown-up children and young grandchildren. Work problems were common, some facing humiliation and despair over redundancy. Many had provoked serious conflict in their complicated relationships, sometimes the result of an extra-marital affair entered into in a desperate hypomanic way to escape from their mid-life depression, often accompanied by diminished sexual performance. These groups showed strong cohesion from the outset, no doubt because of the common shared experience, and as group conductor I also felt very much a part of the group and its preoccupations. It was not uncommon for me to be concerned at a personal level with my own conflict that was identical to the theme of the group.

It seemed that there was a natural life-span of the group of about two years, so that they shifted from 'slow-open' to 'closed' after a year or so, the groups working to termination together over a significant period of time.

Older patient groups

I have made two wholehearted attempts to form a group for the over sixties, but unfortunately without success. On one occasion it was triggered by the fact that there were two or three older patients on the Practice waiting list, none of us having suitable vacancies for them in our general groups at that time. The other was through my conviction that such a group should be part of the Practice range of facilities and that one of us should try to organise it. I wrote or telephoned several colleagues and friends to advise them of my plan, and all were enthusiastic in principle. However, very few suitable referrals were forthcoming, and although I managed to collect three or four people, because of the passage of time they tended to opt out for one reason or another. One retired from work and decided to move abroad. Another became physically ill, preventing him from being able to attend the group. Each time we got near to starting, there were just not sufficient numbers to form a viable nucleus.

In my consultations with older patients, I am particularly concerned to ensure that they are not in the early stages of organic disease. I always insist on a thorough review of their physical state to exclude those common diseases that occur at this time of life. In particular, it is vital to exclude dementia either from Alzheimer's disease or cerebral arterial sclerosis. Although it is possible that patients with early dementia could be helped in groups, the appropriate techniques are more likely to be supportive or behavioural rather than group-analytic. I can remember running groups for geriatric patients in the back ward of a mental hospital, where we did have fun, utilising such techniques as music and movement, but it had virtually nothing to do with analysis. It is also important to be alert to the possibility of a severe depression masquerading as some other condition, such as an anxiety state or even dementia. The old diagnostic category of involutional melancholia is still relevant, and often considerable symptomatic relief can be obtained with appropriate anti-depressant medication.

Some mention should be made of bereavement, an inevitable experience at this time of life. Working with, and hopefully through, the pain and despair of loss of loved ones is vital to those who have been left behind. So often today, the nuclear family is unable to contain the elderly parent, who then becomes increasingly isolated and unsupported – unquestionably a vital area for the continuing application of group methods. For further reading I would suggest *Group Psychotherapies for the Elderly* (MacLennan, Saul and Weiner, 1988) and 'Group Psychotherapy with the pre-Elderly' (Ezquerro, 1989). The former is a comprehensive book divided into two sections – insight-orientated groups, and those which are more supportive and rehabilitative. The latter is an account of a time-limited group for the late middle-aged (55 to 67 years old) over a period of one calendar year. It was a demanding but very satisfying experience for both patients and co-therapists, with particular difficulty during the phase of termination with considerable sadness and vulnerability. Lastly, Martin Grotjahn in a short contribution (Grotjahn, 1989) highlights the problems of old age both for patients and therapists. He insists that the psychopathology of old age is not hopeless, and that psychotherapy with older people does not only consist of preparation for death. He insists that many of the problems of old age such as depression, loneliness, a feeling of neglect by relatives and professionals, can be discussed nowhere better than in groups.

5 Younger patients
Jeff Roberts

For much of the life of the practice there has been one group dedicated to patients between the ages of 17 and approximately 25. I am currently conducting such a group which has been operating now for three and a half years since 1986. This group was started in order to accommodate the youngest of our referrals and also those in their early and mid-twenties judged too immature to go into a more heterogeneous group. Such people tend to fit poorly into the somewhat constraining atmosphere of an analytic group, the majority of whose members are over 25. The issues confronted by these younger and sometimes rather immature people are also different from those of the mid-twenties plus group, and the mode of addressing the issues is certainly rather boisterous and direct.

This is almost by definition a group of youngsters who have encountered difficulty in bringing their adolescence to a satisfactory conclusion. They tend most markedly not to have resolved issues of separation or individuation, despite in many instances being otherwise quite effective people. Others, however, have not satisfactorily established a clear sense of identity. Yet others have emerged from the structured and supportive school environment and encountered problems in making and sustaining relationships owing to schizoid character traits (see section 10 of this chapter).

The group has had a far more rapid turnover than any of my other groups in the practice. This is, I believe, a not unexpected reflection of the characteristics of a significant proportion of the client group; that is, a more or less acceptable impulsiveness and reluctance to make firm or long-term commitments. Moreover, those youngsters who are on a quest for the magical answer to their troubles are not very far into this quest and are likely to be rapidly disillusioned in the slowly acquired and non magical effects of being in an ongoing therapy group. Another contribution to rapid turnover were a number of relatively healthy youngsters who resolved the issues they brought, to their satisfaction, rather more rapidly than a similar adult patient would. These relatively good outcomes achieved in six to nine months were disconcerting and disruptive but probably authentic.

In among this somewhat frenetic activity however some having that element of 'grittiness' in their character, as described by Dennis Brown in Chapter 4, have settled down to work hard in a group which is now beginning to know what it is doing. Some of this group have already left or, sadly for me, are just about to. They have, I believe, mostly made substantial and irreversible gains.

The content of the group has been more or less as expected, with a group of youngsters attempting a somewhat ambivalent separation from parents of variable quality and ability to understand their children. One young woman told her new stepmother, 'You're not my mother', soon after she moved into the household. They have had a stormy relationship ever since. Another young man left home, without a forwarding address, to escape an oppressive home environment, with no emotional expression allowed. Both these people have vigorously explored their continuing angry attachments, and both incidentally are terrified of their dreams. Two other painful areas of discussion have been adoption, why did it happen to me? and then, even more difficult, the working through of feelings regarding the death of parents which occurred prematurely.

The outcome of the group to date appears to fall into three sub-categories. Firstly, there are rather a large number of early drop-outs (leaving the group within ten sessions), who, despite being articulate and apparently strongly motivated, attend the group for no more than two or three sessions, before disappearing and refusing to make further contact. A second sub-group are those with overt schizoid characters who are unable to find a voice in the group and, despite staying for some months, eventually leave, rather than continue to experience their inability to initiate any kind of self-motivated participation in the group process. The final sub-group are those, already discussed, who stay in the group for at least a year, work hard and through their participation achieve the resolution of a number of the key conflicts which they brought with them and thereby mature considerably.

The role I play is that of a robust, permissive and, I believe, rather asexual parent. This enables transference relating to either parent to develop, when conflict in relation to that parent is currently active and near the surface. Despite my permissive stance I also make it clear that destructive acting out is not part of being in an analytic group and strongly discourage damaging extra-group activities. From time to time I find myself making adult or parental judgements as a kind of respected 'adult' role model. This behaviour generally seems to be helpful. My main goal is to promote an analytic process. On the whole this is well received. Recently, however, I had occasion to make a provocative interpretation of some reasonably self evident sexual allusions. A charming young man of the world, who had joined the group a week earlier, went against the tide in the group to protest about the ridiculous thing I had said. Despite previously appearing strongly motivated, he has not attended the group since, nor responded to attempts to contact him.

The younger members of this group, and some of the older ones, continue to live with parents. Approximately half of them have their fees paid by parents. The result of this can be some lack of clarity in this group over financial transactions. Most of the members in fact go out of their way to keep fee paying open and up to date. With a few, however, there is obvious reluctance on the part of parents to pay for therapy. Bills are required and payment is slow. None the less major difficulties are rare. One problem can be that the payer expects reports, which would constitute a breach of confidentiality if given. Another source of difficulty here is when the immature youngster becomes more assertive and apparently even more of a problem than he or she was before starting therapy. Although this is almost invariably improvement, it may not be experienced as such by parents, so that the therapy will not appear to be value for money. A very difficult problem arose over fees when it became necessary to offer an urgent individual session during a summer break. Although mother was away at the time, she felt she should have been consulted over this unnecessary luxury, and was most reluctant to pay for the session.

A final difficulty I have had with this group is of the utmost piquancy. My lively group of adolescents, with a predilection for action rather than talk and talk rather than silence, regularly encounter a depressed, intense and inward-looking group, with a strictly 'analytic' conductor, in the waiting room. The result has been extremely angry encounters which have allowed both groups to explore in some depth issues of youth and youth lost, envy and intensely emotional disagreements between generations. This had led to some uncomfortable encounters with myself and my colleague who conducts the other group. Initially he found it hard to contain his own feelings about what was happening, but after some discussion we agreed that the issue between us and overflowing from him was that of our respective countertransference to our own and each other's groups.

6 Interminable patients
Malcolm Pines

At the initial interview, many patients will ask, 'How long will treatment take?' The reasonable response to such a question is, 'I can't tell you now as I don't know, but two or three years is a reasonable time to think about. That length of time will enable you to get well into your therapy and you will then be able to review your situation and decide how long you want to stay in therapy.' Thus, we make clear to our patients that group-analytic therapy is long-term and we discourage people from thinking that they may only come for a few sessions to 'try out therapy'. Patients who have such doubts should be seen individually until they can make their minds up one way or another.

The majority of our patients come into groups after having had one initial interview, and the therapist is then able to see how the patient involves himself in the group right from the start. There are both advantages and disadvantages for the therapist having only a very broad outline about the patient's personality and dynamics, the advantage being that the field is much more open for the group-analytic experience itself to provide the information; the disadvantage being that the therapist may feel that he does not have access to sufficient information to make him feel familiar with the patient. On the whole we find that the advantages outweigh the disadvantages. The majority of our groups have a stable group membership over at least a few months or even for a year or two. This undoubtedly aids the work, and a good deal of progress can be made during those stable periods. The members can be more trusting, more open, more mutually understanding, as both their conscious and unconscious understanding of one another increases. But sooner or later individuals will decide to leave and endings have to be worked at. The timing of leaving a group may be appropriate or may be premature; which applies should become clear in the working-out process. In any case we ask for a month's notice before a patient leaves a group, and this is made clear when they join a group, but in practice the termination period is much more likely to be two or three months or even longer.

Some of our patients, however, stay on almost as permanent residents in a group. five, six or seven years is not uncommon, and the longest time that anyone has stayed is in the region of 12 to 14 years. Inevitably therapists have mixed feelings towards such long-stay patients. They become part of the core of the group and can be felt as reliable, even helpful members. But the therapist will often feel bothered by a very long-term patient. Does this patient represent a failure of therapy? Has the patient become so attached and so dependent on the group that he or she will never leave? Is there something that the therapist has to work through in the countertransference to release the patient from the need to stay? And it is embarrassing for the therapist when a new patient inevitably asks how long the other patients have been in the group and to have one or more patients reply they have been there for many years! But part of the task of the therapist is to come to terms with this embarrassment, and doing so is a maturational achievement. The therapist has to overcome some of his narcissistic traits and to accept that he is not only going to be seen by others and by himself as an invariably successful therapist whose patients always get better relatively quickly. So much of psychotherapy is very long-term, with patients whose rate of change can be very slow indeed, and much of the strength of the group-analytic situation is that the slowness can be accepted, tolerated and utilised (see discussion of Dr Patrick de Maré's contribution to the Practice in Chapter 3).

The fact is that some patients do seem to need the sense of significant involvement and participation in a group to provide them with a framework for their existence. The 'framework patients' often have some borderline features. Their inner world seems empty or persecutory, and only very slowly do they internalise the group's therapeutic process. Gradually some of the distrust and strong, passive withdrawal defensiveness diminishes and a person begins to participate more actively in the therapeutic process. In the majority of cases the patience of the subject, the therapist and the other group members is rewarded and persons who might seem to be untreatable do benefit.

I came to these ideas from the experience with individual therapy with such patients. I have seen several patients who seem to have fallen to pieces after leaving school. They experience themselves as falling into aimless, despairing, apathetic depressions and defend themselves sometimes with obsessive preoccupations about the meaninglessness of life. Without knowing it they have needed their school, their institution and their place in it as if it were an unacknowledged part of their organised, cohesive self. Against this background they could differentiate themselves and stand out often as rebels or radicals. Removed from this background there was no longer any stable differentiation, no moulding, cohesive pressure that would help to outline the boundaries of the self. Such a person may plunge into the drug scene with its false sense of cohesion, only there to encounter terrifyingly bad trips that leave indelible marks of terror from the experience of disintegration and emptiness which they find there. Many years may pass before the person regains the courage to face his or her inner world.

The treatment of such patients easily produces discouragement in the therapist. Often they will sit silent for hours on end and seem to take very little in. They withdraw their attention from their perceptual boundaries and instead it is concentrated on defensive fantasy. Though feeling mindless and absent from the session, characteristically they cling to the armchair in which they sit and are preoccupied with the boundaries of time. They seem partly diffused, their body boundaries with the supporting chair and their sense of existence with the boundaries of the treatment situation.

The massive denial of involvement and dependency is only shown up by interruptions of treatment, such as in a hospital setting by a change of therapist. This is when the patient experiences enormous anxiety and tension. Showing the patient that his need to cling to the framework of treatment, sharing an understanding that it represents the framework of his existence and that without it he dreads to disintegrate, to fall to pieces, can relieve anxiety in a striking way, though it needs also to be combined with a firm structuring of the treatment situation.

Clinical profiles of very long stay patients

1 Emotionally shallow and inarticulate persons

Some may be classed as alexithymic and present with somatic symptoms. Though relatively inaccessible in individual therapy they often present much less of a problem to their fellow group members than they do to the therapist. The other patients are not as much invested in changing their peers as the therapist might be and this climate of acceptance and absence of pressure helps the target patient to begin to take him or herself more seriously and to see himself in more psychodynamic terms.

Some phobic patients fill the dreaded emptiness of some gaps in their lives by strong attachment to a group. One such patient made several attempts to leave a group over a number of years, but each time was overwhelmed with anxieties which arose from a sense of annihilation. His sense of an inner catastrophe seemed to be related to his fear of destructive feelings towards his father which, projected into the world, made him feel very vulnerable. Eventually he was able to leave the group and to make a successful recovery when the group itself ended. There were several months' notice of the ending, and the fact that the group ended together with him seemed to give him the underlying confidence that his psychic world would not come to an end with the end of the group.

2 Countertransference responses

Very long-stay patients provoke strong countertransference responses in therapists. When these responses are understood and overcome the therapist is better able to continue to accept and to work with the patients' dependence, passivity, hostility, persecutory anxieties or whatever may be the underlying dynamic. Given this climate of understanding and acceptance, the underlying dynamics will gradually emerge. We have seen many persons who have shown little progress over the first three or four years in a group who eventually do quite well given some years more. What must be avoided, though, is the overloading of the group with passive, dependent patients in the initial formation of the group and at stages in its evolution when new members join. When the balance of the group shifts to passive dependency, the arrival of one or more patients with a different character structure is needed to get the therapeutic process moving again.

7 Couples in groups
Robin Skynner

In the early years after we founded the Group-Analytic Practice I was still working half-time or more within the National Health Service. And my work within the practice, though it included an increasing number of stranger-groups as this aspect of our practice expanded, was devoted to intensive individual analytic psychotherapy, either once-or twice-weekly. Over the next twelve years this individual work continued to take up more than half of my time in private practice.

Unlike my other colleagues in the practice I had trained in child as well as adult psychiatry, and my National Health Service work was as a consultant in child guidance clinics and later a children's hospital. During my training I had experimented with groups of children and adolescents, which I was using extensively in my National Health Service work, and also with mother–child couples when the children were under 5, an approach just pioneered by Gordon Stuart Prince. While preparing lectures for some general practitioners who referred cases to one of my clinics I was surprised to note that most of these mother–child couples had responded positively and rapidly to very brief interventions, to a degree I had never encountered with any other form of psychotherapy. This encouraged me to experiment with seeing families together as groups, a new method that had been reported increasingly in journals from the United States during the previous five to ten years, and with which in fact Foulkes had occasionally experimented before World War II.

I was again astonished to observe, in many cases, changes as rapid and extensive as those I had seen with the mother–child couples, occurring within half-a-dozen, and sometimes even within one or two, interviews. The exploration and explanation of this puzzling effectiveness became a major interest of mine and led to the writing of a textbook and to the setting-up of a training within our associated Institute of Group-Analysis, which later became the Institute of Family Therapy.

Increasing numbers of families were referred to me at the Group-Analytic Practice, and later, as the training programmes ensured more adequate provision of this kind within the National Health Service, of couples wanting help with their relationship. Because of this pressure, together with my undiminished interest in stranger-group therapy and the ready availability of psychoanalysis and individual psychotherapy from my colleagues in the Group-Analytic Practice and its associated networks, marital and family therapy has gradually replaced my own previous work with individual patients except for consultations and occasional short-term interventions.

Moving back and forth, several times a day, between natural and artificially constituted groups, I became aware of the different advantages and disadvantages of each. In particular, the natural groups showed rapid and profound responses to appropriate interventions, partly because of the intense interaction which continued between the sessions. On the other hand, the defensive system was hard to observe and penetrate because the whole family shared in it and colluded in its protection. The therapist was heavily outnumbered, as if playing alone against an American football team. The artificially constituted groups, by contrast, provided allies for the therapist in this task, because members did not share the same defensive system (unless the group was badly selected) and each group member's defences could be challenged by all the others as well as by the therapist.

Increasingly I felt that groups of couples might draw on both advantages and offer the ideal form of treatment for problems which either presented, or were most effectively treated, by seeing couples together. Believing also that this might be best accomplished by a pair of co-therapists who were married themselves, I invited my wife, then contemplating returning to work as our children had begun school, to join me. She was interested, but lacked training (she had previously been an advertising executive) and set out to remedy this by attending our introductory course in group work and other teaching experiences in Britain and the United States, and also becoming a member of a therapy group which Foulkes conducted late in his life for senior colleagues who had not had this experience. I have described elsewhere in *Institutes and How to Survive Them, Mental Health Training and Consultation* (Skynner, 1989), a family experience which indicated to us that our relationship could survive such a collaboration, and we began working with our first couples group in 1972. The method has indeed justified the expectation I had of it, and all patients whose problems do not seem likely to be improved to their satisfaction within a few sessions, as judged at the first consultation, or who have been tried in brief couple therapy and have not responded rapidly, are encouraged to join a couples group (arrangements are made for couple therapy with colleagues for those who decline, but most accept if couple therapy is tried first and fails).

We gradually built up to five couples groups. Each contains four couples, which makes it the same size as our stranger groups and also makes it likely that at least three couples will attend. Three or four couples function equally well, but we found five too many and two too few. The duration of each group is one and a half hours and other arrangements are as for the stranger groups, except of course that they are not advised to avoid contact between sessions! All groups meet once-weekly, and, as the between-session interaction makes this a very intensive experience, we have not tried a twice-weekly arrangement.

Because of this intensity, the duration of attendance tends to about half that of stranger groups. Prospective participants are told that they will need to attend for at least a year (the shortest time in which satisfactory change has occurred, in fact in a couple which were turned down by a marital therapy unit as being too difficult to treat) and probably for about two years.

All assessments for couple therapy, and for entry to the groups, are carried out by myself, though colleagues in the practice often refer couples for this purpose where they have seen an individual (or a couple) which suggests this form of treatment might be indicated. Similarly, I often refer a member of a couple, or of a couples group, to colleagues for assessment, or for individual or stranger group therapy, where it appears that the joint therapy they are receiving from me will not be sufficient to meet their needs.

There have really been no practical problems in running these groups within the practice, except for the demand they often make on my colleague's tolerance. They can be very noisy indeed, both in the shouted exchanges that take place – and when they occur must be allowed to take place without restriction – between couples who are breaking through to a less inhibited and more real relationship, and also in the humour and laughter which has proved to be such a rewarding and healing feature of these groups, perhaps the most therapeutic aspect of their functioning. A chapter in my textbook *One Flesh: Separate Persons: Principles of Family and Marital Psychotherapy* (Skynner, 1976), describes some of the principles and practice of dealing with these groups.

8 The patient with somatic symptoms or with psychosomatic illness in the Practice
Jeff Roberts

There is an extensive literature on the relationship between psychological factors and processes and somatic functioning and disorder. The concept of psychosomatic illness has a long pedigree and is now much refined. This is not the place for a review of the literature and the reader can be referred to the following helpful sources: firstly, *Toward a Theory of Psychosomatic Disorders* (Brautigam and von Rad, 1977), which constitutes the Proceedings of the 11th European Conference on Psychosomatic Research, and secondly *Psychosomatic Medicine and Contemporary Psychoanalysis* (Taylor, 1987), which provides a thorough review of the subject.

Like the majority of psychiatrists and psychotherapists, we encounter at Group-Analytic Practice a number of different kinds of somatic symptoms:

1   psychogenic symptoms without somatic correlates, i.e., psychogenic pain;
2   somatic correlates of psychological disturbance or distress, i.e., the various symptoms of anxiety and muscular tension;
3   the somatic consequences of self-abuse and accidental events;
4a the symptoms of an authentic somatic illness (with what is known as cellular pathology),[2] which does **not** have a significant psychological contribution to its onset, course and prognosis;
4b the symptoms of an authentic somatic illness (with what is known as cellular pathology), which does have a significant psychological contribution to its onset, course and prognosis.

Only category 4b contains patients who can be said to have a true psychosomatic illness. Encounters with patients manifesting one or more of these five phenomena are routine at the Practice. It is rare for any patient to escape some kind of somatic condition during the course of his or her time in a group. Apart from the psychosomatic patients, the behaviour and mode of participation in groups of the other patients bearing somatic symptoms does not differ significantly from the broad spectrum of patients at the Practice. Patients with psychosomatic disorder, however, are relatively uncommon and something of a problem in the heterogeneous group. They are likely to suffer from alexithymia (inability to put feelings into words) and manifest *pensée operatoire* (operational thinking). It is also important to note, however, that some patients without overt psychosomatic disorder at the time of presentation may manifest such a deficit. In general terms these people understand poorly the language of feelings and hence, in many ways, the language of the group. They tend to pull conversations towards the mundane and are often quite troubled by their alien brethren. Only slowly can they work towards experiencing feelings and begin to be able to describe these feelings and their significance. They thus tend to feel at times very uncomfortable in a group-analytic group which is working well and are frequently resented by their fellow patients. None the less some patients with this kind of condition have been successfully (and unsuccessfully) treated at the Practice:

A   A young woman in her mid-20s had suffered from a condition which involved swelling of various groups of lymph nodes and pyrexia and had been diagnosed as glandular fever. This condition would invariably develop at times of stress in her life. Prior to admission to her group she had suffered for twelve months from a state of tiredness and general debility, provoked by the least effort, which was diagnosed as 'post influenzal myo-encephalitis'. Psychologically speaking two features were in evidence: a somewhat excessive attachment to mother and a strong tendency towards alexithymia. At first she was resented, in the young mixed group she had joined, for her tendency to talk at length about her symptoms. She slowly gained a foothold however and left the group after 18 months, symptom free. She was far happier with her life when she left and was beginning to build a new circle of friends.

B   A less successful case was that of the quantity surveyor involved in the planning of enormous buildings, and one of the few people with experience in this field. He carried an immense burden. He was admitted to a group specifically for those with somatic symptoms and alexithymic tendencies. On joining he was anxious, irritable, depressed and undoubtedly alexithymic. Gradually in the group he realised the extent to which he was overworking and overworrying. He completed a huge job while in the group and began significantly to improve his life-style. Unfortunately he then developed a severe prolapsed intervertebral disc and required a lengthy period of treatment and ultimately surgery. These events have prevented his continuing in the group and the final outcome remains uncertain.

C   Another member of the same group who moved on into another group, after the first was closed, said recently in his group, 'I feel that I have learned to put my feelings into words, indeed I have also learned to want to.' This was an entirely unexpected and unsolicited testimonial.

There is a case for the more severely disabled psychosomatic patient or patient with marked alexithymia to enter into a slow-moving homogeneous group. Of these, moreover, those who do best will have acquired a 'lacuna' of insight into the relationship between their psychosomatic disorder and their psychological processes. They may thereby be motivated to enter into the long and arduous process which might lead to an acquisition of a psychological world and a life within it, with a concomitant amelioration of the somatic disorder.

It is notable, however, that we receive relatively few referrals of conditions considered to be psychosomatic. This is presumably a reflection of the attitudes of these patients and their physicians towards the somatic illness and its cause. Like Gollum (see section 3 of this chapter) they cling to there being solely a physical cause to their suffering and look forward to a quasi-magical cure through chemical (= pharmacological) or physical intervention.

It is important to remember that the most successful groups for psychosomatic patients have in fact been conducted by the physician in charge of treating that disorder. Among these important examples would be the groups of Pratt (1907, 1908) who set out to offer classes to people suffering from tuberculosis initially in 1905, and Groen and Pelser (1960), who for a number of years conducted successful therapy groups for patients with pulmonary asthma. None the less, selected patients in a tolerant once-weekly or twice-weekly group might begin to make slow progress.

9 The schizoid character in groups
Jeff Roberts

Those with a schizoid personality or character disorder are among the least happy and most tortured of those who consult psychiatrists and psychotherapists. They are essentially a group of people who for constitutional or environmental reasons are unable to enter into a close relationship with others. They will tell a story of never having experienced a warm, trusting and rewarding relationship with any other individual. They tend also to be raw, defenceless creatures who rigidly hold on to the limited protective repertoire which they have acquired. If they use defences other than avoidance, these will be of the more primitive kind; namely, projection, projective identification, denial and splitting. They tend to turn to sources of gratification other than people, although they have established sufficient relatedness to have developed language. This differentiates them from those with early childhood autism who are only able to acquire language with extreme difficulty, in the context of specialised and intensive treatment. Approximately one third of those who will later develop a schizophrenic state appear to have had an clearly identifiable schizoid personality prior to their breakdown.

The most important relationships of the schizoid personality may be with aspects of themselves, with their often narrow and eccentric interests, with material objects such as their motor car or hi-fi system, to sexual part-objects or inaccessible idealised sexual objects, to objects of artistic merit, books and perhaps drugs or food. They may also appear to be creative individuals although the creativity tends to stereotyped and expressed in a highly personal and often idiosyncratic way.

All these individuals embody an enormous fear of relationship and may (if environmentally schizoid) have suffered major deprivation or traumata during the earliest years of their lives. They are usually of an avoidant retreating type, and appear to live their lives according to a motto which says, 'I will only ever allow myself to be hurt once'. Thus if they chance to develop a close relationship with another person, and it ends painfully (as relationships often do), it may be many, many years before any form of relatedness is ventured again. In dyadic or group relationships they often retreat into themselves or present an impenetrable defensive persona. They have a dread of being consumed or consuming and often become fearful, confused and empty headed in encounters with others. They have few social skills and may appear physically as well as emotionally clumsy in social situations.

Such individuals are quite frequently referred for group psychotherapy. The referring person has often despaired of other sorts of therapy and feels that since this person is socially incompetent, being in a group may be of benefit to him or her. Usually this does not work out. Sometimes an apparently schizoid character may be able slowly to test out a group and emerge from his or her shell and if he or she is able to continue coming to the group and struggle with his or her terror, the result can be rewarding. Most such people, however, while accepting the idea that a group could help them, find the pain of being in the group intolerable and leave, often precipitously. In my opinion the degree of success may depend on whether the schizoid character is predominantly due to environmental determinants. This kind of damage is at least potentially meliorable through a psychotherapeutic process.

Since these individuals have rarely, if ever, had a satisfactory, enduring one-to-one relationship, a reparative individual psychotherapy is likely to be a better context to start from, with a view to graduating eventually to a group. If this is not possible or practicable (these patients are painful to be with for many practitioners), then some learning of defensive and coping behaviours may be helpful. This can take the form of social skills training, which can itself be done in a group setting. Following such work graduation to a therapy group might be a useful next step. Unfortunately the analytic process in the group may do no more than threaten to dismantle the newly acquired social skills.

This is an extremely challenging group of patients, not least because they often believe themselves to be entitled to have, by right, the very relationships which they are incapable of forming and which they fear so much. It is the therapist to whom they bring this sense of grievance, about which he must do something! On the one hand it appears that they will be driven mad by their isolation, on the other that they will succumb to the strains imposed by unwanted closeness to others.

We do not yet have a clear, routine strategy for these patients although some have done well in their groups. One young man sat in his group in almost total silence for years. He then announced that he was ready to leave now, that he had made great gains in all areas of his life and – thank you very much! Others I have seen struggle painfully for long periods of time to make intermittent and often inappropriate contributions to their groups, leaving perhaps slightly improved but none the less having learnt to survive. Others go through a similar experience and leave having gained nothing beyond a reinforcement of their painful awareness of the difficulty of human encounter.

A number of factors will influence the decision to place a person with schizoid traits in a group. A key consideration will be motivation. Positive motivation, in the form of a strong desire to change, through insight and new experiences, materially improves the prognosis of the most difficult psychological disorders. It would be unusual at any stage in our assessment and selection process to turn down a really strongly motivated schizoid patient.

If the withdrawal and schizoid defences are understandable in terms of traumatic or depriving early life (or perhaps later life) experiences, then we would be more likely to offer group analysis with hope of success. We quite often encounter poorly motivated, probably constitutionally schizoid characters, perhaps pushed into therapy by relatives, or on a quest for a magical solution to their discomfort. These people we may place in groups out of a reluctance to turn them away or let down a colleague. Generally they do badly, however, and should probably be seen as not likely to be helped by group analysis.

This is also a group of patients who are significantly helped by adjunctive therapies. A concurrent individual therapy can be helpful. Also in selected patients some form of therapy involving non intrusive 'body work' can be helpful. Some of my patients have found Alexander lessons extremely useful. Indeed, one of my patients who evidenced disturbance from a very early age has been transformed completely by his group experience, and some work with an Alexander teacher, which he undertook during the middle period of his time in the group.

These, then, are among the more difficult people to help in any way with psychotherapy or indeed with any form of treatment. They are tortured beings who want to feel better and yet who cling to their 'precious' way of life with a ferocious intensity. Therapy often fails. One could feel that there is an incorrigible obstinacy here which must be confronted. This is a dangerous attitude. Slowly, at their own pace, these people may gain salvation. The truth is, however, that although they are terrified and indignant about the barren social life they describe, anything more exciting or intimate carries the threat of disintegration and psychosis. Some people in the interests of sanity and health are condemned to live within the constraints of an extremely narrow band of external stimulation. This is inevitably experienced as a prison, but the sad truth is that we have no sure way of enabling release from this confinement. A well-planned group analysis, with or without adjunctive treatments can sometimes help.

10 The psychotic patient
Lionel Kreeger

Are there dream rooms that we decorate ourselves?

I will kill myself leaving a note incriminating you for the evil things you have done to me. You will have to kill yourself. I will dance on your grave!

These two verbatim quotes exemplify the enormous divergence of the clinical manifestations of psychotic illness. The first demonstrates the rich, creative and innovative contribution of a talented young woman struggling through her madness towards sanity and a fulfilling life. The second is typical of a raging and destructive psychotic process, pervading the transference, necessitating her leaving the group to be seen individually over a period of many stormy and disruptive years; truly a psychotic transference of malignant proportions.

Psychotic illness is classified as follows:

1 The functional psychoses
  (a) Affective disorders
      I Unipolar – depression, hypomania and mania
      II Bipolar – manic-depressive illness
  (b) Schizophrenic and paranoid states
2 The organic psychoses, for example, the results of severe chronic alcoholism, epilepsy, drug-induced and other physical illness that lead to major psychological disturbance.

In the present context, we can disregard the organic psychoses, as patients with these conditions will normally be treated in hospitals or psychiatric centres, where groups may be employed, but probably as adjuncts to the total therapeutic regime, often utilising behavioural rather than group-analytic techniques, although there have been some groups for alcoholics within the Practice. The late Fernando Arroyave had a particular interest and skill in this area. It is probably better for them to be treated in departments which have the facility for admission to hospital for drying out and the establishment of set routines. It is the functional psychoses which concern us here, the affective disorders and schizophrenic states.

Affective disorders

The modern classification into unipolar and bipolar presentations may be more technically acceptable, but I still tend to prefer the use of the term 'manic-depressive psychosis', which immediately transmits the dramatic impact of this illness. Its presentation may be essentially depressive or manic, with little or no admixture, or truly manic-depressive with alternating episodes of depression and mania in cyclical form.

On the whole, these patients tend to be referred by psychiatric colleagues, often having had periods of inpatient care in a psychiatric hospital or clinic. They may well be on drug therapy including anti-depressants, major tranquillisers, and possibly a mood stabilising lithium salt. It is essential that the monitoring of the drug regime is left to the referring psychiatrist with the co-operation of the patient's general practitioner, and although it may be appropriate at times for the group conductor to offer his view on the state of progress in relationship to the dosage of drugs, it is undoubtedly best to leave the decision making to one's colleagues. In my experience it can become restrictive or even paralysing for the group conductor to be left with the responsibility of drug administration. It can be difficult to judge when it may be possible to reduce or even stop the drugs, but that would be the time for particular vigilance on the part of all the professionals involved in the patient's care.

On the whole, it is easier to cope with a deeply depressed person in a group than one who is manic or hypo-manic. The depressive will create concern and anxiety, particularly risk and fear of suicide, but it is mostly containable. The manic patient is a trial, and may be uncontainable in the group setting. The few times in my professional life when I have had to take action and remove a patient from the group because of the disturbance have been because of a florid manic episode.

Schizophrenia and paranoid states

Freud's classical psychoanalytic theory included the concept of the narcissistic disorders, as against the psychoneuroses, with failure of reality testing and inability to form a transference within the analytic setting. He believed that such patients were unsuitable for psychoanalytic treatment. In later years, other psychoanalytic theories, such as those of Melanie Klein, have taken our understanding of psychotic states much further and deeper, and, apart from helping us all in appreciation of the dynamics of these conditions, including familiarity with 'psychotic mechanisms' in 'normal' persons, have led to psychoanalytic treatment of the psychotic patient. Such analyses can be prolonged and disruptive, often requiring periods of inpatient care while analysis is continued. When I was at Halliwick Hospital as a Consultant Psychiatrist back in the 1960s, Beech Ward became quite well known for accepting psychoanalysands during episodes of disturbance or regression, particularly at holiday breaks. It is sad that such refuge or asylum is becoming so difficult to find within the National Health Service in recent times.

Nowadays schizophrenic patients are often on anti-psychotic drugs, such as the depot neuroleptics at the time of referral for consultation, and my experience has been that while it may be comparatively easy to obtain significant reduction in dosage of the drug over a period of time, it is less simple to determine if and when the injections can be terminated completely. I have known patients doing extremely well on minimal doses of maintenance drugs, but who became overtly psychotic again once the drugs were stopped, and had to be restabilised on the drug. It is always most gratifying when this does not occur, and the patient becomes able to function well without chemical containment.

The decision has to be made whether the patient should be treated in a specially selected group, or in a general mixed one. We have had special groups in the past at the Group-Analytic Practice, one run for many years by the late Ronald Casson, taking younger patients who mostly had been through an overt psychotic illness, but were sufficiently improved and stable to be able to make a commitment to group therapy on a long-term basis. My own first group at the Group-Analytic Practice starting in 1967, was an all-male one, when I took all those who had been lingering on the waiting list and who had not been offered vacancies elsewhere. Half of them had psychotic illnesses, the others very serious neurotic and personality disorders. With my initial enthusiasm and energy, things went quite well over the first year or so, and when vacancies occurred through people leaving, I was able to introduce some young women, again quite disturbed, and the group continued to function for many years, basically in a supportive and containing way, and I had warm feelings towards 'my young damaged group'.

Within the usual mixed groups, care must be taken to judge the impact of one who has been or is psychotic. He must be capable of forming a therapeutic alliance, be able to communicate in a fashion which even if strange or bizarre at times, can be comprehended, accepted and worked with. Sometimes a twice-weekly group is to be preferred to once-weekly, and should there be a combined group available in which the patient can be seen individually as well as in the group, this might well be the most satisfactory therapeutic modality. I have not myself run such a group, and I remember the late Harold Kaye saying to me while having coffee in the kitchen of the Practice that I was rationalising when I offered my difficulties about time commitment for such a venture. The nearest I ever came to participating in a combined group was at the Paddington Centre for Psychotherapy back in 1976, when I began to discuss with a co-therapist a basic plan for each of us to see four patients individually in preparation for the group, and to continue seeing these patients regularly after its commencement. Fortunately, this never got going. My potential co-therapist became one of the protagonists in the opposing staff faction during the threatened chaotic disintegration of the unit a year or so later; and working alongside this person in a group would have proved difficult.

Two particular problems of working with psychotic patients are the potential disruption not only within the group, but also outside it, and the risk of suicide. Patients who become deeply disturbed during sessions can be both noisy and destructive, threatening to wreck both the therapeutic task and even the consulting room and its contents! This can be most difficult at times requiring more active intervention and containment than interpretive skill alone. It can be embarrassing when complaints about noise emanating from one's consulting room are made by one's colleagues, and even worse, from neighbours in the adjoining flats. There have been moments when I dearly wished to be back in a hospital setting, where noise and destructive acts were tolerated as a normal part of everyday institutional life.

Attempted suicide, or its rare successful outcome, is a continuing threat if one works with psychotic patients. In the same way that a surgeon knows there is a risk of death in any surgical procedure, an in-built mortality rate, so the group analyst must accept that deeply disturbed patients do kill themselves when beyond hope, or when overwhelming anger is turned back against the self. I remember in one of the seminars for the Qualifying Course, Dr Foulkes commented that he had never had a suicide. As his co-seminar leader I said that he must have been either extremely careful about selection, or incredibly lucky. I consider myself fairly fortunate in having had only one suicide in a group, and that was about seven years ago, a deeply depressed young man whose own mother and maternal grandfather had both committed suicide, his mother taking her life when he was 14 years of age. In talking to my colleagues at the Practice, it seems there have been four suicides over the past 20 years. From my own personal involvement, I know about a man in his 50s, a brilliant philosopher, who had suffered from manic-depressive psychosis through most of his adult life, had been in a once-weekly group with me for some two years, but clearly needed much more help than could be offered in that setting, and he transferred eventually to a twice-weekly group with the late Jim Home, unfortunately only to take his life a year or so later.

To end this short and incomplete contribution, my feeling about treating psychotics in groups is that with careful selection, impeccable provision of both professional and personal support, and with realistic aims, much can be achieved. In some, radical changes allowing major resolution of the psychotic part of the personality with profound improvement in all areas of their lives can occur. In others, at least a holding and containing compromise can be reached, permitting a limited but significant improvement.

It can be most gratifying when after years of struggle a real breakthrough occurs. One day in his group a patient announced, 'I am no longer mad, no longer schizophrenic.'

Notes
1 Gollum, a fallen hobbit, is a creature of J.R.R. Tolkien. He appears as a shadowy figure in Tolkien's lengthy fantasy novel, *The Lord of the Rings*, and is essential to the working out of the plot.
2 'Cellular pathology' is a term adopted by pathologists and physicians, which means there is a demonstrable microscopic abnormality in the tissues of an organism, which can be correlated with the physical illness from which the organism is suffering. An example of this would be the clot of blood, and the tissue necrosis which has resulted from the occlusion of blood supply, caused by the clot, found in one of the coronary arteries, of someone who has died from a myocardial infarction (heart attack).

Chapter 8

Destructive phases in groups

Jeff Roberts

Did he live his life again in every detail of desire, temptation and surrender during that supreme moment of complete knowledge? He cried in a whisper at some image, at some vision – he cried out twice, a cry that was no more than a breath – 'The horror! The horror!'

(Conrad, 1902)

The offing was barred by a black bank of clouds, and the tranquil waterway leading to the uttermost ends of the earth flowed sombre under an overcast sky – seemed to lead into the heart of an immense darkness.

(Conrad, 1902)[1]

Kurtz, the speaker of the first quotation above and mysterious anti-hero of Joseph Conrad's (1902) novelette *The Heart of Darkness*, was claimed by T.S. Eliot as 'standing for the dark heart of the twentieth century'. Sigmund Freud also explored the dark heart of the twentieth century. One of his deepest and most fundamental works is *Beyond the Pleasure Principle*. The core hypothesis of this book is that the human being has internal drives towards both creation and destruction. The language Freud chose to use to describe these motivational sets was that of 'instinctual drives'. This was compatible with the main body of his theoretical work and the state of biological science at the time of writing the book. He hypothesized the existence of a 'life instinct' and a 'death instinct', which he named Eros and Thanatos. At the core of his argument was a quasi thermodynamic point of view, which in effect points out that human consciousness is a pinnacle of achievement from which descent is inevitable. In other words, implicit in the development of a conscious self is a tendency to disintegrate either wilfully or by default.

The psychoanalytic school which picked up on these difficult notions was founded by Melanie Klein. The work of the 'Kleinians' takes us to the very heart of human destructiveness and appears to many to insist arbitrarily that although a proportion may be reactive, much that is nasty about the human being is innate and must be confronted in the interest of

the health and maturity of the individual. Moreover, the Kleinians i
that this innate destructiveness becomes active in very early infancy.
work of the Kleinians is marred by dogmatic presentation, a lack of
willingness to engage in research and discussion and a tendency towards
a somewhat rigid therapeutic technique. None the less, the Kleinian
group's work on primitive defensive manoeuvres and the human being's
relationship with his or her destructive drives and impulses is seminal.

The fact that destructive processes in group settings can be long term
and destructive to members of the group has been brought into focus over
the past 15 years. Prior to this, pointers to these phenomena were given
by W.R. Bion (1958). He reported in his *Experiences in Groups* how
primitive and destructive modes of functioning emerged in groups whose
attempts at developing defensive or co-operative solutions to the problems
of being in a taskless group were relentlessly undermined by their conductor. These destructive modes of functioning he termed 'basic
assumptions'. Bion had no intention that his groups would be therapeutic,
and this appears to have been the experience of most of their members.
However, groups which are conducted in a more nurturing and less
anxiety provoking manner than Bion's have repeatedly proved to be
able to transcend the destructive forces within them and produce good
outcomes for most committed and well-motivated patients. The group-
analytic technique is one such method, which on the whole, we
confidently expect to facilitate the creative management of destructive
trends in our groups in the Practice.

Two important works have been produced by group analysts. The first,
by Zinkin, identifies a phenomenon which he names 'malignant mirroring'. The second, by Nitsun, invokes the 'anti-group', and is a scholarly
review of the processes whereby groups set up with therapeutic intent
enter phases in which darker motivations emerge.

Malignant mirroring

The group-analytic therapy group has been poetically compared to a hall
of mirrors (Anthony, 1957). In most writings on mirroring the assumption
is made that the effect of finding oneself in such a hall of mirrors is
beneficial to the individual and contributes to the positive development
of the group. That this is not always the case was pointed out by Zinkin
(1983) in his article on malignant mirroring. He makes the point that the
view of oneself gained in the 'hall of mirrors' can be experienced as
intensely persecuting. The results of this opportunity for outsight to
become insight can be joy, transformation and growth; it can also be rage,
panic, denial and flight. As Zinkin suggests, the sight of oneself in a mirror
can be an intrinsically alienating, rather than affirming experience.
As indicated in his article, peculiar and terrifying phenomena can be

associated with this quasi-magical reflector of images. However, mirrors also display the truth (Garland, 1983). The ultimate horror for some may not be contained in the mirroring process itself nor yet in the distortions which may be present in the image. The hated and truly dreadful experience, often repudiated with amazing violence, is almost certainly an experience of the difference between what is perceived in the mirror and the individual's expectation of what he or she will see. A patient in a group of mine is, in effect, transfixed, for much of the time (as was Narcissus) in front of a mirror he holds up to his life and self. He is transfixed however, not by the beauty of what he sees, but as was Kurtz, by 'the horror, the horror'.

The psychoanalyst and group analyst are, I believe, engaged in a quest for the truth, with the expectation that an uncovering of the truth will facilitate healthy growth and development in the individual and the group. Some people, however, are not ready to face the truth about themselves, when it arrives, and indeed may never be ready to encounter their truths. These people are likely to react catastrophically if the truth arrives, too soon, too explicitly or in too large a quantity. The likelihood of a catastrophic reaction to experiencing this truth will also vary according to the mode of its delivery and the context in which it arrives. A tactless confrontation in a new group is entirely different from the slow emergence of truths in an established and caring matrix. The effect on a group of the catastrophic reaction to self-discovery through mirroring is likely to be the initiation of a destructive phase or the amplification of destructive processes already in train. One such destructive phase is vividly described by Zinkin in his article.

Awareness of these issues has important implications for the selection and composition of groups and also for the timing of interventions in the group process. It also gives food for thought about those patients who suddenly leave groups, whatever the manifest reason for this. It is likely that such patients are having problems facing truths about themselves, which are being exposed in the group. The more energetic the departure the more likely it is that the truth will never be faced. After all, Kurtz's confrontation with his truths was on his death-bed.

The anti-group

Nitsun (1989) points out that the belief that the group is intrinsically creative and hence therapeutic can only be the consequence of a blinkered idealism. In his experience, particularly in a new group, and particularly if errors in selection have been made, an anti-group will develop whose 'aim' is to fragment and undermine the group, thereby defeating its integrative and therapeutic potential. He also makes the crucial point that balance between group and anti-group is far more precarious than we would wish to believe. Indeed I suspect that a feather might tip it either way. I would like to think that Foulkes would agree with me that at the right moment the feather is in fact the intervention of the conductor, which gently tilts the process in favour of group rather than anti-group.

The central thesis of this chapter is that there are groups in which for significant periods of time the death instinct gains the upper hand and that in most groups there will be transient destructive phases. The problems in such groups may appear to be located in one destructive individual or be manifest in the group as a whole.

In the following section of this chapter a number of anecdotes from group analysts working in the Practice will be presented as examples of the type of destructive phases we encounter in our practice groups. In each the conductor will present his or her moving from hope to despair and back to hope again, as the destructive phase develops and is resolved. The conductor will outline the problem he or she experienced and then talk of the way he or she intervened to facilitate a resolution or maybe observed as his or her group found its own resolution. Each of the anecdotes is presented below in the conductor's own words. It is necessary in the interests of confidentiality that the conductors are anonymous.

1 The group conductor of a group-analytic group would view one of the markers of a healthy group to be a capacity to engage in a free floating conversation. Moreover, this conversation would tend to re-semble creative human thought, as if in some way the group were an organism manifesting a mind of its own. This phenomenon is a significant contributor to the group's potential as a therapeutic instru-ment. The 'group mind' is, according to Foulkes (1973) embedded in the network of communication or 'matrix', established by the interac-tion of the members. Some groups appear to resist with remarkable tenacity the development of a free-floating conversation. I have an experience with a once-weekly group which consistently behaves in this way. The group was originally started 25 years ago. It has estab-lished a way of working which is normally seen in the early months of a group's life. Each member takes it in turn to present a problem, which the others then compulsively and attentively work on. In the course of two recent meetings, attention was given to the transfer of money from one country to another, how *x* might arrange the sale of her house, how *y* was having legal difficulties with an inheritance, how *z* was losing money through others taking advantage of his lack of business sense. Each of these issues was discussed in turn at some length, in an entirely concrete way with a conscientious attention to the niceties of points of law, and principles of banking and accountancy, as misunderstood by successive contributors. There was a complete avoidance of attention to emotional implications, little personal interaction and no attempt to

consider any latent meaning in communication. The conductor felt unable to intervene in any way to promote a more healthy process. The group tends for the majority of its life to be fixed in this type of interaction. The group is a Tower of Babel in which eight individuals apply themselves diligently to solving problems, while retaining their individuality and hence resisting the development of an integrated group. This group is dysfunctional.

2 The events to be described occurred in a once-weekly group, which was tending to be supportive rather than analytic. The group comprised a number of youngish, quite damaged individuals. Over a period of a year, there developed more and more contact outside the group, even though the members knew that this was not encouraged. People started meeting in a planned way, until eventually one of the members had a birthday party and decided to ask the other members of the group and their spouses or partners to it. This was not reported until after the event, and I was faced with a *fait accompli*. I had tried previously to deal with things in an interpretative way, looking at the sense of deprivation and frustration within the group which was being more practically satisfied through contact outside the group. Clearly this intervention had failed. I felt that I had to make a decision on the spot and came down heavily on the side of confrontation and authoritarian prohibition. I said that this could not continue, that they had to choose whether they wanted friendship with continuing contact between them all and their partners outside the group, or group psychotherapy. If they desired the latter, I said, they had to agree to make a commitment to cease meeting outside the group, and particularly to avoid involving their partners. This was accepted, the acting out ceased and the group continued thereafter in a more conventional style.

3 I was conducting a training group in which two members, male and female, started meeting outside the group. They began to consider whether to develop full relationship and become sexually involved. This was brought up on several consecutive meetings of the group and it seemed as if they were moving inevitably towards the reality of accepting their mutual attraction and the gratification which could be achieved through an intimate relationship. I felt that this would happen if I did not intervene. I decided again [the same conductor as in anecdote 2, ed.] to confront the situation, and said that the contact outside the group must cease, but if they felt they could not continue in the required state of abstinence, they would both have to leave the group. This was accepted, they remained in the group and things went well thereafter.

4 A slow-moving, once-weekly group containing a man and a woman

who had been members for more than ten years, found it difficult to move from 'fire-fighting' and concentration on one member at a time, especially following the summer break, when I returned with a bad back, which necessitated my missing several group sessions. This restriction of group functioning seemed to be an attempt to satisfy deeper longings for individual attention, which at the same time was feared, especially by the women. All of them had conflictual and disappointing relationships with their fathers, one of whom had abandoned her at birth and another abused her sexually. When I came back to more reliable attendance, there was a period of repeated intense attacks on me by the women; firstly, for favouring the two long-term members, and secondly, for sexism. So fraught did the group become that fears were expressed that it could not continue. Not only was I so unfair and discriminatory, but the violence in the group made it too uncomfortable for people to feel they could continue in it.

My destructiveness was seen as obvious by the women, while the more diffident men on the whole seemed at times to collude with this belief and its exploration in terms of unconscious conflicts, and transference was resisted.

The situation only changed when, staying firm and flexible, I put it to them that they consider what was happening in transference terms. At the same time I showed a preparedness to think how I had contributed to the situation through countertransference problems. I also indicated my belief that they all needed parental reassurance and comforting, a need which had been exaggerated during my period of illness. Subsequent concern about my health had promoted jealousy of me and denial of their own needs. This enabled one woman to turn from her 'spiky aggressiveness' to grief at the loss of an important mother-figure (she had been abandoned by both her parents at birth), and another (the one who had been sexually abused by her father) to share a dream in which I had sexually exploited her. The group began then to work more as a group again. In the session before the next break, one woman gave me a card in which she had written, 'It is only after we have accepted our rage that we can CHOOSE to love. It is only after we have accepted our rage that we can CHOOSE to be more understanding. Otherwise we are just pretending to be nice.'

5 For over two years I had a female patient in a group whose diagnosis was that of a borderline character. She was a very intelligent woman with university education, but whose personal and professional life had deteriorated considerably. Within the group she became increasingly bitter and destructive towards most other members, but particularly towards, men upon whom her attacks became overtly castrating. Although she was responded to with considerable warmth and under-

standing in an attempt to get behind her destructive envy, she continued
to escalate her attacks. At times this led to violent confrontation. On
one occasion she added some strong racial comments, to which a
sensitive member responded with such anger that he could scarcely
contain a physical attack. Though temporarily contrite, the offending
patient was not able to make reparation or to take adequate responsibility for her provocative stance. As therapist I eventually asked her to
leave the group. This is the only time I have ever done this and it was
a great relief for both the patient and the group that I finally took this
action. She left owing a considerable amount of money, which she
promised to pay, but never did. I did, however, hear from her some
months later, when she had left London and was setting up in a
handcraft industry in the country. Her letter was reasonably balanced
and appreciative of the care she had received.

6 Another very destructive patient was a woman whose aggressive
behaviour increased to such a point that she was marching out of the
group in mid-session and locking herself in the lavatory. Sometimes
she would refuse to open the door at the end of the session and disturbed
everyone by very loud, agitated sobbing. I attempted to deal with this
by offering individual sessions, which was clearly a mistake, since her
behaviour became even more regressed during these sessions. She
eventually decided to leave the group and go into individual therapy.

Conclusions

The examples above give some valuable insights into the group-analytic
process as it is influenced by a variety of destructive processes. These may
be grouped as follows.

1 Collusive activity in the group, whose goal appears to be to prevent
the development of a group (or group matrix). This collective resistance can be assumed to be a manifestation of the 'anti-group'. The
anti-group is determined to maintain neurotic and psychotic defences
and is an enemy of the truth.
2 Energetic and usually destructive responses to the emergence of more
truth than can be borne.

Various phenomena may be identified which played an important part
in the events described.

splitting	fragmentation
projection	shortsightedness
projective	bad faith
identification	ill will

callousness	meanness
narcissism	murderousness
lack of empathy	perversity
lack of cohesiveness	collusion

These little dramas, as one might expect, manifest all the usual components of humans' nasty and tragic behaviour. The truth of the matter is that human beings are both destructive and creative. Not entirely surprisingly the the extent of human destructiveness is not generally accepted and our groups are no exception to this. Members of the groups individually and collectively avoid confrontation and exposure of destructive motivation and often choose destructive modes of behaviour to achieve this. In destructive phases in the group, then, it often appears that the group is delicately poised between collusive avoidance of the nasty truth and a traumatic individual experience of it.

The role of the conductor in these destructive phases of the group's life is, on the one hand to encourage the group to continue its voyage of discovery, while on the other helping it to live with what it finds – With 'live' here meaning among other things that the group retains its integrity.

In the examples above it is possible to identify various ways in which the conductors succeeded and failed in their task. The techniques adopted include: *confrontation* (examples: 2 and 3); *holding* (example 1); *letting go* (examples 5 and 6). Foulkes's notion about destructiveness in the group was that the members of the group would apply their aggression to attacking one another's neuroses, rather than one another. With this in mind he could afford to sit back and allow the group process to continue in a self-analytic fashion. Group analysis is, according to Foulkes, 'analysis of the group, by the group, including the conductor'. When a group enters a destructive phase this I believe no longer holds true. What one may then see is 'destruction of the group, by the group, including the conductor'. We are increasingly aware of this and are now prepared to be as active as is necessary to maintain optimally safe and creative groups. None the less the most difficult task for the conductor is actually to face the truth about the destructiveness of his group when it emerges.

Note
1 This is the final paragraph of Conrad's novelette *The Heart of Darkness*.

135

Chapter 9

Individual and group therapy combined

Roger Hobdell

The group-analytic process is flexible enough to adapt to other settings, including hospital and community. The group described in this chapter is an adaptation that has been running at the Practice for over two decades. It provides a treatment of combined individual and group analysis. The chapter will include a brief description and history of the group and some of the dynamics that will be encountered in a practice like ours or a hospital outpatient setting. Because of the flexibility and permutations of such a group, there will be no hard and fast guidelines suggested. Indeed, this treatment allows a tailor-made therapy for a wide range of people.

To the best of my knowledge, the first reference to combined therapy using a group-analytic group was by Foulkes (Foulkes and Lewis, 1944) in the *British Journal of Medical Psychology* which was reprinted in his third book, *Therapeutic Group Analysis* (Foulkes,1964). The original paper does not expand on the advantages and disadvantages of combined therapy, and one gets the impression that Foulkes had not at that time worked out a position with regard to the combination. However, when the paper was reprinted in *Therapeutic Group Analysis* he was not in favour, summing up, 'our bias has on the whole been to leave the group situation uncomplicated while the patient participates in a group'.

Foulkes' position, however, fluctuated on this point and it is difficult to burden such an exploratory thinker with a definitive statement. Basically, his whole thrust was to make the group experience complete in itself and, with increasing knowledge and ability, this has largely been achieved in the classic group, so that only occasionally may members of the group need to be seen individually to work on something for which there is insufficient time in the group. Most of his statements follow this direction. He also felt that if someone needed individual analysis, this should preferably take place after the group treatment. On this point I disagree with him, in that for some people it is the right sequence but not for others. I have had several people join this group after individual therapies with fair success. In a personal communication to me, Foulkes stressed how important it was that when individual treatment followed group treatment, it should not be too long. Again, my own experience over the years has been that while this is a helpful attitude to adopt, in practice it is not nearly so clear cut.

Later, Foulkes developed a combined approach where members in the group were seen individually in turn, one per week, so that each member was seen approximately once every two months. It would be interesting to know what led him to such a combination because the group described below was probably started with something similar in mind.

Description of the group

History

It is not certain when the group began, but probably it was in the mid sixties. I have a belief but no proof that it was started as a joint venture between Foulkes and Harold Kaye. Nor do I know when it was combined with individual therapy. I joined it in 1974 as a co-therapist with Harold Kaye when I had just qualified as an individual analyst and had been an Associate of the Practice for only a year. The understanding between Harold and myself was that this would partly be a learning experience for me, partly an experiment between ourselves in combined work which we would write about, and partly a convenience that one or other of us could occasionally be absent to go to the theatre! (Neither of us did.) Much to my chagrin, I received no money for my contribution, though it was understood that I would do so in the future.

Harold Kaye was an American with group experience in New York who came to England to train under Foulkes and also became an analytical psychologist. When I joined the group, the numbers were large – about 12 members – and most were seen weekly on an individual basis by Harold. It was assumed that the next new member would be seen individually by me. It was not easy coping with the splitting that inevitably occurred between the two of us. He was the established group conductor and I was the intruder who, confusingly, was not only new to the group and therefore ignorant of the complexity of its communications but also had some mysterious closer link with Harold than the other members, which no matter how many years they knew him, they could not share. The tension thus set up meant that I received most of the projections of the bad and Harold the ones of idealisation. For my part, this took some difficulty in sitting through.

Sadly, six months after I joined the group, early one morning following the evening group meeting, Harold suddenly died. Ours was the last group he sat in and I remember well the attention he paid to hidden aggression within the group that evening. I now became the sole group conductor and took on a few of the patients for their individual therapy, including one or two who had previously been most vociferous in their attack. At first I met them for individual sessions at the Practice, but later at my own consulting rooms.

Strangely, the group has had a low profile at the Practice. At the time of Harold's death, no one realised the large number of groups that he was conducting, and I think it true to say that the presence of a combined group was unknown to his colleagues. Over the years, the group seems to pass in and out of the collective perception of the Practice. If it was raised at long intervals at the Members and Associates meetings, pleasant surprise would be expressed that such a group existed. It has occasionally met with the criticism that it was neither fish nor fowl, since in a true combination group all the members would be seen individually, unlike this group where it is optional. I believe this hesitation in accepting it has arisen out of a corporate awkwardness in the Practice about group or individual treatment. This group blurs the boundaries, and one uncomfortable implication may be that a group analysis alone may be insufficient. (I do not personally subscribe to this view, but the question of group versus individual treatment was also to be found beyond the confines of the Practice.) Demarcation and territoriality in the London analytic world until the 1980s was excessive. Different dynamic therapies were jostling one another for credibility and respectability, as well as having to fight against a medical, organic model. When I joined the Practice, one condition was that I should cease to work with a co-conductor from another organisation because of their uncertain reputation. Conversely, I know of an individual analytic body that advised a staff member of the Practice that they would never become a training analyst of that institution unless they first left the group practice.

Thus I believe that the macro-culture of the London analytic scene is reflected within the micro-culture of this practice. Every institution has its shadow side, and it would be naïve to suggest that the Practice did not have one. The art is to know approximately where it lies.

I add these remarks on the history of the group for instructional purposes, because any combination group will meet conditions of one sort or another, good and bad. As they say of agriculture, you can't farm without weather.

Present structure

The group meets once-weekly and, at the time of writing, has eight members, four men and four women. This is fairly typical of its history. Three members see me for individual therapy once-or twice-weekly. One of them sees another therapist once-weekly, as others have done in the past. I am quite satisfied with this and would encourage it, but with limitations. If a patient has not been referred specifically for combined treatment, I advise them at the pre-group meeting that they have the option of seeing me or another therapist individually and that other members already do so. I do not, I hope, give the impression that this is a condition of joining. They are informed that if they wish to take up this option later, they should first talk about it in the group where the decision is reached. I cannot recall any difficulty with this procedure, particularly as it gives time for the group to evaluate the motives for individual treatment and it does not usually come as a surprise.

In all other respects, the group's composition resembles a typical slow open group with an age range of 30 to 60 years. I try to eliminate those who have life experience that might not be appropriate, and not to have a group with too many single or too many married people in it. We went through a bad patch some years ago when new referrals repeatedly left after a few weeks or months. We had to work on this within the group and at present new members seem to stay.

I would never have more than two borderline or narcissistically damaged patients within the group at any one time, mainly because of the imbalance within the group dynamics that this would cause. At present we have no one who would fit that category, and in consequence the group seems rather too quiet. Two people in the past at different times suffered from alcohol abuse. The severity of their illness had not been picked up at the diagnostic interview and they both failed rapidly within the group. (The Practice at one time had its own specialist in alcohol abuse.)

The group has had, however, a range of people who have stayed for a shorter or longer time and inevitably been changed by their experience in the group. Sometimes they have felt that this was sufficient, sometimes not. But the cases I have chosen to illustrate this group seem to me to have benefited because it was a combined group run along the very flexible principles I have indicated.

Case 1 The vicar

The patient at the time of the following dream was in his mid-forties. He had been referred to my individual practice via a group for clergy, where it was felt he needed more specific therapy. In his work, he had a fair amount of difficult pastoral counselling to perform. When he had the dream, he had been in combined therapy for two years, after being in individual therapy with me for some years previously. The dream was as follows:

A Devonshire vicar and a woman were in the room. The vicar was in great distress and anxiety. He didn't know how he could continue with the work. The woman was quite unable to help him. The patient in the dream then counsels the vicar, saying that if he went into psychotherapy, it would be all right.

The patient's association to the dream was that it reminded him of when he first started in analysis after years of anxiety kept at bay with diazepam. He remembered the years before the group when he came to see me for individual treatment, the feelings of isolation and climbing unending staircases to a bare waiting room, then going in to see a doctor who was a complete stranger. He said the real beginning was when he started the group. That was when he began to feel part of the world. There he could see me as a person. People called me by my first name and he realised then that others too had difficulties and he was not alone.

Because he lived so far out of town, problems of travel and duties meant that he could only see me once-weekly individually. I had tried to increase this and met a lot of defensiveness. Each week it was undone a little, only to return for reasons of survival in the outside world before the next visit. I knew that the problem was not solely practical, but we could not make progress. After I had been in the group five or six years I suggested he should have a second weekly session which might be in a group that met in the evening. After seven years he joined the combined group. I knew that problems of transference to me were involved, and I hoped that this could be side-stepped to some extent in the group.

If I had been thinking of the predictive element in the dream, I might have interpreted it as meaning that the Devonshire vicar was still not managing with combination therapy and that his patient-self was urging himself to go further. In fact, two years after the dream, he became acutely anxious, fearful and regressed. He had to stop work for a period and we increased our individual meetings to twice-weekly. The other members of the group were somewhat anxious themselves because of their natural concern and because they felt a therapeutic responsibility had been placed upon them to a much greater degree than in the past. Indeed, but for the holding capacity of the combined therapy, many people in his condition would have been admitted to hospital. However, over the weeks, the crisis passed, to the mutual benefit of patient and group, and the work continued in a quieter way.

This is a lengthy treatment history, longer than most in the group, but looking back, I do not think it could have been achieved without combined therapy. The patient is now working towards an ending.

Case 2 Valerie

This brief study is included because it illustrates the ways in which a combined group can fail, though not, I hope, disastrously.

Valerie was in her mid-thirties, was employed at management level, but was not making relationships. Her father had died when she was about 3 years old and there was an older and a younger brother. Her last boyfriend had left her five years previously and she could feel life slipping by her. She had already had some individual treatment and the previous therapist felt that a group might help where he had not. Valerie's world view was of men who did ruthless things to women and then callously left them. Her actual experiences unfortunately confirmed that men could be like that. I had high expectations that the group could modify this rather harsh picture, for it was at the time full of men who had shown sensitivity and concern both in the group and in their lives. This of course was a naïve view for it failed to take account of the early level of Valerie's disturbance and of her rage which was not confined to men.

Confrontation after confrontation took place in the group. All the men, and some of the women, confessed that there was something about the violence of Valerie's attack which frightened them. She became a scapegoat for the rest of the group's hostility and a sub-group of one. After two years, she asked for an individual therapist, by which time she had actually become less hostile and could listen to the group. She asked for a female therapist and took well to her. After a few months, Valerie discussed in the group her wish to see her other therapist more often and to leave the group.

I think it would have been in the group's interest and probably hers to stay, but she did eventually leave. It would be easy for a purist to argue that letting her see an individual therapist would dilute her own and the group's experience. That cannot be denied. But over the years I have taken an overall picture of the individual's treatment, and undoubtedly Valerie needed to explore her unconscious thoughts and fantasies within a one-to-one relationship. Needless to say, when she left, the next few sessions were spent by the members fighting one another after they had taken back their projected rage.

Theory

In conducting combined groups I have always worked from the major premise that the group is primary and comes before everything else. The welfare and integrity of the group has to be maintained at all times. Initially, in the early stages of a group, this may be difficult, but once started and the basic parameters understood, it seems to work from generation to generation. Such an attitude does not mean that the individual's needs (for example Valerie's needs) are neglected but that decisions are reached through the group, not via the individual therapy situation. To follow this procedure allows patients to be introduced from individual practice (the conductor's or someone else's) without loss to the group as an instrument of change. The self-image of the group must remain the one of foremost therapeutic significance, and not be experienced as a mere adjunct to individual therapy. However, some members may not experience it in this way. For them, individual sessions may feel more intense and significant.

In relation to the main group, I would like to call the individual therapist–patient interaction a 'satellite group'.

The satellite group

The term 'satellite' is used to denote a group attached to the main one but in contrast to a sub-group which arises within and out of the main group.

In this sense, a sub-group is a pathological acting out (or acting in), though it is still grist for the analytic mill. The satellite group, on the contrary, is consciously set up to enhance the total therapeutic aim, albeit apparently directed towards only one member. The role of the conductor is to prevent the satellite from becoming pathological, which happens only too easily in a way unconscious to the group and often to the therapist.

Foulkes was not in favour of laying down group rules but of allowing the group to explore different possibilities, committing errors on the way which could be analysed for meaning. Most of the errors caused by the presence of a satellite tend towards fragmentation of the group. What holds the group together is the group matrix, which as defined and described by Foulkes has transpersonal connotations.

As an analytical psychologist, I find the group matrix very similar if not identical to Jung's collective unconscious. (Jung termed it thus in opposition to a 'personal unconscious'). The matrix for Foulkes and the collective unconscious for Jung are the source of healing.

The planetary metaphor of a satellite seems to fit the group described above in several ways, though there are several satellite moons belonging to the group. Their significance varies at different times in the group's life. At the risk of repeating what is said elsewhere in this book, I wish to enlarge on the matrix and the combined group.

In the combined group, the boundary enclosing the area of influence of the matrix extends to include the satellite group. It can be compared, therefore, to the force of gravity reacting on the moons, holding them within the larger system which for the group could be described algebraically as:

[group + satellite]

Like gravity and the archetypes, the matrix cannot be seen or touched, but its effects can be observed in the group. Foulkes from the group-analytic position described the *force*. Jung, from the position of analytical psychology, described the *structures* of the matrix. These structures may appear as images in dreams or in art or in cultures; for example, the contrasexual archetypes animus and anima. The transpersonal nature of the matrix in both Foulkes' and Jung's taxonomies is of paramount importance. It allows human beings to be meaningful to one another and I do not see how a group could function without it.

The matrix as described above was called by Foulkes the 'static' or 'foundation matrix'. One can use various incomplete images to describe it. It 'passes through' the individuals or the individuals are 'embedded' in it or 'rise out of it'. Jung poetically described the 'collective unconscious' as a rhizome out of which the individual flowers grow. After the death of the flower, the rhizome remains, as does the group matrix after the departure of any one member from the group. The static matrix stays the same for all mankind, through all the ages, hence the recurrence of symbols worldwide, from so-called primitive through to modern man.

As opposed to the foundation matrix, Foulkes also drew attention to the dynamic matrices operating within the group (the dynamic matrices change and develop during the course of the group). I list three, followed by the Jungian equivalent in parentheses.

1 Face value, public image (persona)
2 Transference – family, mother, father (transference)
3 Projective level; narcissistic. Group represents fantasy objects of the self; for example, themes, such as abandonment; parts of the body, and so on (No single Jungian equivalent, though a large proportion of Jung's work was devoted to pre-Oedipal and self-psychology.)

I believe the psychology of the [group + satellite] system is nearer to matrix number 3 than number 1. In the planetary system, centrifugal force would spin the moon away from the planet if it were not for the force of gravity. The [group + satellite] system would likewise be torn apart but for the foundation matrix. My experience with combined groups is that there is considerably more wobble in the psychological system than the planetary one! Within certain limits, this wobble is a reason for analysis, not necessarily for concern. The healthy, working, combined group could therefore be expressed thus

[Group ⟷ Satellite]

where the upper line represents the dynamic matrices and the lower the foundation matrix.

The pathological combined group could be expressed in this way:

[group] + [satellite]

The first formulation has coherence, tension and meaning. The second does not.

I have given this brief comparison between Foulkes and Jung to show not only that a dialogue is possible between group and individual analysis but that there is a rationale of the combined system that need not distort the theories and practice of either discipline. Freudians, Kleinians and others will no doubt be able to make their own formulations.

In a combined group, the role of the conductor is obviously the same as any other group with additions. Initially, a major task is to show the group its tendency to fragment. As time passes, the group itself is better able to take this task on itself and becomes sensitive to lapses. This can be observed particularly in therapeutic communities where keeping the form can become a bit of a religion. The following are the main areas of which to be aware. For exploratory purposes, they are broken up into sub-divisions which are not always apparent in practice.

Sub-grouping

A particular form of sub-grouping has occasionally appeared in the group described above between those who are seen individually and those who are not, or, more usually, between those who see me and those who do not. I have always tried not to know too much about my own individual patients in the group and not to neglect the rest. I do not bring in facts about a patient's life that have only been obtained in the satellite setting, though I take steps to make sure those facts are brought into the group as soon as possible by the patient. Sub-grouping has usually been dealt with satisfactorily by pointing out that it is happening and allowing the group processes to take their course.

Enactment within the group

Any psychotherapy group is liable to choose a nominal patient and for the rest of the meeting to sit back and act as the problem-free therapist. This is even more likely in a combined group. The group under discussion has had long periods in this mode. As a group analyst, I find this irritating, but have come to accept it as an inevitable aspect of a combined group, where the individual interview may take on mysterious powers of healing, and so on especially as in this group, where the individual interviews take place in a different location. The mysteriousness can be reduced somewhat by giving the phone number of the other location to the members who do not go there or by seeing them there for one-off interviews when necessary. The other members therefore have at least the ability to communicate with the therapist there, reducing the tendency to make it a prohibited area.

Enactment of the satellite couple outside the group

Again, this is not confined to the combined group. The form it has taken in this group has mainly been lifts home and a rather unsuccessful Christmas meeting in a pub. An understanding of it can usually be achieved within the group. About ten years ago, two members fell in love and after much debate and a guideline from me, one of them left the group. They married and are still together. This was a technical failure but a victory for life.

Sub-grouping and enacting the therapeutic couple are group phenomena that can and should be worked through in the group setting. The management of the following are more difficult, since they include material that often relates to the group or its state of functioning, yet are brought to the individual setting.

Projection

The satellite group is used to evacuate affects into it from the main group. Such affects may include anger, depression, feelings evoked by abandonmentm, and so on. For example, a member may sit quietly through the group meeting but bring his anger to the individual session. Shame can also be sidestepped in the large group. The individual in his session then says, 'I couldn't discuss this in front of others.'

Splitting

With projection and splitting, the group processes are operating at the third level of the dynamic matrices. Instead of the total system [group + satellite] holding the tension of the ambivalent feelings, these develop a split so that one aspect is located in one part of the system and the opposite aspect in the other part. The following are just a few of the splits encountered:

Good – bad
Idealised – despised
Bad container – good container
Nourishing – starving
Free expression (loving/hating) – controlling
Potent – impotent
Secret – public

Mad – sane
Fullness – emptiness

The management of splitting and projection requires more subtlety than that of sub-grouping and enacting, since although one should consider them as group phenomena, the evidence of their occurring usually manifests itself first or only in the individual setting. In this case, I invariably say that the subject should be taken back to the larger group, and although I have sometimes spent a few nail-biting weeks waiting for this to happen, it invariably does. The conductor is put in this difficult position because I feel he should not speak for the patient. If the atmosphere in the group is not right to say something there and then, it has to be worked on in the group. If the individual cannot say it, then he or she has to be analysed further. In practice of course, it is not nearly so clear cut.

I would be the first to admit that a fair proportion of splitting and projection escapes my attention, but when it has been confronted it has always been beneficial.

Co-conductors for combined groups

In an ideal world, the co-conductors (such as Harold and myself, as described earlier) would be balanced more or less for age and experience and possibly of opposite sex. In a hospital setting, this is easier to achieve. The kind of training they have had obviously has to be compatible. The balance in experience means to me an equivalent ability to

1 interpret and tolerate symptoms (group and individual);
2 tolerate anxiety;
3 'hold' patients' externalisations and projections.

It is not that these need always be identical, but if one conductor is vastly more experienced and can go into areas of anxiety the other cannot, a skew develops in the group, with one conductor ineffective.

Satellite therapists

The above qualifications apply for the individual analysts who work with members of the group other than the conductor, though in my experience, a much wider range is tolerable. There are, however, individual analysts who will not work with a split transference. However, anyone else who is trained psychodynamically – analyst, therapist or counsellor – usually gets on well enough. I have rarely had to communicate with the other therapists once the combined treatment has started and would certainly not make a habit of it or do so without the patient's knowledge. I have relied on the patient to inform the group of the basic direction of the outside work and get hints of what the other therapist is doing. I would avoid other therapies where touching, massage, and so forth are the norm.

Selection of patients for the combined group

In practice, it has almost always worked out that someone who is already in treatment, whether it be group or individual, is deemed by a referring therapist to need combined treatment. I find very few referrers thinking in terms of a combined group for a first-time patient. In my experience, some patients referred only to the group immediately take up the option of being seen individually when they start in the group. These could be successful referrals, for a combined group. Foremost among reasons for referrals to the group from individual therapists has been one that the patient is 'socially inhibited'. I would, I think, accept this more easily if it was put that an introvert may need encouragement to see the advantages of a more extrovert attitude to life.

Transference problems or difficulty in forming a transference may be improved by joining the group at the same time as remaining with the individual therapist. The mirroring capacity of the group helps the patients to see aspects of themselves an individual analyst may not supply. Otherwise, all the usual advantages of a group can be anticipated.

The reasons for advising a group member to seek individual sessions as well as joining a group may be that

1 once-weekly is insufficient for the level of anxiety present;
2 early material cannot be sufficiently explored;
3 frequent dreams need unravelling, but not at the expense of the group;
4 problems of individuation (I purposely leave this vague).

I hope this chapter will encourage those who are thinking of, or those who have just started, a combined group. I hope it will raise a wry smile of recognition on the faces of those who are practised in the strange art of the combined group. I hope also that some of my enthusiasm, frustration and belief in its creativeness is expressed here.

Chapter 10

Training for and trainees in group analysis

Lisbeth Hearst and Meg Sharpe

A special feature of the Group-Analytic Practice is the inclusion in its twice-weekly groups of potential and approved candidates for the Qualifying Course of the Institute of Group-Analysis, London. The groups into which such applicants and trainees are put are conducted by training group analysts. Although the Institute of Group Analysis has appointed several training group analysts who are not Members or Associates of the Practice, only a few have at present twice-weekly groups regarded by the Institute as suitable for trainees. This is a situation which is changing rapidly. To date the advantage to the Institute as a training body is that the Group-Analytic Practice, due to its well-established reputation and wide referral network, can and does offer a wide range of suitable patient groups which the candidates and trainees can enter for their group analysis. Practice members would welcome the establishment of twice-weekly groups in other settings: sometimes there can be considerable pressure on the Practice's group conductors to give priority to Qualifying Course students.

The predominance in the Group-Analytic Practice of suitable groups is the outcome of the historic development of the Practice and the Institute of Group-analysis. Group analysis, the Group-analytic Society, the Institute of Group-Analysis were conceived of and developed by a group of psychiatrists and psychoanalysts who were colleagues and close professional intimates of Dr S.H. Foulkes, the founder of group analysis. Much of the theoretical work, the formation of the Society, the planning and shaping of the Institute, took place on the Practice's premises and with the co-operation of the original members. It is poignant that Michael Foulkes died while conducting a peer group in the Practice with these his colleagues and co-founders of the Institute of Group-Analysis. The present situation – namely, that almost all candidates for training in group analysis have to come to the Practice – has certain practical and professional implications of which the training analyst and the Practice are well aware.

Once accepted for training, the candidate is obliged to remain in his or her group throughout the training period. (In the event, most stay on for long periods after qualification; some leave as soon as they are qualified.) This may mean considerable expenditure in time and money. Some students come from far afield, others have to cross the vast expanse of Greater London twice-weekly for years. All have to pay the relatively high fees which a London West End practice must charge, though, since the fees are paid to the group analyst, he or she may decide to adjust them should this be considered appropriate. The trainee–patient, unlike other patients, cannot 'shop around' for his or her group analysis. His or her choice is limited to training analysts and to what the Practice offers. However, the choice of day and time of day, as well as of group analyst, is considerable, due to the large number of twice-weekly groups the Practice runs.

Ethical considerations emerge when one considers that the group analysts' life-affecting influence and at times power, considerable with regard to all patients, is increased with trainee–patients. The therapist will periodically report to the Training Committee about the state and progress of the trainee's group analysis, thus influencing the Committee's decisions on the qualifying process and its outcome. In view of the dual position of the trainee as a patient and a student and future colleague in the Institute, the group training analyst will be especially alert to use the power thus conferred wisely and, ultimately, solely in the service of the trainee–patient.

The inclusion in patient groups of candidates and trainees is the result of a well thought-out decision. There has been much discussion, nationally and internationally, about whether it is preferable for trainees to be placed in groups made up entirely of trainees (T groups). It is the view of the Institute that such groups, though undoubtedly therapeutic, are in their very nature not therapy groups. In the former, the aim is training through experiential participation. In the latter, the patient group, the aim is personality exploration in the service of deep and lasting change. The Institute and the Practice consider that only participation as a patient in a patient group offers a group analysis, parallel to, though necessarily different from, the personal analysis the trainee in psychoanalysis undergoes. At present, the Practice has 12 training analysts and treats on average two to three trainee–patients in each twice-weekly group.

An attempt is made to place not more than two or three trainees in one group and these should be at different stages of their training courses. Too many trainees in one group unduly alter the constitution of the therapy group. At times trainees in the same therapy group find themselves also in the same theory seminar group, in spite of an effort to prevent this. They may have their training analyst as a seminar conductor at some stage during their training course, since some of the training analysts, though by no means all, are engaged in teaching on the Qualifying Course. This poses a considerable strain on the trainee–patient, since it requires an adaptation in quick succession to different modes and levels of relating to a fellow group member and to the group conductor and to tolerate changing boundaries in the settings of the different groups in which the trainee is engaged. To some degree the field in which the transference unfurls is enlarged to include other groups, such as the supervision group and the theory seminar group, or indeed the entire training course and the Institute itself.

One trainee–patient who encountered his group analyst in the theory seminar for one term found it impossible to take part in the seminar, indeed to utter one coherent sentence throughout the whole term. He was, however, able to take this up in the therapy group and, through its exploration, to reach a new intensity of experiencing his relationship with his father during his early childhood and in his school years with certain teachers. The group conductor who also met the trainee in the theory seminars and in the group was able to understand the trainee's difficulties and assist in the therapy group with the process of experiencing, understanding and working through the childhood neurosis which had been influencing the man's professional life and preventing the full utilisation of his considerable intellectual ability. Another trainee–patient expressed the use she was able to make of the emotional proximity in the triangular structure of therapy, supervision and theory, thus: 'In my therapy group I had gained insight into my childhood feelings of helplessness and hopelessness when trying to keep my family together in wartime Europe; but it was the initial period of conducting my therapy group and its supervision that provided the opportunity of a corrective emotional experience.' (The training group is the group the trainee conducts and presents for supervision.)

The training analyst has this special situation in mind when meeting the trainee–patient for the initial pre-group interview. At this stage it is still possible to decide that a particular person will not be suitably placed in the group which has been considered for him or her, often due to a particular phase in which the group is at that moment. If this is so, the trainee–patient goes back on to the waiting list. Usually the information obtained in the previous diagnostic consultation will make this the exception rather than the rule. It is one of the features of the Group-Analytic Practice that, because of the many groups and group conductors, there is an excellent chance of placing the trainee–patient in the right group, at the right time for the trainee–patient and the group.

One important feature in the pre-group interview will be the motivation with which the new group member approaches his entry into group analysis. The motive of the trainee–patient at this stage may not be symptom relief or a distressing disturbance in functioning for which he or she is seeking an urgent solution. Disease, neurotic solutions to everyday problems and, at times, deep personality disorders will often be disguised by training preoccupations, used as a defence against entering therapy as a needy patient (Hinshelwood, 1985). This defence will be addressed in the diagnostic and pre-group meetings, but it well may persist for a considerable time into treatment before the trainee–patient will be able to drop it and experience the previously denied status in the group, as someone seeking deep rooted change in many vital areas of his or her pattern of relationships and personality manifestations. Other trainee–patients come into group therapy fully aware of their need of and yearning for a mutative therapeutic experience. For them, the training requirement of group analysis acts as the final incentive to overcome the resistance to therapy present in all patients. As one trainee–patient put it: 'As I walked down Baker Street to my first group session, it felt like walking voluntarily towards a prison.... I saw the prison gates closing behind me, and I was beginning a long, long sentence.' The 'long sentence' represented the time she would 'have to' stay in the group; that is, throughout the training course. But it also meant the long time it would take to discover and deal with what she perceived as powerful 'bad' personality traits.

In our experience, the training aspects recede usually fairly early on in the group analysis, helped by group members who are sensitive to anyone who is 'not a real patient'. They feel observed, used, exploited and rejected. False communications are uncovered and attacked in the service of ever widening and deepening true communications. This is especially the case where a trainee–patient tries to defend himself or herself with previously acquired knowledge of group processes and uses what he or she thinks is the appropriate language. Trainee–patients often try to show their competence in and suitability for being a group analyst by acting as co-therapists. This may arise out of a wish to demonstrate how good and hard-working they are and how valuable to the group and especially to the conductor. Such patients often come into the group with a strong positive transference to the parent–conductor whom they may have encountered professionally in lectures and for whose groups they may have waited for a considerable time before a vacancy occurred. There is a wish to become the favourite group child. It takes some time to realise that this procedure is not only unnecessary but actually achieves the opposite to the desired effect. The mutative experience of being accepted, appreciated, even loved for the person one is and for what one has to bring to the group is one of the strong and lasting emotional insights which group analysis affords.

Later in the life of a group, and after the trainee has become a true patient, the group and indeed the conductor welcome the therapeutic insights which the trainee may display as one welcomes those from any patient in the group. Time and again, this also gives the conductor the

151

opportunity to contain his or her envy of the talent and expertise a trainee often has. In the negative transference phase, a weapon often used by the trainee–patient is to cap an interpretation of the conductor's with another one; or he or she would rephrase the analyst's comments, or openly reject them and offer alternative interpretations to a group member.

The ploy of the trainee as a co-therapist has another aspect; it affords the conductor an early insight into the likely development of the trainee as a therapist. For instance, a withholding trainee–patient who would interpret in a grudging manner was obviously *en route* to becoming a withholding therapist. His behaviour in the group allowed this to be explored and worked on and a change to be effected. Another competitive trainee offered interpretations urgently, 'as if there were no tomorrow', as the group put it. This could be experienced by fellow members as a psychical or even physical assault. The conductor's intervention allowed insight into the motivation and a resulting change to take place, which paved the way for a more constructive style of intervention in the trainee's future role as a conductor. Again, a gifted and emotionally open and honest patient who had not yet been accepted for training showed early signs of becoming a gifted therapist.

Seen from the point of view of the non-trainees in the group and the group as a whole, one of the earliest experiences that surface, especially when there are more than two trainee–patients in the group, is the division of the group into an 'in group' and those outside it. The 'in group' is experienced as forming round the conductor by the trainees, who are seen as his or her special cohort. Does the trainee not aspire to become a conductor and heir to the group conductor, a member of the Institute (or Practice) like him or her? And is not the 'ordinary' group member forever excluded from this intimacy? The situation evokes strong transference experiences of exclusion from the proximity of mother or father, of being of less importance to the parent figure than another sibling, of deeply resented and envied intimacy another sibling is seen to have with a parent. In reality, the meetings a trainee–patient may have outside the group, in the Institute, in academic seminars and supervision will be with the teaching staff, which by no means includes all the training group analysts.

Nevertheless, these meetings (real or imaginary) can increase the transference experience of the other group members to a near delusional level. A near paranoid dimension may be added when fears arise and are being voiced in the group that trainee–patients discuss their fellow group members in these academic meetings, thus using them as guinea pigs; can one really trust them to keep the basic rule of complete confidentiality? One man who seemed to have dealt with the experience of an 'in group' from which he was excluded in an earlier stage of his group life, burst into an uncontrollable rage when a trainee–patient referred to the period after the Easter break as 'the summer term'. The group and the conductor were unprepared for the strength of the rage expressed, having thought that much of a sense of exclusion had been worked with successfully earlier on. This incident offered an occasion for working through once more on a deeper level, this man's central childhood experiences in his large family with father absent in the war and surrounded by five siblings, all of whom seemed to him to be more important, more lovable, to mother than he could ever hope to be. There seemed no time, no place, no emotions which were special for him from mother.

Another manifestation of envious, negative, destructive feelings directed against a group conductor which is specific to the trainee–patient is an insistence on stereotyped, textbook-bound understanding of a reaction to group processes. The trainee knows 'how it should be done'. One trainee–patient frequently accused the conductor of not interpreting 'properly' or at all, because the conductor failed to use 'Freudian terms' and because it was his or her style to wait for the group to find its own meaning, while all the time moving the group along in that direction and intervening only where it was necessary. It often takes the trainee–patient longer than others in the group to experience what Foulkes meant when he gave the admonishment 'to follow the group and interpret only when understanding does not come from the group itself'.

There are as many variations of the trainee–patient themes as there are individual trainees. Some are expressed less aggressively than others, but are no less angry or competitive with the conductor–parent. Some are very clear in their wish for approval and the need to be the favourite special child–patient.

One trainee–patient reported a dream in which he found himself in the group but only three other faces were recognisable. One was that of a younger man in the group who sees himself as the sick boy child of the group; his symptoms are the most intransigent in the group. His rage is there, just under the surface, but shut off by a massive, impenetrable wall. It was his face that the dreamer saw clearly and also the face of a woman whom the dreamer frequently attacks.

There was also the group analyst. The dreamer dreamed that he gave the woman an interpretation which felt correct and helpful. Yet the conductor shook her head sadly in disapproval and took the woman outside the group room clearly to redress the damage done by the dreamer's interpretation.

Upon this the dreamer took the hand of the young man and together they left the group room. The group was told how miserable the dreamer felt on waking up and how the feelings of failure and inadequacy stayed with him all through the day. (One important feature of the dream is the denial of rage with the conductor, which, however, is expressed in the dream by the use of the young man who represents unexpressed rage with parental figures for the group.)

On the opposite side of the scale there is the experience of the group as being well-fed and enriched by the presence of trainee–patients. They are seen to bring all of themselves to the group, and this includes their knowledge and experience of psychotherapy, and group therapy and to share it with the group. One patient said, 'I am really glad we have trainees – I benefit from their knowledge.' There is often a sense of great loss when a trainee–patient leaves the group appropriately; that is, when his or her therapy comes to an end and not necessarily when the training course is completed. There is of course often a great sense of loss and mourning when a patient leaves the group, but at times, though by no means always, the loss is felt most acutely when the trainee–patient leaves and takes with him or her not only his or her patient contributions and personality features but also the qualities of a new fully fledged group analyst.

This extended sense of loss and mourning can be an obstacle when the departing group member is in due course replaced by a new patient, especially when this patient is not also a trainee. It may make entry into the group and acceptance by the group more difficult than it normally is. On one such occasion a group member who, for reasons which had to do with his history, took the departure of a trainee–patient who had been in the group for seven years with special grief and a deep sense of loss, exclaimed with great vehemence, 'Someone precious is gone, I don't want anyone in his place, I don't want to start all over again.' This reception was not easy for the newcomer to take, but others in the group were able to voice different experiences with the departed member and the new arrival so that, as so often in groups, the whole experience emerged in its entirety and was available to the newcomer. There was no need for the group conductor to protect a new patient and, by doing so, evoke more resentment and jealousy.

The presence of trainee–patients in a patient group brings with it special manifestations, group problems and dynamic constellations for everyone in the group including the group analyst. The additional requirement – namely, that the progress of the trainee–patient be reported to the Training Committee – creates a therapy situation that is delicate and at times difficult to negotiate. There are some training schemes in psychoanalytic training where such reporting has been dispensed with as interfering unduly with therapy. The experience of the training group analyst and the Training Committee is different. Difficult though it may be, it is found to be productive in the therapeutic process which, as Foulkes formulated, is a process of ego training in action.

Chapter 11

Starting a group at the Practice: an Associate's view

Jason Maratos

In its formative years, the Practice was the part-time commitment of a group of psychiatrists – most with psychoanalytic training – who also had a substantial commitment to the National Health Service through appointments in London teaching hospitals. With the leadership of S.H. Foulkes they were pioneers in group psychotherapy and, as such, were interested in developing group analysis as a discipline. These three elements of private practice, parallel National Health Service work and academic interest have shaped the Practice. The Practice's patients had to pay fees but these were, as they still are, relatively small and affordable by a large number of people. At that time formal, written knowledge of group analysis was comparatively small and a major source of development and learning was these early groups. Although we are aware that our groups are our best teachers (and often good therapists of the conductors), the attitude of the conductors then and now must be different; I do not think this is idealisation or nostalgia. The enthusiasm which led to the creation of the Institute of Group-Analysis (and contributed to the creation of the Institute of Family Therapy) in my opinion is likely to have influenced the selection of patients and the attitude of the Practice towards them.

One of the most important aspects of my experience as a patient at the Practice is the sense of partnership between conductor and group. At one stage Robin Skynner recorded the sessions. This was perceived in many different ways, but a powerful dynamic was the feeling that we, the patients, were teaching him something which he could use in educating others. We were not the 'have nots' expecting to receive; we had a lot to receive but we also had something to give, something worth preserving, something worth telling others about. Some of us had slightly grandiose ideas about the group being so superb that it was worth preserving in this way. On the whole we learned something from the experience.

The willingness, the interest, the wish of the conductor to learn from us made it easier for us to learn from one another. For the trainees, being co-patients with 'real' patients became such an asset that very few of us would now accept that therapy in a group composed of trainees only can have the same therapeutic value.

In my wish to make this chapter representative of the practice of the Practice [*sic*] I approached all Members for some reminiscences. What follows contains to some extent experiences of Practice colleagues.

One Member's account of his first group at the Practice reflects and describes the ethos which was prevalent at that time.

I started my first once-weekly group with Group-Analytic Practice back in January 1968 when it was suggested to me that perhaps I might become an Associate of the Practice; I was delighted. I was so delighted, that I undertook to clear the waiting list! There had been quite a number of rather damaged, or psychotic young people on the waiting list, many of them having been lingering there for a long time, I believe up to about a year. They were mainly young men, and so it was expedient to start an all-male group. I believe that all the men on the waiting list were contacted, and seven of them were able to manage the time and make the commitment to starting.

I nicknamed this group my 'young damaged group'. Understandably it was a very tricky group, highly defended, extremely anxious, but it nevertheless developed a sense of containment and support. Slow progress was made over a period of about 18 months, with two or three drop-outs replaced by new men, one as I remember a stabilised schizophrenic, the other one of the worst obsessive-compulsive characters that I have met, outside hospital. Round about June 1969, two other men were stopping, and I was able to introduce two young women, albeit with some ambivalence towards them. One of the women was a difficult and highly defended anorexic, with very little capacity for insight, but with whom we struggled along in a supportive and more counselling way for several years. Gradually over the next year the group took on a more group-analytic quality, with a balance of four men and four women. Although it was possible to do some analytic work in the group, it remained extremely defended, and I used to say to my colleagues about this group, that if I made one transference interpretation a month, we were becoming quite dynamic!

The young people did quite well in a reality sense, the schizophrenic started and successfully ran a small business, and was even able to make an important relationship, possibly leading to marriage later. The anorexic girl was able to hold down a simple secretarial job, and again found it possible to begin to explore her sexuality. By the autumn of 1972 there were seven members of the group, but frankly I had a sense of stagnation. There seemed to be the indication of a natural point of termination of the group and I believe I gave six months' notice of the group ending, and the last session was held on 11 December 1973.

They were able to get in touch with their sense of loss and sadness at its ending, and, surprising to me, not one of them got in touch with me again after the end of the group, even though they know they were free to do so if they needed further help.

I decided after this group experience that I would never again take a group of a waiting list without seeing people individually myself for 'assessment'.

The whole process, from initial referral, through assessment to allocation to a group, has now become much more organised and structured than in those early intuitive days. Patients are assessed by a medical member of the Practice who is also a training group analyst. Agreement is reached with the patient regarding the form of treatment most suitable for him or her. Group treatment is recommended to only about half of the candidates. A wide range of interventions is proposed, from psychoanalysis and individual psychotherapy to psychiatric treatment and even autogenic training. Some patients are referred to non-medical members and later seen for a medical responsibility interview at no extra cost to themselves.

The assessor records factual information and his opinion on a structured form (see Chapter 6). If the patient is advised to join a group at the Practice he or she may find an immediate vacancy or his name is put on the waiting list. When a vacancy arises, the conductor interested in filling that vacancy will be given the assessment form to study. On the basis of that form he will decide whether or not to proceed with this particular patient.

The waiting list is mirrored by the vacancies or expected vacancies list. Information is fed into these lists by the Clinical Secretary and all Members and Associates. For example, 'My Thursday evening once-weekly group will have a vacancy for a woman in her forties in three months' time' or 'Two youngish men will be needed for a twice-weekly group after Christmas – not trainees, please'. Allocation to groups, though, does not always happen in this impersonal manner; the Clinical Secretary will get in contact with another member personally if he thinks that a patient has special needs or might pose particular difficulties. Also, during the termly practice meetings it is possible to point out if there are any special requirements for a particular group. Members may also discuss their intention to establish groups with a more homogeneous membership; for example, an older persons' group or a 'psychosomatic' group or one for severely damaged or borderline personalities. With this kind of information, the Clinical Secretary, knowing what groups are available, attempts to match patients with suitable groups as 'accurately' as possible.

Communication between the Clinical Secretary, members of the Management Committee and Associates has not always been as good or open as it is today. Up to 1988 the Associates did not have access to the waiting list. In earlier days it was more difficult for Associates to maintain a full complement in their groups. This situation in my perception inevitably led to negative feelings and to some tension between the Members and the Associates. A feeling that the Members kept the 'better' patients (better attenders, wealthier ones, ones with better prognosis) prevailed and was considered unjustified by the Members.

The Practice does not have a unified attitude about selection of patients. Some believe that the absence of contact of the conductor with patients before they join his group might have advantages – indeed, believe that one of the reasons why training groups work well is because the members are not selected. Others are more careful about selection; in the early days conductors would meet informally for about 20 minutes with the prospective members but now some meet for about one hour and others more than once.

This meeting was given the somewhat undignified epithet of 'pregroup chat' by a former secretary-administrator. The meeting is far from a frivolous, superficial, quasi-social encounter in which only unimportant matters are discussed. As this is the first occasion in which conductor and prospective group member meet, it is full of significance and importance.

Both conductor and patient need each other; the conductor has a vacancy which needs to be filled while the patient is in search of therapy. Both invest a lot in making this meeting a successful one. Deeper and often unconscious aspects of the two personalities will colour the atmosphere of the interview and might determine the final outcome. There is little doubt that therapists can learn a lot from patients whom they do not like, but offering a place to such a patient needs to be a conscious and carefully thought-out decision and not dictated by the needs of the group to replenish its 'numbers'.

The therapist needs to be cautious not only about patients he dislikes but also about those towards whom he experiences strong feelings – not only negative but positive as well – even though research suggests that therapists are more beneficial to patients they like than those whom they don't.

The first meeting is an opportunity for the patient to pull out if he feels that he can't work with the therapist. This is a two-edged process, however. The patient may see correctly that he or she and this particular therapist will never form a useful therapeutic alliance. On the other hand, he or she may perceive, however, that this therapist understands him only too well. The patient's decision may be coloured by having waited a long time for this encounter. Again this is a two-edged phenomenon. He or she by now may be so desperate that any offer may be perceived as a good one. Alternatively the accumulated anger from so much waiting may be displaced on to the one who finally offers therapy – by now far too late!

Some misconceptions about group therapy become evident even at this stage. People have a mental picture of group therapy from television or films and expect anything from a discussion group to scenes which could have been created by Edward Albee or Eugene O'Neill.

During the first meeting, questions about group therapy being the right choice may emerge both in the conductor and the candidate and convert what was set up as a single hour-long session to either a longer one or a series of sessions; it is better not to include someone in a group rather than have an early drop-out or premature termination. The outcome of a psychiatric assessment at the Practice is occasionally unexpected. One patient, presenting with somatic symptoms, disclosed to his potential therapist that he had been so terrified by the psychiatric assessment and the prospect of joining a group that he had been unable to sleep. Since the assessment he was constantly being awakened by nightmares. I offered to see him for a second meeting but he cancelled, saying that he was a lot better since seeing me and had decided not to join a group!

A borderline patient with intense sensitive ideas of reference was offered as a potential group member to me. It became obvious that he would not be able to communicate with (understand or be understood by) the other group members of that particular group; this was explained to him. Another, more suitable group, was found for him, but after a few sessions he moved to another part of the country, possibly in flight from perceived persecution and threat, in this group.

I used to be but am no longer surprised to find, when seeing a new group patient, that he or she asks about fees and how they are paid – even though this information is explained to prospective group members at their psychiatric assessment and contained in a printed leaflet given to them during the meeting. Even though the leaflet makes it clear that the fee is an 'annual' rate for a minimum of 40 sessions and that it is to be paid in twelve monthly instalments in advance, the 'in advance' is often 'forgotten' and complaints about having to pay for the holiday month of August arise with some regularity.

The above examples are only a few of the many which illustrate that even when one takes the utmost care to screen, select, match and prepare patients many continue to maintain a staunch resistance to developing a therapeutic alliance, despite continuing to claim a desire for therapy. Unconscious processes operate continuously, and will sooner or later either surface and become the subject matter of therapy or they will lead to action. This acting out can be either within the group context (lateness, poor attendance, non-payment of fees) or occasionally an act of sudden withdrawal and an angry departure from the group. Naturally there are patients who value the opportunity to meet the prospective group conductor, who ask for literature about group therapy, who appreciate that they are not being charged for that session and also feel that Group-Analytic

159

Practice is an institution which is thorough in its approach, thoughtful about its patients and liberal in its attitude, as it gives its patients the opportunity to assess and reject a therapist for whatever reason.

The variety of responses of patients to the first interview reinforces the view of a few practice members that it is an unnecessary and even anti-group process. One believes it is preferable that the patient should not meet the conductor before joining the group. The selection of trainees is a more extended process. They too undergo a psychiatric assessment, but the psychiatrist prepares a report which is considered by a Board of Assessors of the Institute of Group-Analysis. The candidate also undergoes an extensive assessment by the fore mentioned Board, which consists of three established group analysts who, in turn, report through their chairperson to the Training Committee of the Institute of Group-Analysis.

The prevalent practice is for a slow-open group; when a vacancy arises it is filled from the waiting list. This process had led to a number of groups in the Practice to continue for many years, though it is extremely rare for a group member (other than the conductor) to have stayed with the same group for such a length of time.

There is a further area in which the Practice will not come across as homogeneous: the way in which members believe one should conduct the early phases of a group. Where there is consensus is in the belief of the autonomous personality of the group.

Lionel Kreeger writes:

I never cease to be amazed at the qualitative differences between groups. Issues such as punctuality and regularity of attendance vary enormously from group to group. There are groups where from the beginning people seem absolutely committed to regularity and punctuality and others where from the very first session people are late or just don't turn up for the groups, the whole experience being both ragged and frustrating at times.

Another colleague confirms this view by stating:

I have started two twice-weekly groups at the Practice. One of these groups has never looked back; it immediately understood its task, had some conflict with me which was resolved and finally became a most rewarding and creative experience. The other group has been quarrelsome and reluctant to pay; it had trainees who appeared to hate patients or to hate being patients – as well as patients who resented being in the same group with trainees.

Personally, like some parents who never cease to be amazed by the independent personality development of their children, I continue to be

surprised when my groups remind me that, important though I am, I am only one member of an organism which 'has its own life'.
Different conductors at the Practice approach the beginning of a group differently. Most would agree with Lionel Kreeger, who is prepared to increase the temperature of the group, heighten the arousal level, tolerate long silences, make early transferential interpretations in a twice-weekly analytical group, while he would tend to be supportive, encouraging more didactic and perhaps offer counselling at the early stages of a once-weekly group. Again, much depends on the group; the analyst who can tell if a silence he encounters is stimulating change rather than overwhelming anxiety or terror before it is too late is a wise man indeed. Some of us still discover the nature of some silent periods only with hindsight.

I have had two extreme cases of silent members in a group. The first remained totally silent for the first group session, left and never returned. The second, a predominantly silent (and erratic) attender, has blossomed in the group and speaks out in its defence when it is attacked, to the surprise of other members – and initially, of the conductor. This member, who found the fact that he was allowed to be a part of the group and remain silent as a non-intrusive acceptance of him, appreciated that he was allowed to progress in therapy at his own pace. Other silent members perceive the group silence as rejection and as a sign of lack of interest on the part of the group. Group silence, like analyst silence, often forces deep anxieties to emerge to near or actual consciousness – what happens then is, of course, a matter beyond the scope of this chapter. What is almost certain is that it demands particularly sensitive handling at the early and formative stages of the group.

Readers of this chapter are probably well aware of the large literature on groups' phases of development, from Foulkes (1957) onwards. The beginning of a group has special significance and is not only a formative period but also a time when the group is fragile and likely to evoke primitive responses in its members (Nitsun, 1989). The members of a slow-open group re-experience some of the feelings of the earliest phase of the group's life each time a new member joins. Insecurity, rivalry and wishes to extrude the new member re-surface and will be strong under-currents, however neutral or even welcoming the old members seem. I would like to conclude with a personal opinion about the dynamics of starting a group. Patients who are all new to a group are exposed to a threatening situation. If they are to pursue this situation for personal growth, they need not only to develop trust, but also security. It is sometimes difficult for the new group to achieve this from the start. If a member does not feel secure, he or she runs a high risk of 'dropping out', becoming a therapeutic failure and further influencing the feelings of the remaining group members. Similarly, a new member to an established group cannot be expected to relate to the 'matrix' and to feel the group as a secure base. Transference to the group is a phenomenon which might develop – it is not invariably present from the start. It seems to me that before a patient joins a group it helps if he or she feels safe with his or her conductor and that he or she has a special relationship with him. This attachment will serve as a transitional relationship (Winnicott, 1971), and will enable the patient to tolerate the inevitable frustrations which are inherent in a group situation – as in real life.

As we are trying to help people who are so different from one another we cannot expect one and the same method of induction to be optimal for all. We need to be flexible and receptive to each prospective patient's particular needs. Some will be mature enough to begin to use and develop through the group experience, but others might need long preparation by the conductor and yet others may need continuous and concurrent individual (that is combined individual and group) therapy (see Chapter 9). Because of these factors, when assessing a candidate for group therapy we need to decide not only if the person is likely to benefit but also what degree of preparation he needs prior to joining the group and, furthermore, if he is likely to require any concurrent additional therapy. With these measures one hopes to reduce the likelihood of therapeutic failures and to broaden the range of patients suitable for this particular form of psychotherapy.

Chapter 12

Death and the Practice

Meg Sharpe

S.H. Foulkes, the father of group analysis, died 'in action' conducting a group of colleagues at 88 Montagu Mansions. Some of those colleagues who are now Members of the Practice acknowledge their difficulties in dealing with such a loss, and many feel they never worked it through sufficiently, or as thoroughly as the patient groups, facilitated in the working through of other deaths in the Practice. This group was unique in 'dying' with its conductor, unlike any other groups I shall be discussing.

In any analytic group the transferential relationship between the analyst and the group is centrally important. What happens when this relationship is severed either in the short term or permanently, by death, illness or departure of the conductor? The first part of this chapter will illustrate different aspects of this problem and how they have been dealt with in the Group-Analytic Practice. The second part looks at the other side of the coin, and illustrates some experiences from groups at the Practice where patients' deaths had to be dealt with.

In the process of becoming established as a group-analytic practitioner I have assumed responsibility in various circumstances for several different groups from other analysts. The variety of reactions of these groups to this trauma is, it seems to me, linked with many factors, the more prominent of which are discussed here. All the 'change-overs' were clean breaks – that is, with no overlapping co-therapy. I use the term 'change-over' rather than 'takeover' throughout the chapter, since the process is more akin to the change of a pilot or navigator than a change in management or control.

The main change to be coped with is the integration of the new conductor. The group is not the problem in that it has its own continuity – the conductor is the discontinuity. How well the integration proceeds depends on the circumstances. How did it happen? How prepared were the group? How sudden was the change? How long have they been with the departing conductor? For the new conductor the question is, how does one get into a full boat without rocking it too much, without shipping too much water, without tipping everyone overboard or being thrown overboard oneself? The boat will lurch or lose direction if the group (crew) becomes mutinous. Feelings of alienation or pointlessness may emerge and patients could even attempt to abandon ship. The conductor's effectiveness in making it safer to stay rather than leave determines how well the boat is brought back under control.

The new conductor needs to 'read' the personality of the group and merge with and adapt to it. He or she should follow the process and be aware that he or she may be experienced as a sudden and perhaps unwelcome intruder.

It is important to be sympathetic towards the analytic outlook of the departing conductor, and it can help if the replacement has a style that is not too dissimilar. The orientation of the group is more crucial than that of the conductor, who should already have expertise in reading and understanding groups. His or her philosophic orientation may dictate how easy or difficult he or she finds it to take charge. My own personal style has been to move in quietly, observe and listen until I begin to get some understanding of the group's character. There is no easy way; there is always a great need for persistence, patience and control of personal anxiety.

There are several different change-over situations which fall into two main categories:

1 Planned:
    retirement (change is permanent);
    resignation (change is permanent);
    scheduled absence (change is temporary); for, e.g., an operation.
2 Unplanned:
    death (change is permanent);
    illness (change may be permanent or temporary).

In either category the process can be confusing, disturbing and difficult for the analyst and the group. In general, unplanned change-overs are the most traumatic and planned ones are just traumatic or difficult. The actual degree of difficulty experienced is determined by:

length of association with previous analyst;
degree of similarity of orientation between the new and the previous analyst;
the group's reading of the analyst's potential for ensuring their survival.

These different factors present themselves in widely different proportions, as the following clinical illustrations will indicate.

1 Planned change-overs

(a) Retirement or resignation

The conductor may have strong feelings about who should take over his or her groups, and arrangements are usually made months (even years) ahead and the groups are prepared. The group also has time to plan resistance and so may be more subversive when the new conductor arrives. The responsibility for a planned change-over lies with the group conductor.

As an illustration, one Member who was very ill in his last year was anxious that I should look after his groups, and during his remaining months at the Practice, he needed constant affirmation and reassurance from me that I would be available. I had been 'caretaker' for him some years previously when he had had minor surgery. As he had been my supervisor during my own training, I was very familiar with his work and analytic attitude.

Another group, well-prepared by a Member who had resigned, was welcoming. They had worked on their separation reasonably well and were therefore more open to a change than they might have been. The change-over went smoothly and it proved to be a lively and talented group which continues ten years later to give me considerable pleasure and satisfaction.

One Member who planned his retirement two years in advance prepared his groups and they were secure in the knowledge that they would be looked after by two of the Associates and had ample opportunity to voice feelings before the change-over. A current Member who is resigning has also planned well ahead, and again the groups will be fully informed as to who will be their new conductor.

(b) Scheduled absence

A scheduled absence is altogether a simpler situation to deal with. The conductor will appoint a locum, the group know the length of the gap and who will be looking after them, and the date the conductor will be returning. In our experience this is not too disturbing for groups and can often be an insight-promoting event for all parties.

A scheduled absence is one of several weeks, not a short one where usually the group will meet on its own.

2 Unplanned change-overs

(a) Change-over due to death

My own entrance to the Practice was a direct result of the death of one of the Members in 1974. This sudden and unexpected invitation left little time to prepare; the evening following his death I walked into a room not knowing what to expect. As I had not personally known the dead conductor I did not carry any grief with me, and felt freely open to whatever experience the group might be going through. Foulkes' words – 'go in, sit down and see what happens' – stood me in good stead.

I inherited a group with a particular personality, an extremely depressed collection of 'individuals' who did not communicate with one another; they were unconcerned both about their fellows and to a great extent about the death of their analyst. There was considerable hostility that he had died – why couldn't he stick around? Very little sorrow or guilt was expressed and there was general indifference to the change-over. One male member told me, with a shrug of his shoulders, that two weeks before his death the conductor had told them that if he had a heart attack in the group he did not believe any member would lift a finger to help him. I surmise he was absolutely accurate on this point.

A member who had just joined the group a week before was the exception; he was depressed too, but not so hostile. He remained with the group for some six years, long after the original members had moved on, and he still sends me an annual letter to check that I am alive.

One week after I joined this group, our room was changed without notice. The lack of time to prepare for this provoked an outburst of anger. The environmental change produced psychic change, namely, anger, a displacement of anger about the death on to the room change. The group were displaced persons with an unwanted stepmother. Although it was experienced as an unthoughtful action on the part of the management (by me) and on my part (by the group), I later reflected that it could be a good idea deliberately to change the setting to trigger off otherwise bottled-up anger and grief.

The group was filled with negativity, dreariness and punishment for the first year. People were slow to pay their fees, but they did not come late or miss sessions. One sole member who professed to care about my predecessor did not settle her debts with his estate (fees owing for two years or more) and neither did she pay me. Any interpretations were ignored. Eventually I had to ask her to leave.

This, my first private group, remains in my mind as the most stressful and difficult group I have conducted in some 20 years. Any new member introduced by me was infected by the *malaise,* and it took four years to work through the depression and then rage (with me carrying most of it for a long time) and for the culture to change and some optimism to be injected into it. Eventually, after hard labour on all our parts, there was an upsurge of hope and the start of a renaissance. In the group transference I continually shifted between being the Wicked Stepmother and the Bad Dead Father, and through constant interpretation finally enabled a mourning process to start.

I learned to respect my predecessor, and I later heard to my relief that he himself had classed it as an extremely difficult group. Fifteen years later this group is most lively, hard-working and rewarding.

Another group which the analyst left shortly before he died followed a different process in the transference. His death and funeral were shared with the group, and some patients attended the memorial service. This was restorative and binding – patients and new conductor shared the mutual loss.

In one group, some years after the conductor had died, one of his ex-patients rejoined his old group, now very different. He frequently refers to the previous conductor who has become a beloved ancestor of present members. They experience the continuity of the group's history and enjoy legends about the archetypal Good Father. We have a metaphorical chair for him in the group. And of course there are echoes of his death on anniversaries.

(b) Change-over due to illness

A sudden illness may give the locum conductor some leeway because emotions are disturbed and the group usually responds well to holding. One Member who was ill invited me to be a locum in his group for a lengthy period, and after some six months asked me to continue as conductor as he felt unable to cope with all his work. This was a painful decision for the group members who were not the chosen ones; the rejection also reflected some members' individual history. Again I was experienced as a step-parent and new members I introduced were seen as my 'real' children as opposed to step-children. I was angrily told once that not only did I not sound like the old conductor, I didn't even look like him. Positive and negative feelings about the departing analyst also were expressed, and the culture made this possible. He was much loved and respected, there was deep sadness as well as anger about his departure. He was the super-human, godlike 'Wise Old Man' and the group felt it was left to the mercy of the unknown 'Mother'.

Group-Analytic Practice policy

In unplanned change-overs the responsibility lies with the Practice Management Committee. In the case of a death, a Member personally informs the deceased's groups and then may leave them to their private grief. A replacement conductor will be moved in almost immediately. If the illness is sudden, the Practice also goes into action at once. Locums are provided but are not imposed on the group. The group is consulted and, if possible, the conductor is consulted. One Member takes responsibility for informing a particular group and being available for consultation. If it is likely to be a lengthy separation, then locums are deemed necessary.

The mourning process

Whatever the reason for the change-over and however well the group is prepared, this process gets into motion. After the initial flicker of interest in the new conductor, the inevitable negative feelings arise. Bowlby (1974) discusses three phases of mourning: (1) protest (grief, separation anxiety, denial, weeping, aggression); (2) despair (disorganisation, nothing is any good); (3) detachment from the lost object (reorganisation: after this attachment capacities are released).

This loss cycle is repeated at intervals and needs constant attention on the part of the new conductor. Unresolved mourning hinders the development of creativity and individuation, and it is vital that the group is helped into this natural process. The group may feel responsibility for the analyst's death, and this omnipotence needs to be challenged. There is additional stress if the conductor has been involved with the previous analysand and has to work through his or her own grief. In the group, concentration must be on the group and the individuals' grief – not on the conductor's grief, although of course there should be no denial of shared grief. The analyst must also deal with any personal feelings of inadequacy for not being so clever, so kind, and so on. The advent of new members, the real children, as opposed to step-children always repeats the loss cycle.

Surviving the change-over

Taking over someone else's group is a potentially perilous situation for the conductor as well as the group, and one needs a survival kit. My Jungian background and generally optimistic outlook have been helpful to me in these circumstances. Repeated experiences have enabled me to survive: survival breeds confidence and greater ability to deal with the situation. Perhaps the most important message one can project unconsciously into the new group is one's own inner conviction that it will turn out all right because it has done so in the past.

The size of the group has an effect on the change-over. There are different strategies for dealing with groups that are under-strength at the change-over. If the original patients are nourished for too long, there is a greater resistance to new members. Moving them in fairly rapidly produces quicker integration. For example, one group of mine had four members at the change-over. I moved them from their old room to a complete change of scene and added two new members. The group adapted well and continued without much ado. Another group had enormous resistance to each one of the new members who was added. Three years later, resistance to any new admission from the original nucleus of three still continued. Another group numbered six at the change-over and although I quickly built it up to eight, it was rare to have eight people all together – someone was always missing. Were they leaving space for the ghost of my predecessor? Another group took a long time to settle because it took me time to organise my own space; I had to hold alternate sessions in a different room.

There are different forms of behaviour for different groups. We can speculate on what this behaviour means, and indeed interpret it, but the main point is that it is distinct behaviour and different behaviour.

The Group-Analytic Practice is in a unique position because of its size when dealing with the change-over of conductor. All the groups are slow-open groups; when a member leaves, a new one joins. Similarly, when the analyst leaves (for whatever reason) a new analyst is appointed, usually from the Members or Associates. If this is not possible, the Practice has access to a wider circle of graduates of the Institute of Group-Analysis, a high quality professional organisation, which can offer security that our groups will be in safe hands.

It is a salutary antidote to the egotism of the conductor to realise that he or she is not immortal and that the group's continuity is more important than his or hers. In the Group-Analytic Practice, groups do not die when the conductor dies – they survive.

Death and the patient group

Jung (1931) believed that the goal of the first half of life is a strong ego and the goal of the second half is reconciling the ego to the meaning of life in the face of inevitable death. Rosemary Gordon (1978), a Jungian analyst, has made a special study in her excellent book *Dying and Creating: a Search for Meaning*. She states Jung's belief that there is a natural and innate disposition in man to concern himself with death and to prepare himself for it as life moves forward.

As an analyst, one cannot avoid dealing with death both personally and professionally. We may need to help our patients to cope with a past or present death – or indeed to prepare them to face an impending death. The analyst cannot escape – he or she has to cope with personal loss that inevitably occurs during his or her professional life. An example of this is a personal event.

Some time ago my father died, early one morning in the last working week before a three week holiday. I was just about to enter a group when I heard the news. One of my colleagues informed the group that I could not attend owing to a 'family bereavement' and he instructed the Secretary to leave notes to that effect in my room for my other groups. Dealing with the matter in this way ensures some privacy for the analyst and also facilitates the exploration of any possible fantasies later.

When I returned, I was met with various responses. One group discussed the death immediately and revealed many preoccupations and fears for me. It took a few sessions for the group to settle. Another group – the one I had to abandon the day my father died – showed some aggression and expressed their difficulties in coping without me. It was particularly poignant that a young woman was due to leave the group that day and could not say goodbye to me as planned. Her mother had killed herself years before. The discussion was on mothers who let you down, who are not there when needed. A third group, a fatherless group (most patients had lost their fathers) offered strong support and expressed relief that it wasn't my husband or child. I had received five cards from this group of eight. I then discovered that one of them had asked the Secretary who had given them details of my father, how old he was, that I was in France, and so on. I was told crossly that the Secretary talked too much. After the initial sympathy, hostility, support or otherwise had been expressed, the group quickly settled down to normal and work continued.

The first part of this chapter attempted to describe some particular experiences of the Practice in coping with the loss of a Member. Arrangements to cope with such an event are largely determined by Practice policy and may be far from typical elsewhere. The remainder of this chapter therefore looks at the more generally experienced difficulties arising from death within the patient group itself.

Many of our patients, both young and old, encounter death in one form or another during their time in a group. I do not have personal experience of a group patient dying by his or her own hand. Others in the Practice have had to deal with this traumatic event – I believe there have been two such deaths during my sixteen years as a Member.

I will illustrate three different 'deaths' in patient groups.

L, a young Norwegian woman (in her twenties), joined my group after a lengthy period of once-weekly individual psychotherapy with me. She originally presented as very depressed. She had discovered, when getting a passport to travel to England, that she was adopted: her mother was her natural mother, but her 'father' was not her natural father. He had adopted her at the age of two. This secret had been kept from her. She was then told by her mother that her real father was dead and her mother was not prepared to talk further. This information caused L considerable distress while at the same time it helped her to make sense of childhood feelings – that is, that she was second-best in the family, and her younger sister (half-sister) was sent to private school and had other favours bestowed on her. She had little physical resemblance to either parent and always felt the odd one out. An unsatisfactory love affair with a kindly Norwegian man in his late fifties prompted her to seek help. Her unspoken agenda was to search for her true father in herself. In the course of her analysis, and after much pressure, her mother told her that he was in the Danish Navy and died when she was a baby. Mother's responses to questioning were aggressive, but finally she told L she was conceived on a ship and that it was a 'one night stand'.

Mother herself felt bitterly ashamed about this, and had tried unsuccessfully to have an abortion. So L was plunged once more into depression, not only was she not wanted, but her very identity was in question. She was not Norwegian but Danish.

Time passed and the wound healed. L wrote to the Danish naval authorities to find out where her father was buried so that she could visit his grave. To her astonishment (and mine) she discovered that he was alive, a widower and living in Copenhagen. They met and it was good – she was much welcomed. Her joyful father introduced her to four half-siblings she did not know existed. He told her he was already married when the ship's encounter took place, that he had sent money for her upkeep all through her childhood, that he had repeatedly asked for photographs, but had been denied all contact by her mother.

About this time, L joined my group and began to flourish. She formed strong bonds with the other group members, simultaneously forming bonds with her new Danish family. She made plans; she left her Norwegian lover sadly but optimistically. Her need for him was over – she had a 'real' father. She changed her work to a more interesting and better-paid post so that she could visit Denmark more often. She was in the process of deciding whether to live in Copenhagen when illness struck. One day I had a call from her that she was sick, 'probably 'flu', and that she would see the group in a week. A second call from her – she was in hospital under investigation; she felt very weak but hoped to see us soon; she sent her love to the group. The following week, her Norwegian friend rang to tell me she was dead.

Needless to say this totally unexpected death shocked the group and myself and confronted us all with the harshness of reality and with our own mortality. Together we mourned her, the group drawing very close for many months. (Was the main purpose of her life to place herself in her family and then to die? She coped with the resurrection of her father before she died.) On the day she was buried, I was working in Copenhagen where her new-found father lived and also mourned.

The next illustration is of a patient who left the group to die.

I experienced from another position, in my own personal group analysis, a fellow group member who was in the process of dying. S was a severely depressed woman in her forties who was always complaining, about her analyst, the group, her physical condition, and so on. Over two years her state of mind improved considerably – she also had twice-weekly individual analysis with the group conductor.

In the third year, S complained increasingly about feeling tired and listless and indeed she began to look ill. The group urged her to visit her general practitioner, which she eventually did, albeit reluctantly, stating that he would not give her much attention as she was labelled 'neurotic'. He told her nothing was wrong – no doubt she had exasperated him in the past, as she had the group, with her constant moaning.

Weeks passed. S began to get noticeably thin and drawn. The group was seriously worried and pressed her into seeing a particular general practitioner, known to be extremely thorough. Cancer was diagnosed and she was immediately hospitalised.

S's sudden departure was not prepared for – she was unable to say goodbye and this left unfinished business and guilt in the remaining members. Why had we got so angry with her for complaining? Why did we not insist she saw another doctor earlier? Had we caused her illness? A few months later, and after I had left, this group had a further devastating blow – the analyst died suddenly. S died some months later, sadly after his death.

My final illustration is about a different kind of death that had to be dealt with in a group.

H, a talented illustrator, was very ambivalent, and indeed hostile, about group analysis. His previous group analyst had left the group and I took over. He felt abandoned to the dreaded 'mother' figure. He attended regularly and promptly, pointing out my shortcomings and the group's inadequacy.

One evening, the group started and he was absent. This was most unusual. During the group's meeting I was aware of an unusual and increasing anxiety about his whereabouts. This became so pressing I shared it with the group and found that others had similar feelings. We could not understand the significance of this. Five minutes before the group was due to end, the door burst open and an ashen H fell inside. On the way to the group he had had a car accident and knocked down and killed an old lady. It was a dark, very wet night and he did not see her step on to a pedestrian crossing. His anguish and horror pervaded the group. We continued for a further half hour or so, while H was in a state of shock. The group sustained him for many months and even years, and coped with his varied mood swings. He was prosecuted and banned from driving, and needed the encouragement and firm containing of the group to enable him to live through his terrible guilt. The group also needed strong support to cope with his accusations that it was the group's fault: that he had been mentally so disturbed by them that he had had the accident. After four years, the group helped him to face the fear of driving and to start again, and to let the past rest.

Summary

These different events show how vital it is for a group to be helped by the conductor to work through the mourning process appropriately. The analyst must provide sufficient support to let the group 'be' – that is, miserable, angry or tearful – and be prepared to stay close by its side for as long as it takes. However well the analyst can cope with his or her personal (inevitable) death and his or her personal losses, so will he or she be able to assist others to cope by not shirking the task of facing death.

Jung sees life as an energy process. 'Like every energy process it is in principle irreversible and is therefore directed towards a goal. That goal is a state of rest.'

Chapter 13

Administration of the Practice

Meg Sharpe

The Group-Analytic Practice has been established legally and administratively with great care. This chapter, which outlines these aspects, is of necessity different from the others in that it deals with matters which are not clinical or theoretical, but none the less important. This importance is perhaps not always immediately apparent. while we (the Members) readily acknowledge that the Group-Analytic Practice provides a substantial proportion of our livelihood, it is difficult to engender the same sense of purpose and commitment towards the successful operation of the business as to our professional work.

For this reason the running and management of the Practice can be both difficult and frustrating, as analysts would far more willingly have a clinical discussion than work out how to reduce the phone bill. As we are not necessarily gifted with financial expertise and business acumen, it can be a struggle, on joining as a Member, to grasp the intricacies of a surprisingly complex arrangement. (The Associates have a different responsibility, so that participation is not so complex for them.) Outside professional help is sought when necessary, and internally we arrange for a constitutionally appointed chairperson to co-ordinate the organisation. Not an easy task!

Constitution

The Practice is an association of members and its essential nature is that of a non-profit-making association. It is not a partnership nor a private company. Its Members join together for the purpose of sharing the administration and management of its premises, the lease of which they jointly own, and where they practise as individuals within the terms of a licence which forms part of the lease. Under the licence, Membership is restricted to seven, but up to a further nine Associates are also permitted to practise on the premises. Associates were originally appointed to deal with an increasing workload and also to form a possible pool from which to draw future Members. There are important differences between Mem-

174

bers and Associates in their professional, legal and financial responsibilities.

The activities of the Practice are regulated by 'Rules' which were drawn up in consultation with the Practice lawyer and which are legally binding on Members. Any Member wishing to resign must give six months' notice to the Committee of Management. Associates are invited to renew their Associateship on a yearly basis and to sign a relevant extract from the Rules as advised by lawyers. This has no legal connotation and is an agreement freely entered into by both parties.

Members' duties

Members form the Management Committee and have certain responsibilities. The major ones are as follows:

(a) to ensure that the Practice is managed and run on a sound professional and financial basis;

(b) to secure sufficient new business to maintain the progress and financial security of Members, Associates and staff;

(c) to maintain and improve its prestigious central London premises for the comfort and well-being of patients, staff and colleagues;

(d) to manage the staff and ensure efficient administration of patient files, appointment services, assessment interviews, room allocation, relationships and communication with the outside world and professional bodies, accounts and budgets, housekeeping and cleaning, and 24-hour telephone cover;

(e) to ensure that all patients are adequately covered medically at all times (Members themselves provide 24-hour medical cover) and to provide locums for vacation periods, sick or absent Members and for Associates;

(f) to provide professional support and advice to other Members and Associates as required;

(g) when required, to select and appoint new Members and Associates who will enhance and reinforce the reputation of the Practice;

(h) in the event of loss or serious damage to the Practice premises, immediately to arrange alternative accommodation to ensure continuity of work and to rearrange group schedules if required;

(i) to answer legally for acts commissioned in the name of the Practice whether by Members, Associates or staff;

(j) to discharge without limitation as to liability all financial debts of the Practice and to provide adequate working capital.

Members elect from among themselves three officers annually. An officer will usually serve for three years before rotation takes place. The officers and their responsibilities are as follows:

(i) The *Chairperson*, who is required to convene and preside over the Monday meetings and meetings with lawyers, accountants, financial advisers and Associates. The Chairperson must also monitor the overall running and welfare of the Practice and ensure that the Practice Rules are followed. In addition, the Chairperson has to represent the Practice at certain professional functions to the outside world. Located as it is in a large residential apartment block with large numbers of patients coming and going between the periods of 7.30–9.30 a.m. and 6–9 p.m. it is essential to be conscious of the potential irritation to other residents and maintain support of the Residents' Association.

The Chairperson also prepares the agenda for the weekly Monday meetings and has responsibility for organising locums at vacation times or if a Member or Associate is suddenly ill.

(ii) The *Clinical Secretary* who has to deal with referrals to the Practice (which might come into the Practice rather than to individual Members) and to allocate assessment interviews to various consultants and to look after the waiting list. Members and Associates inform the Clinical Secretary of any vacancies they may have. Associates are encouraged to check the waiting list for themselves too. If there is a need for a new group, the Clinical Secretary will inform the Members.

(iii) The *Treasurer* who is responsible for liaising with the accountant and the financial adviser, for keeping Members in touch with the financial situation and for ensuring that contributions to overheads are correctly set, collected and monitored.

Associates

Associates are not Members of the Association and as such do not have the same rights, privileges or responsibilities. Their responsibilities are:

(i) to practise group analysis with patients referred to them from the Practice, conscientiously and to a standard which will maintain and enhance the standing of the Practice;

(ii) to keep the Practice fully informed as to vacancies in their groups, and any developments in relation to the Practice with a bearing on the reputation or security of the Practice;

(iii) to pay promptly the contributions levied by the Practice in return for use of the premises and the services, protection and support provided by Members.

Change of membership

Arrangements for dealing with this have been drawn up legally, and all Members are bound by these. In replacing a Member or Associate there has to be a unanimous decision by the Management Committee (Members do not have to be unanimous on other decisions). The procedure for dealing with a change of Member is complicated and lengthy as the sale of a share in the lease is involved, in addition to a share in the working capital. It can take several meetings before a decision is reached.

The office

This is staffed full-time by a practice manager/senior secretary and a secretary. Part-time staff are used from time to time; in addition, a permanent 'door and telephone sitter' is employed every evening, plus a domestic cleaner. The Practice manager is in charge of staff and takes ultimate responsibility for housekeeping, flower arranging (very important – the Practice always has beautiful flowers which delight many patients), co-ordinating any redecoration and the annual spring clean. She also masterminds the large Christmas party and other social events.

'No-door' policy

This is an unusual office and calls for special qualities in staff over and above the usual secretarial skills – in particular, great flexibility. The office has no door, and this is symbolic of the office philosophy – always open to whomever wishes to walk in, in complete contrast to all the other closed doors of the consulting rooms. Complete confidentiality of all its activities is vital to the security of the Practice, and the secretaries sign an agreement to uphold this totally and at all times.

The office is the nerve centre of the Practice – all lines meet here. The telephone and door bell are constantly ringing, and the secretaries have to deal with referrers and enquiries as well as patients who may be distressed and difficult. At peak hours when groups have ended (often seven groups exit simultaneously) the office is often full of people wanting receipts, and so on, and Members and Associates who may wish to obtain or convey information.

A well-run office with a good atmosphere is vital to the well-being of the practitioners, who may often need sustenance themselves. This has not always been the case and it can be a major headache if this area is not functioning well.

We endeavour to choose staff carefully and to look after them. while the operational workload is often intense, the staff have the compensations of light duties and short hours when the Practice is closed for vacations three times a year.

Practice meetings

1 The Monday meeting

This is a clinical meeting held by the Management Committee weekly primarily to discuss new patients and allocate them into appropriate groups. An agenda is drawn up by the Chairperson and any urgent administrative matters are raised for discussion. This can sometimes be a frustrating meeting owing to the urgency of the waiting list, which must have priority. There is little time for extended clinical discussion, although steps are being taken to provide for this. Associates have an open invitation to attend this 2 p.m. meeting but rarely do owing to their own commitments. They are encouraged to check the waiting list themselves to see if there are any suitable people for their individual groups, and the Members also refer a particular patient to a particular Associate or group – for example, a young persons' group.

The Monday meeting is an essential meeting for Members to attend, as it is the one time that everyone is together and management matters can be dealt with. It endeavours to ensure good communication between Members who otherwise may only meet individually in the brief intervals between sessions. Monday between 2 and 3 p.m. is the only time in a normal working week that Practice affairs take precedence over individual timetables. Members constitute a group of highly individualised people with a common purpose – to uphold Foulkesian tradition and principles. Our own interpersonal relationships are rarely discussed unless there is something vital; it is very much a task-oriented work group.

2 Other meetings

Members are expected to attend extra meetings in the evenings as and when required. This may be on average three to four times a year. In addition, there are regular meetings with the solicitor, accountant and financial adviser. An AGM is held by Members to elect officers.

3 Lunch meetings

Members instigated these thrice-yearly meetings for Members and Associates as a forum for open discussion. Not enough use was being made of the vast clinical expertise available, but to orchestrate this kind of event is exceedingly difficult. Analysts tend to be working morning, noon and night. The two-hourly lunch meetings, which have replaced poorly attended evening meetings, are principally intended for clinical discourse and exchange, with time put aside for any matters pertaining to organisation and running of the Practice. There are usually one or two absences, which may reflect some antagonism about the two-tier structure of the Practice earlier referred to. Nevertheless, Members hope by eating together to promote a healthy interchange in spite of these unavoidable inequalities, and conflict is surprisingly rare.

4 Annual party

This function is held at Christmas-time primarily to meet and thank the large numbers of referrers and others associated with the Practice. This has proved to be a very popular event which has become an 'institution' of the Practice. It is also the only public relations activity that we have at present.

Finance

The Practice makes use of the services of a management consultant who is familiar with its business details and acts as financial adviser. He monitors expenditure and income at intervals throughout the year and assists the Management Committee in the preparation of forward forecasts and the annual budget.

Accounts

The books of account are straightforward daybooks recording all revenue receipts and expenditures by calendar months. Capital transactions are only noted in these books and are separately incorporated into the annual accounts at the year-end.

Income derives almost exclusively from contributions to overheads paid by Members and Associates. The fees are based on the number of weekly groups conducted by each individual and are worked out as a monthly amount which is paid by standing order. Because the analytic working year is one of 40 weeks, monthly fees are one-twelfth of (40 x contributions). This provides a regular monthly cash flow. Patients are correspondingly required to pay Members and Associates monthly in advance every month whether or not their groups are actually conducted every week of that month.

Expenditure is classified under about ten broad headings. The major items are property-related costs and office salaries. All ten headings are analysed towards the end of the year in order to identify trends and to assist in the formulation of the next annual budget (see below).

Although the character of the Practice is that of a non-profit/non-loss association, in reality there is always some imbalance between income and expenditure at the year-end. This difference, usually a deficit, is carried into Members' current account. Members as distinct from

Associates are of course totally responsible for the financial circumstances of the Practice, and any debt not covered by income is debited pro rata to each Member's separate share of this account.

Forecasts and budgets

Forecasts are used to check progress against planned budget figures as required, but not less than twice-yearly. A forecast is always made near the year-end to anticipate the annual accounts (not usually available before 3 months after the year-end) and the net result in Members' current account. A surplus will allow some offset against cost increases in the coming year; a deficit will require a larger proportionate increase in fee income requirement. This is a necessary preliminary to the preparation of the annual budget.

The budget is an estimate of results for the coming financial year. It is based on the end-of-year forecast (see above) and best estimates of expected changes in costs in the ten main categories over the next 12 months. In addition, Members are asked to decide what major non-revenue expenditures they expect to incur during the year, such as new equipment for the office or major refurbishment of consulting rooms.

These decisions are usually developed at an annual review meeting with the financial adviser. He indicates the consequences of different options in terms of the contributions to overheads necessary to achieve a balanced result. Once decisions have been reached, advanced notice of next year's fee structure is passed on to Associates by the Treasurer. Members usually at this time also decide what change, if any, they will make in patient fee rates. It is unfortunately becoming increasingly costly to run a practice in central London, and it is a struggle to keep group fees at a level that does not exclude the less than wealthy.

Chapter 14

Guidelines for setting up a similar Practice

Jeff Roberts

It may seem somewhat presumptuous to set out guidelines for the development of a similar practice. The Practice, after all, as must be evident from the preceding chapters, was not at any time designed to take its current shape. It has, rather, evolved as an organic entity of a unique kind.

We do not have complete knowledge of all the group-analytic groups which are currently conducted privately in the United Kingdom It is certain, however, that the Group-Analytic Practice is unique in the number of practitioners conducting groups under its umbrella, and consequently in the number of patients in treatment in its groups. London has one other centre for group psychotherapy: the North London Centre for Psychotherapy. This is approximately one-eighth the size of Group-Analytic Practice. Additionally, there is a substantial referral network, the 'Group-analytic Network', whose members meet, but practise independently. Finally there are a number of entirely independent group analysts conducting groups in London and Greater London. So far as we are aware, there are no similar enterprises in the remainder of the United Kingdom. Moreover, at the time of writing the authors are not aware of any twice-weekly groups offered outside London. Much the same applies internationally, with a few small (1–3) partners' practices which we know of in Athens, Thessalonica and Rome.

A key component of the Group-Analytic Practice is the twice-weekly group. This is an important contribution which we have made to psychotherapy practice. As emerges in Chapter 3. the first of these was conducted by Robin Skynner and the second by S.H. Foulkes in response to pressure from his younger colleague.

These groups have now become the *sine qua non* for the training of qualified group analysts. Thus as well as offering therapy of greater intensity and depth with more containment than the once-weekly groups, our twice-weekly groups also enforce an encounter between a body of people who regard themselves more or less psychologically healthy with another group who tend to regard themselves as psychologically ill. The absence of twice-weekly groups outside London is we believe, a great loss to those thereby deprived. This is not quite the same phenomenon as the tendency of psychoanalysts to live within 5 miles of 20 Maresfield Gardens, since there are quite a number of qualified Members of the Institute of Group-Analysis who live and work in provincial towns and cities. None the less, these colleagues have not grasped the nettle of the twice-weekly group and indeed have not to our knowledge developed once-weekly group-analytic therapy to the extent that must be possible. If there were twice-weekly groups conducted in some of the larger cities away from London this would also make the training of group analysts at centres outside of London a practicable proposition.

It is important to ask why there are so few group-analytic therapy groups outside London and no organisation which resembles the Group Analytic-Practice. The following reasons may be proposed:

1 The vision and determination of Foulkes and his followers in working to establish their initial groups was of a rare quality, as was their ability to conduct groups which actually worked.
2 There are in fact far more group analysts living in London than elsewhere; thus only in London could an aggregation of therapists of the type who have come together in the practice occur.
3 There are more people who are sufficiently aware of their needs and ready for group therapy in London than in other parts of the country.
4 In less densely populated parts of the country it might prove difficult to locate sufficient people who were strangers to one another to start developing groups.
5 There is a quite strongly held emotional belief that individual psychotherapy is a superior form of therapy.
6 It is now more than 40 years since Foulkes started his first group in London. Rome was not built in a day!

Each of these arguments has a degree of validity but does not mean that the task is impossible. Indeed, it may be pertinent to remember that Foulkes started his first groups in Exeter, not London, in 1939. It is however, not necessary to be discouraged by fears of people not being strangers in smaller towns. An approach to this problem might be to avoid setting up in a small town, and seek a convenient large centre, readily accessible from smaller population centres. People are prepared to travel considerable distances for their therapy.

I must acknowledge that it has been far easier to remain in London and take advantage of the hard work of the founding fathers of the Practice than it would have been to be a pioneer in Manchester, Birmingham or Glasgow. In order to do this a number of steps have to be taken, each a formidable effort in its own right. Thus to arrive at the kind of practice we now have at 88 Montagu Mansions in another British city, the following would be necessary:

1 to set up as a private therapist;
2 to start ones' first group(s), once-weekly;
3 to associate with like-minded colleagues (the stimulating context of the Maudsley Hospital and the Institute of Psychiatry attached to it played some part in the initial associations which led to the development of the Practice);
4 to find and fund premises;
5 to start twice-weekly groups.

Each of these steps takes courage and determination and involves an element of risk. These steps are all theoretically within the reach of newly qualified graduates of the Institute of Group-Analysis. In fact many graduates of the Institute never intend to practise in the private sector and a proportion do not seek to work directly with patients. Rather surprisingly, however, even among those graduates of the Institute who intend to conduct private groups there are substantial hurdles to clear before embarking on a career of full-or part-time private group analysis. Issues of self-belief and lack of access to suitable premises and to regular referrals are likely to present obstacles. There may indeed be a need for post-qualification seminars and support to enable erstwhile students to turn their proudly acquired qualification into a genuine economically viable professional competence.

There is another important step towards being a well-rounded group analyst (and in practical terms, a training analyst) which our Institute does not appear to have addressed at all. This is the conducting of twice-weekly groups. As was pointed out in Chapter 5, the twice-weekly group differs both quantitatively and qualitatively from the once-weekly group. It is a more intensive experience for all involved and, in my opinion, requires a higher order of skill and analytic competence from its conductor than the once-weekly group. An anomaly in the training and supervision of group analysts is that this is almost entirely directed towards the once-weekly group. It is thus possible to become a training group analyst[1] without ever having had supervision or practical and theoretical seminars directed towards understanding and conducting twice-weekly groups. This lack of provision will, I suspect, soon be addressed, if only because the consciousness of it has become clearer in the preparation of this book and the undertaking of the somewhat presumptuous task of writing this final chapter. It might be addressed by revising the content of the qualifying course, inevitably thereby making it longer and more arduous than it already is. Alternatively, the example of some psychoanalytic institutes could be followed and an advanced post-qualification course be established. Only those who successfully completed this course could apply to become training analysts.

I would suggest that newly qualified group analysts intending to start a similar practice to the Group-Analytic Practice should ideally locate or establish some seminars in the practical issues involved in becoming a competent, ethical provider of 'treatment' in groups. At the same time they would gain further by finding a way of obtaining advanced supervision and teaching particularly aimed at conducting twice-weekly groups. These graduates would find both support and invaluable further development of their personal and professional selves in pursuing this pathway.

Those who consider themselves to have reached a more advanced stage of personal and professional development, who might be training analysts of the Institute of group analysis, for instance, will wish to address more practical tasks of building a practice. The first step would be to identify a group of like-minded colleagues who have a strong desire to work together in the way we do in the practice. An unequivocal agreement to go into partnership would presumably follow. Next, and this is perhaps the biggest step, premises are required which would provide sufficient group rooms, plus a comfortable staff room and a convenient office. There would follow financial and legal arrangements which would bring the partnership into being, purchase the property and enable it to be used as premises for 'medical practice'. At the same time the partnership would need to find ways of alerting referrers and clients to their presence and intent, without overstepping ethical guidelines regarding advertising of medical or psychotherapeutic practice. Doctors are, I believe, required to restrict their advertising to the fixing of a brass plate with their name and qualifications to the outside of their premises.

In the chapter on administration of the practice Meg Sharpe has outlined our current position with regard to these various practical matters. Realistically, however, it is important to remember that the Group-Analytic Practice has evolved very slowly from Foulkes' original single-handed venture begun in the immediate post-war years.

Any thoughts of starting a new practice in one quantum leap are probably unrealistic and would certainly provide a culture quite unlike that arising from a 54-year history.

Conclusions

In the guise of offering guidelines, this chapter has actually served other (perhaps far more useful) purposes. Firstly, it has partly reiterated and certainly reframed much of what was described in Chapters 1 and 13. It must also be placed alongside a careful ingestion of Chapter 3. Secondly, this and parallel chapters have identified ways in which the Practice might have, or might still, develop differently. It has also identified blind spots of the Members of the Practice and also a major area of omission of our training body, the Institute of Group-Analysis, in its attitudes towards training of conductors for twice-weekly groups.

It can be said without much expectation of contradiction that Group-Analytic Practice is a successful small organisation. It has been successful for a number of reasons, including good fortune. An important factor in the genuine working together which is part of this success could well be our background. We are all deeply interested, indeed fascinated, by groups and have had therapy and training in this field. This brings with it, on the whole, good will towards one another, and an ability to work together for the good of the group. Moreover, key members of the practice once conducted the large group on the 'General Course' together, in the manner of a skilled American football team (as Robin Skynner suggests in Chapter 3). We have had, and indeed still have a strong team. The strength of this team is clearly partly due to the considerable skills of individual members, but it is underpinned by the essential ingredient of all authentic teams – namely, an ability and willingness on the part of *all* players to subordinate their own narcissistic needs to that of the needs of the team as a whole, when necessary.

Finally, I would like to suggest that if the Practice is in any way exceptional, this is because some quite exceptional people have worked, and indeed are still working, with us. Past members of the Practice with short biographical notes are listed in Chapter 3: the first of these was S.H. Foulkes. His ideas, imaginativeness, flexibility of attitude and, most of all, a most extraordinary capacity to facilitate, are qualities on which the Practice is founded. His willingness to bring people and ideas together, thus bridging splits, countering regression and encouraging synthesis, is a continuing inspiration for the Practice which remains one of the living tributes to him. If learning from Foulkes is continuing in the Institute of Group-Analysis and through the Institute, other similar practices in centres throughout the United Kingdom and further afield will undoubtedly develop.

Note
1 A training group analyst is one who regularly conducts twice-weekly groups which are recognised by the Institute of Group-Analysis as suitable for the therapy of trainees of the Institute.

Bibliography

Introduction

Foulkes, S.H. (1948) *Introduction to Group-Analytic Psychotherapy, Studies in the Social Integration of Individuals and Groups*, London: Heinemann,1948; New York: Grune & Stratton, 1949. (Reprinted London: Karnac Books, 1983.)

Foulkes, S.H. (1964) *Therapeutic Group Analysis*, London: George Allen & Unwin. (Reprinted London: Karnac Books, 1984.)

Foulkes, S.H. (1975) *Group-Analytic Psychotherapy, Method and Principles*, London: Gordon & Breach. (Reprinted London: Karnac Books, 1986.)

Foulkes, S.H. and Anthony, E. J. (1957) *Group Psychotherapy, the Psychoanalytic Approach*, Harmondsworth: Penguin Books. (New editions 1965, 1968, 1971, 1973. Reprinted London: Karnac Books, 1984.)

Chapter 1 A view of the current state of the Practice

Foulkes, S.H. (1948) *Introduction to Group-Analytic Psychotherapy, Studies in the Social Integration of Individuals and Groups*, London: Heinemann, 1948; New York: Grune & Stratton, 1949. (Reprinted London: Karnac Books, 1983.)

Foulkes, S.H. (1964) *Therapeutic Group Analysis*, London: George Allen & Unwin. (Reprinted London: Karnac Books, 1984.)

Foulkes, S.H. (1973) 'The Group as Matrix of the Individual's Mental Life', in L. R. Wolberg and E. K. Schwartz (eds), *Group Therapy* (pp. 211–20), New York: Intercontinental Medical Book Corporation. (Reprinted in S.H. Foulkes, *Selected Papers, Psychoanalysis and Group-analysis* edited by E.T. Foulkes, London: Karnac Books, 1990.)

Foulkes, S.H. (1975) *Group-Analytic Psychotherapy, Method and Principles*, London: Gordon & Breach. (Reprinted London: Karnac Books, 1986.)

Foulkes, S.H. and Anthony, E. J. (1957) *Group Psychotherapy, the Psychoanalytic Approach*, Harmondsworth: Penguin Books. (New editions 1965, 1968, 1971, 1973. Reprinted London: Karnac Books, 1984.)

Knight, L. (1986) *Talking to a Stranger*, London: Fontana.

Skynner, R. (1976) *One Flesh: Separate Persons, Principles of Family and Marital Psychotherapy*, London: Methuen.

Skynner, R. (1987) *Explorations with Families: Group-analysis and Family*

Therapy, edited by J. Schlapobersky, London: Methuen; published in paperback by Routledge in 1990.

Skynner, R. (1989) *Institutes and How to Survive Them: Mental Health Training and Consultation*, edited by J. Schlapobersky, London: Methuen.

Skynner, R. and Cleese, J. (1983) *Families and How to Survive Them*, London: Methuen.

Chapter 2   Group analysis and psychotherapy services

Foulkes, S.H. (1964) *Therapeutic Group Analysis*, London: George Allen & Unwin. (Reprinted London: Karnac Books, 1984.)

Chapter 3   A history of the Group-Analytic Practice

Anthony, E.J. (1983) 'The group-analytic circle and its ambient network', in *The Evolution of Group Analysis*, pp. 29–53, edited by M. Pines, London: Routledge & Kegan Paul.

Bion, W.R., (1958) *Experiences in Groups*, London: Social Science Paperbacks.

Foulkes, E.T. (1990) 'S. H Foulkes: a Brief Memoir', in *Selected Papers, Psychoanalysis and Group-analysis*, edited by E.T. Foulkes, London: Karnac Books, 1990.

Foulkes, S.H. [Fuchs] (1936) 'Zum Stand die heutigen Biologie. Dargestellt an Kurt Goldstein: Der Aufbau des Organismus', Imago, 22: 210–41. (Extracts reprinted as 'Biology in the light of the work of Kurt Goldstein', in *Selected Papers, Psychoanalysis and Group-analysis*, edited by E.T. Foulkes, London: Karnac Books, 1990.)

Foulkes, S.H. (1937) 'On Introjection', *International Journal of Psychoanalysis*, 18: 269–93. (Reprinted in S.H. Foulkes, *Selected Papers, Psychoanalysis and Group-analysis*, edited by E.T. Foulkes, London: Karnac Books, 1990.)

Foulkes, S.H. (1948) *Introduction to Group-Analytic Psychotherapy, Studies in the Social Integration of Individuals and Groups*, London: Heinemann,1948; New York: Grune & Stratton, 1949. (Reprinted London: Karnac Books, 1983.)

Foulkes, S.H. and Lewis, E. (1944) 'Group-analysis, Studies of the Treatment of Groups on Psychoanalytical Lines', *British Journal of Medical Psychology*, 20: 175–84. (Reprinted in *Therapeutic Group Analysis*, London: George Allen & Unwin, 1964; London: Karnac Books, 1984.)

Home, J. (1966) 'The Concept of Mind', *International Journal of Psychoanalysis*, 47: 43–9.

Skynner, R. (1984) 'Institutes and how to survive them'. 8th Annual S.H. Foulkes Lecture, published 1984 in *Group-Analysis*, XVII/2.

Chapter 4   Assessment and selection for groups

Balint, M. (1968) *The Basic Fault: Therapeutic Aspects of Regression*, London: Tavistock Publications.

Bion, W.R. (1962) *Learning from Experience*, London: Heinemann.

Bibliography

Brown, D. (1987) 'Change in the Group-Analytic Setting', *Psychoanalytic Psychotherapy*, 3, pp. 53–60.

Brown, D.G. (1988) 'Confrontation in the Group-Analytic Matrix: Towards a Classification', *Group*, 12, pp. 191–7.

Brown, D. and Pedder, J. (1979) *Introduction to Psychotherapy*, London: Tavistock Publications.

Clarkin, J.F., and Frances, A. J. (1982) 'Selection Criteria for Brief Psychotherapy', *American Journal of Psychotherapy*, 36, pp. 166–180.

Clarkin, J.F., Frances, A. J. and Moodie, J. L. (1979) 'Selection Criteria for Family Therapy', *Family Process*, 18, pp. 391–403.

Foulkes, S.H. (1964) *Therapeutic Group Analysis*, London: George Allen & Unwin. (Reprinted London: Karnac Books, 1984.)

Foulkes, S.H. (1975) *Group-Analytic Psychotherapy, Method and Principles*, London: Gordon & Breach. (Reprinted London: Karnac Books, 1986.)

Frances, A.J. and Clarkin, J. F. (1981) 'No Treatment as the Prescription of Choice', *Archives of General Psychiatry*, 38, pp. 522–5.

Frances, A.J., Clarkin, J. F. and Marachi, J. P. (1980) 'Selection Criteria for Outpatient Group Psychotherapy', *Hospital and Community Psychiatry*, 31, pp. 245–50.

James, D.C. (1984) 'Bion's "Containing" and Winnicott's "Holding" in the Context of the Group Matrix', *International Journal of Group Psychotherapy*, 34, pp. 201–13.

Rayner, E.H. and Hahn, H. (1964) 'Assessment for Psychotherapy', *British Journal of Medical Psychology*, 37, pp. 331–42.

Rutan, J.S. and Alonso, A. (1982) 'Group Therapy, Individual Therapy or Both', *International Journal of Group Psychotherapy*, 32, pp. 267–82.

Skynner, A.C.R. and Brown, D. G. B. (1981) 'Referral of Patients for Psychotherapy', *British Medical Journal*, 282, pp. 1952–5.

Sloane, R.B., Staples, F. R., Cristol, A. H., Yorkston, N. J. and Whipple, K. (1975) *Short-term Analytically Oriented Psychotherapy versus Behaviour Therapy*, Cambridge, Mass.: Harvard University Press.

Strupp, H. and Hadley, S. W. (1979) 'Specific Versus Non-specific Factors in Psychotherapy: A Controlled Study of Outcome', *Archives of General Psychiatry*, 36, pp. 1125–36.

Winnicott, D.W. (1960) 'The Theory of the Parent-infant Relationship', *International Journal of Psychoanalysis*, 41, pp. 585–95. (Reprinted in *The Maturational Process and the Facilitating Environment*, London: Institute of Psycho-analysis and Hogarth Press.)

Chapter 5 The twice-weekly groups

Foulkes, S.H. (1964) *Therapeutic Group Analysis*, London: George Allen & Unwin. (Reprinted London: Karnac Books, 1984.)

Foulkes, S.H. (1975) *Group-Analytic Psychotherapy, Method and Principles*, London: Gordon & Breach. (Reprinted London: Karnac Books, 1986.)

Freud, S. (1910) *The Future Prospects of Psychoanalytic Therapy*, Standard Edition, vol. XI, pp. 141–51, London: Hogarth Press.

Freud, S. (1912) *Dynamics of Transference*, Standard Edition, volume XII, p99, London: Hogarth Press.

Heimann, P. (1950) 'On Counter-transference', *International Journal of Psychoanalysis*, 30.

Laplanche, J. and Pontalis, J. B. (1973) *The Language of Psychoanalysis*, London: Hogarth Press.

Yalom, I.D. (1985) *Theory and Practice of Group Psychotherapy*, 3rd edition, New York: Basic Books.

Chapter 6   The once-weekly groups

Foulkes, S.H. (1948) *Introduction to Group-Analytic Psychotherapy, Studies in the Social Integration of Individuals and Groups*, London: Heinemann,1948; New York: Grune and Stratton, 1949. (Reprinted London: Karnac Books, 1983.)

Foulkes, S.H. (1975) *Group-Analytic Psychotherapy, Method and Principles*, London: Gordon & Breach. (Reprinted London: Karnac Books, 1986.)

Freeman Sharpe, E. (1930) 'The technique of Psychoanalysis. The Analysand', *International Journal of Psychoanalysis*, 11, in M. Brierly (ed.) (1978), *Collected Papers on Psychoanalysis by Ella Freeman Sharpe*, London: Hogarth Press and Institute of Psycho-analysis.

Mittwoch, A. (1982) 'From Fantasy to Reality: Case History of a Silent Borderline Patient', *Group-Analysis*, 15, (1), pp. 15–16.

Yalom, I.D. (1975) *The Theory and Practice of Group Psychotherapy*, 3rd edition, New York: Basic Books.

Chapter 7   Special categories of patients in groups

1   The borderline patient

Bion, W.R. (1962) *Attention and Interpretation*, London: Tavistock Publications.

Pines, M. (1984) 'Reflections on Mirroring', *International Review of Psychoanalysis*, 11, pp. 27–42.

2   The borderline patient, an alternative viewpoint

Bion, W.R. (1961) *Experiences in Groups*, London: Tavistock Publications.

Bion, W.R. (1962a) *Learning from Experience*, London: Heinemann.

Bion, W.R. (1962b) *Attention and Interpretation*, London: Tavistock Publications.

Bion, W.R. (1962c) 'A theory of thinking', *International Journal of Psychoanalysis*, 43, pp. 306–10.

Fairbairn, W.R.D. (1941) 'A revised psychopathology of the psychoses and psychoneuroses', *International Journal of Psychoanalysis*, 22, pp. 250–79.

Fairbairn, W.R.D. (1952) *Psychoanalytic Studies of the Personality*, London: Tavistock Publications.

Bibliography

Foulkes, S.H. (1964) *Therapeutic Group Analysis*, London: George Allen & Unwin. (Reprinted London: Karnac Books, 1984.)
James, D.C. (1984) 'Bion's "Containing" and Winnicott's "Holding" in the Context of the Group Matrix', *International Journal of Group Psychotherapy*, 34. pp. 201–13.
Rey, H., (1968) 'Personal communication'.
Sutherland, J.D. (1989) *Fairbairn's Journey into the Interior*, London: Free Association Books.
Winnicott, D.W. (1953) 'Psychoses and Child Care', *British Journal of Medical Psychology*, 126, pp. 68–74. Reprinted in *Collected Papers: Through Paediatrics to Psychoanalysis*, London, 1958: Tavistock Publications.
Winnicott, D.W. (1960) 'The Theory of the Parent Infant Relationship', *International Journal of Psychoanalysis*, 41, pp. 585–95. (Reprinted in *The Maturational Process and the Facilitating Environment*, London: Institute of Psycho-Analysis and Hogarth Press.)
Winnicott, D.W. (1969), 'The Use of an Object and Relating through Identifications', *International Journal of Psychoanalysis*, 50, pp. 711–16. (Reprinted in *Playing and Reality*, London: Tavistock Publications, 1971.)

3 The patient with gender problems and other sexual difficulties in groups

Tolkien, J.R.R. (1954–55) *The Lord of the Rings*, published in 3 volumes, London: George Allen & Unwin.

4 Older patients

Ezquerro, A. (1989) 'Group Psychotherapy with the Pre-elderly', *Group-analysis*, 22.
Gordon, R. (1977) 'Death and Creativity: a Jungian Approach', *Journal of Analytical Psychology*, 22 (2).
Gordon, R. (1978) 'Dying and Creating: a Search for Meaning', a volume from The Library of Analytical Psychology, London and New York: Academic Press.
Grotjahn, M. (1989) 'Group-analysis in Old Age', *Group-Analysis*, 22.
MacLennan, B.W., Saul, S. and Weiner, M. (eds) (1988) *Group Psychotherapies for the Elderly*, Madison, Wis.: International Universities Press.

7 Couples in groups

Skynner, R. (1976) 'Multi Family and Couples Groups', chapter in *One Flesh: Separate Persons: Principles of Family and Marital Psychotherapy*, London: Methuen.
Skynner, R. (1989) *Institutes and How to Survive Them, Mental Health Training and Consultation*, edited by J. Schlapobersky, pp. 110–12. London: Methuen.

8 The patient with somatic symptoms or with psychosomatic illness in the Practice

Brautigam, W. and von Rad, M. (1977) *Toward a Theory of Psychosomatic Disorders*, Basel: Karger.

Groen, J.J. and Pelser, H. E. (1960) 'Experiences with, and Results of, Group Psychotherapy in Patients with Bronchial Asthma', *Journal of Psychosomatic Research*, 4, pp. 191–205.

Pratt, J.H. (1907) 'The Class Method of Treating Consumption in the Homes of the Poor', *Journal of the American Medical Association*, 49, pp. 755–57.

Pratt, J.H. (1908) 'Results Obtained in the Treatment of Pulmonary Tuberculosis and the Class Method', *British Medical Journal*, 2, pp. 1070–1.

Taylor, G. J. (1987) *Psychosomatic Medicine and Contemporary Psychoanalysis*, Madison, Wis.: International University Press.

Chapter 8   Destructive phases in groups

Anthony, E.J. (1957) 'The Phenomonology of the Group Situation', p. 150, in Foulkes, S.H. and Anthony, E. J. (1957) *Group Psychotherapy, the Psychoanalytic Approach*, Harmondsworth: Penguin Books. (New editions 1965, 1968, 1971, 1973. Reprinted London: Karnac Books, 1984.)

Bion, W.R., (1958) *Experiences in Groups*, London: Social Science Paperbacks

Conrad, J. (1902) *The Heart of Darkness*, Harmondsworth: Penguin Books (1973).

Foulkes, S.H. (1973) 'The Group as Matrix of the Individual's Mental Life', in L. R. Wolberg and E. K. Schwartz (eds), *Group Therapy* (pp. 211–20), New York: Intercontinental Medical Book Corporation. (Reprinted in S.H. Foulkes, *Selected Papers, Psychoanalysis and Group-analysis* edited by E.T. Foulkes, London: Karnac Books, 1990.)

Freud, S. (1920) *Jenseits des Lustprinzips*, Vienna: G. S., 6, 191; G. W., 13, 3. (Trans. : Beyond the Pleasure Principle, Standard Edition, 18, 7; I.P.L., 4.)

Garland, C. (1983) 'Commentary on Zinkin's "Malignant Mirroring" paper', *Group-analysis* 16 (2), pp. 126–9.

Nitsun, M. (1989) 'The Anti Group', paper presented at the 10th International Congress of Group Psychotherapy, Amsterdam.

Roberts, J. (1983) 'Foulkes's Concept of the matrix', *Group-analysis*, 16 (2), pp. 111–26.

Zinkin, L. (1983) 'Malignant Mirroring', *Group-analysis*, 16 (2), pp. 113–26.

Chapter 9   Individual and group therapy combined

Foulkes, S.H. (1964) *Therapeutic Group Analysis*, London: George Allen & Unwin. (Reprinted London: Karnac Books, 1984.)

Foulkes, S.H. and Lewis, E. (1944) 'Group-analysis, Studies of the Treatment of Groups on Psychoanalytical Lines', *British Journal of Medical Psychology*, 20: 175–84. (Reprinted in *Therapeutic Group Analysis*, London: George Allen & Unwin, 1964; London: Karnac Books, 1984.)

Chapter 10   Training for and trainees in group analysis

Hinshelwood, R.D. (1985) 'Questions of Training', *Free Association*, 2, pp. 17–18.

Chapter 11   Starting a group at the Practice: an Associate's view

Foulkes, S.H. and Anthony, E. J. (1957) *Group Psychotherapy, the Psychoanalytic Approach*, Harmondsworth: Penguin Books. (New editions 1965, 1968, 1971, 1973. Reprinted London: Karnac Books, 1984.)

Nitsun, M. (1989) 'Early Development: Linking the Individual and the Group', *Group-analysis*, 22 (3), pp. 249–60, 1989.

Winnicott, D.W. (1971) *Playing and Reality*, London: Tavistock Publications; paperback (1974), Pelican Books, Harmondsworth: Penguin.

Chapter 12   Death and the Practice

Bowlby, J. (1974) 'Attachment Theory, Separation Anxiety and Mourning', in *American Handbook of Psychiatry*, vol. VII.

Jung, C.G. (1960) [1931] 'The Stages of Life', *Collected Works*, vol. 8, chap. VI, London: Routledge & Kegan Paul.

Gordon, R. (1978) *Dying and Creating: a Search for Meaning*, Library of Analytical Psychology, vol. 4. Madison, Wis.: Academic Press.

Selected bibliography of the Group-Analytic Practice

Mr B. Boswood: *Selected Bibliography.*

Boswood, B. (1988) 'Thoughts on the selection of candidates for professional training in group analysis', *Group Analysis*, Vol 21: pp. 345–52.

Dr D. G. Brown: *Selected Bibliography.*

Brown D. G. (1959) 'The relevance of body image to neurosis', *British Journal of Medical Psychology*, Vol 32: pp. 249–60.

Brown, D. G. (1976) 'Listening to eczema: deductions and predictions', Chapter 7 in H. Maxwell (ed.) *Integrated Medicine*, pp. 89–102, Bristol: Wright.

Brown, D. G. (1977) 'Drowsiness in the counter-transference', *International Review of Psychoanalysis*, Vol 4: pp. 481–92.

Brown, D. G. (1979) 'Some reflections on Bion's basic assumptions from a group analytic viewpoint', *Group Analysis*, Vol 12: pp. 204–10.

Brown, D. G. and Pedder, J. R. (1979) *Introduction to Psychotherapy: An Outline of Psychodynamic Principles and Practice*, London: Tavistock Publications. (2nd edition due 1991, Routledge.)

Brown, D. G. and Skynner, A. C. R. (1981) 'Referral of patients for psychotherapy', *British Medical Journal*, Vol 282: pp. 1952–5.

Brown, D. G. (1982) 'Text, context and texture: free speech in the service of health and healing', *Group Analysis*, Vol 15: pp. 207–18.

Brown, D. G. (1985) 'Bion and Foulkes: basic assumptions and beyond', in M. Pines (ed.) *Bion and Group Psychotherapy*, pp. 192–219, London: Routledge & Kegan Paul.

Brown, D. G. (1985) 'The psychosoma and the group', *Group Analysis*, Vol 18: pp. 93–101.

Brown, D. G. (1986) 'Dialogue for change', *Group Analysis*, Vol 19: pp. 25–39.

Brown, D. G. (1987) 'Change in the group-analytic setting', *Psychoanalytic Psychotherapy*, Vol 3: pp. 53–60.

Brown, D. G. (1987) 'Context, content and process: interrelationships between small and large groups in a transcultural workshop', *Group Analysis*, Vol 20: pp. 237–48.

Brown, D. G. (1988) 'Confrontation in the group-analytic matrix: towards a classification', *Group Analysis*, Vol 12: pp. 191–7.

Brown, D. G. (1989) 'A contribution to the understanding of psychosomatic processes in group', *British Journal of Psychotherapy*, Vol 6: pp. 5–9.

Mrs Caroline Garland: *Selected Bibliography.*

Garland C. (1976) 'An ethological study of chimpanzee play', in J. and S. Bruner (eds) *Play: Its Role in Development and Evolution*, London: Penguin.

Garland, C. and White, S. (1980) *Children and Day Nurseries*, London: Grant McIntyre/SSRC.

Garland, C. (1981) 'Widdershins: theories and resistance', *Group Analysis*, Vol 13: pp. 42–3.

Garland, C. (1982) 'Group-analysis: taking the non-problem seriously', *Group Analysis*, Vol 15: pp. 4–14.

Garland, C. (1991) 'External disasters and the internal world: working with survivors of disasters', in J. Holmes (ed.) *Psychotherapy Techniques in Psychiatry*, London: Churchill Livingstone.

Mrs L. E. Hearst: *Selected Bibliography.*

Hearst, L. E. (1988) 'The restoration of the impaired self', in N. Slavinska-Holy (ed.) *Group Analytic Treatment in Borderline and Narcissistic Patients in Therapy*, Madison, Connecticut: International University Press, Inc.

Hearst, L. E., Pines, M. and Behr, H. L. (1982) 'Group analysis', in G. M. Gazda (ed.) *Basic Approaches to Group Psychotherapy and Group Counselling*, Springfield, Illinois: Charles C. Thomas.

Hearst, L. E. (1990) 'Transference, counter-transference and projective processes in training course block sessions', *Group Analysis*, Vol 23: pp. 341–6.

Dr R. A. Hobdell: *Selected Bibliography.*

Hobdell, R. A. (1988) 'The lost ones: studies on patients with multiple therapists', *British Journal of Psychotherapy*, Vol. 4.

Dr D. C. James: *Selected Bibliography.*

James, D. C. (1981) 'W. R. Bion's contribution to the field of group therapy: an appreciation', in L. Wolberg and M. Aronson (eds) *Group and Family Therapy*, New York: Brunner/Mazel.

James, D. C. (1982) 'Transitional phenomena and the matrix in group psychotherapy', in M. Pines and L. Rafaelsen (eds) *The Individual and the Group*, New York and London: Plenum Press.

James, D. C. (1984) 'Bion's "containing" and Winnicott's "holding" in the context of the group matrix', *International Journal of Group Psychotherapy*, Vol 34: pp. 201–13.

Dr L. C. Kreeger: *Selected Bibliography.*

Kreeger, L. C. (1974) 'Psychotherapy in the past, present and future'; 'Psychotherapy with adults', in V. Varma (ed.) *Psychotherapy Today*, London: Constable.
Kreeger, L. C. and de Maré, P. B. (1974) *Introduction to Group Treatments in Psychiatry*, London: Butterworths.
Kreeger, L. C. (ed.) (1985) *The Large Group. Dynamics and Therapy*, London: Constable, USA: Peacock, and London: Maresfield Reprints.

Dr J. Maratos: *Selected Bibliography.*

Maratos, J. (1986) 'Feeding disorders', in I. Tsiantis (ed.) *Child Psychiatry – Modern Approaches*, Athens: Kastaniotis Publications.
Maratos, J., Bowlby, J. and Kohut, H. (1986) 'Where science and humanism meet', *Group Analysis*, Vol 19: pp. 303–9.
Marotos, J. (1988) 'Self psychology', *Current Opinion in Psychiatry*, Aldershot: Gower Academic Journals.

Dr P. B. de Maré: *Selected Bibliography.*

de Maré, P. B. (1972) *Perspectives in Group Psychotherapy*, London: George Allen & Unwin. (Translated into Italian and Brazilian.)
de Maré, P. B. and Kreeger, L. C. (1974) *Introduction to Group Treatments in Psychiatry*, London: Butterworths.
de Maré, P. B. (1975) 'The large group', Chapter 4 in L. C. Kreeger (ed.) *The Politics of Large Groups*, London: Constable.
de Maré, P. B. (1976) 'Spheres of group analysis', Chapter 6 in T. E. Lear (ed.) *Large Group Perspectives*, Kildare: Leinster Leader.
de Maré, P. B. (1982) 'Koinonia', *International Journal of Therapeutic Communities*, Vol 3.
de Maré, P. B. (1985) 'Large group perspectives', *Group Analysis*, Vol 18, No 2: pp. 79–92, Ninth S. H. Foulkes Annual Lecture.
de Maré, P. B. (1989) 'The history of large group phenomena in relation to group analytic psychotherapy', *Group*, Vol 13.
de Maré, P. B. (1990) 'The development of the median group', *Group Analysis*, Vol 23: pp. 113–27.
de Maré, P. B. (1991) *Koinonia*, London: Karnac Books.

Ms Adele Mittwoch: *Selected Bibliography.*

Mittwoch, A. (1982) 'From fantasy towards reality. Case history of a silent borderline patient in group analysis', *Group Analysis*, Vol 15, No 1: pp. 15–16.
Mittwoch, A. (1987) 'Aspects of guilt and shame in psychotherapy', *Group Analysis*, Vol 20, No 1: pp. 33–42.
Mittwoch, A. (1987) 'Getting better, staying well', *Group Analysis*, Vol 20, No 4: pp. 335–42.

Dr D. H. Montgomery: *Selected Bibliography.*

Montgomery, D. H. and Hartnup, T. B. (1982) *A Search for the Lost Mother: A Significant Psychodynamic Factor in the Aetiology of a Case of Puerperal Psychosis*, Proceedings of the Conference of Le Centre Regional pour l'Enfance et l'Adolescence Inadaptées, Toulouse.

Montgomery, D. H. and Jubuni, B. (1989) 'Editorial: sex reassignment surgery', *British Journal of Hospital Medicine*, Vol 41, No 1: p. 15.

Dr M. Pines: *Selected Bibliography.*

Pines, M. (1976) 'Group psychotherapy with difficult patients', in L. Wolberg and M. Aronson (eds) *Group Psychotherapy*, New York: Stratton Intercontinental Books.

Pines, M. (1978) 'The contributions of S. H. Foulkes to group-analytic psychotherapy', in L. R. Wolberg, M. L. Aronson and A. R. Wolberg (eds) *Group Therapy*, New York: Stratton Intercontinental Books.

Pines, M. (1981) 'The frame of reference of group psychotherapy', *International Journal of Group Psychotherapy*, Vol 31: pp. 275–85.

Pines, M. (1984) 'Reflections on mirroring', *International Review of Psychoanalysis*, Vol 11: pp. 27–42.

Pines, M. (1985) 'Mirroring and child development', *Psychoanalytic Enquiry*, Vol 5, No 2: pp. 211–32.

Pines, M. (1986) 'Coherency and its disruption in the development of the self', *British Journal of Psychotherapy*, Vol 2, No 3: pp. 180–5.

Pines, M. (1986) 'Psychoanalysis, psychodrama and group psychotherapy: stepchildren of Vienna', *Group Analysis*, Vol 19: pp 1–12.

Pines, M. (1987) 'Change and innovation, decay and renewal in psychotherapy', *British Journal of Psychotherapy*, Vol 4, No 1: pp. 76–85.

Pines, M. (1988) 'Mirroring and group therapy', in N. Slavinska-Holy (ed.) *Borderline and Narcissistic Patients in Therapy*, New York: New York International University Press.

Pines, M. (1989) 'The group-as-a-whole approach in Foulkesian group-analytic psychotherapy', *Group*, Vol 13, No 3/4: pp. 212–16.

Pines, M. (1989) 'Group-analysis and healing', *Group Analysis*, Vol 22: pp. 417–29.

Pines, M. (1989) 'On history and psychoanalysis', *Psychoanalytic Psychology*, Vol 6, No 2: pp. 121–35.

Pines, M. (1990) 'An English Freud?', *Psychoanalytic Psychotherapy*, Vol 5, No 1: pp. 1–9.

Pines, M. (1990) 'Group-analysis and the corrective emotional experience: is it relevant?', *Psychoanalytic Enquiry*, Vol 10, No 3: pp. 389–408.

Pines, M. (1990) 'Group-analytic psychotherapy and the borderline patient', in D. E. Roth, W. N. Stone and H. D. Kibel (eds) *The Difficult Patient in Groups*, Monograph 6: American Group Psychotherapy Association, Monograph Series, New York International University Press.

Pines, M. (1990) 'Psychological aspects of energy', *Holistic Medicine*, Vol 5: pp. 5–15.

Books (edited)

Pines, M. (1983) *The Evolution of Group Analysis*, International Library of Group Psychotherapy and Group Process. London: Routledge & Kegan Paul.

Pines, M. (1985) *Bion and Group Psychotherapy*, International Library of Group Psychotherapy and Group Process. London: Routledge & Kegan Paul.

Joint authors

Pines, M., Hearst, L. E. and Behr, H. L. (1982) 'Group analysis', in G. M. Gazda (ed.) *Basic Approaches to Group Psychotherapy and Group Counselling*, Springfield, Illinois: Charles C. Thomas.

Jackson, M. and Pines, M. (1986) 'Borderline personality: concepts and criteria', *Neurologia et Psychiatria*, pp. 54–67.

Jackson, M., Pines, M. and Stevens, B. (1986) 'The borderline personality: psychodynamics and treatment', *Neurologia et Psychiatria*, pp. 66–88.

Dr J. P. Roberts: *Selected Bibliography.*

Roberts, J. P. (1977) 'The problems of group psychotherapy in psychosomatic patients', in *Towards a Theory of Psychosomatic Disorders – the Proceedings of the 11th European Conference on Psychosomatic Research, Heidelberg, 1976. Psychotherapy and Psychosomatics*, Vol 28: pp. 305–15.

Roberts, J. P. and Kennard, D. (1978) 'Learning from experience in a therapeutic community', *Group Analysis*, Vol 11, No 3: 222–3.

Roberts, J. P. and Kennard, D. (1980) 'Therapeutic community training. A one year follow-up', *Group Analysis*, Vol 13, No 1: pp. 54–6.

Roberts, J. P. (1982) 'Destructive processes in a therapeutic community', *International Journal of Therapeutic Communities*, Vol 1, No 3: pp. 159–70.

Roberts, J. P. (1982) 'Foulkes' concept of the matrix', *Group Analysis*, Vol 15, No 2: pp. 111-26.

Roberts, J. P. (1983) 'The group analyst as consultant to a therapeutic organisation', *Group Analysis*, Vol 16, No 3: pp. 187–91.

Roberts, J. P. with Kennard, D. and U.K. Information Section (1983) 'Training for therapeutic community work', chapter in *An Introduction to Therapeutic Communities* by D. Kennard. London: Routledge & Kegan Paul.

Roberts, J. P. (1984) 'Resonance in art groups', *Group Analysis*, Vol 17, No 3: pp. 211–19.

Roberts, J. P. and Meinrath, M. (1984) 'On being a good enough staff member', *International Journal of Therapeutic Communities*, Vol 3, No 1.

Roberts, J. P. (1986) 'Inpatient group psychotherapy', *British Journal of Hospital Medicine*, Vol 36, No 5.

Roberts, J. P., Kennard, D. and Winter, W. (1990) 'What do group analysts say in their groups? Some results from an IGA/GAS questionnaire', *Group Analysis*, Vol 23: pp. 173–90.

Mrs M. Sharpe: *Selected Bibliography.*

Sharpe, M. and Harrington, J. A. (1967) 'A technique for music therapy', *The International Mental Health Research*, Vol 9, No 2.

Sharpe, M. and Dickens, G. (1970) 'Music therapy in the setting of a psychotherapeutic centre', *British Journal of Medical Psychology*, Vol 43: pp. 83–94.

Sharpe, M., Rimmer L., Lingar, T., Whan, M. and Evans, P. (1977) 'A visit to Le Havre Psychiatric Services – Centre Pierre-Janet', *Group Analysis*, Vol 11, April.

Sharpe, M. (1978) 'Group themes in a district general hospital psychiatric unit', *Group Analysis*, Vol 12.

Sharpe, M. and Blackwell, D. (1987) 'Creative supervision through student involvement', *Group Analysis*, Vol 20: pp. 195–208.

Dr A. C. R. Skynner: *Selected Bibliography.*

Skynner, A. C. R. (1969) 'A group-analytic approach to conjoint family therapy', *Journal of Child Psychology and Psychiatry*, Vol 16: p. 81. (Reprinted in *Social Work Today* (1970) and in *Developments in Family Therapy*, Routledge & Kegan Paul (1981), S. Walrond-Skinner (ed.).)

Skynner, A. C. R. (1972) 'Implications of recent work in conjoint family therapy for group analytic theory', *Group Analysis*, Vol 5: p. 153.

Skynner, A. C. R. (1974) 'Boundaries', *Social Work Today*, Vol 5: pp. 290–4.

Skynner, A. C. R. (1974) 'Group psychotherapy', in V. P. Varma (ed.) *Psychotherapy Today*, London: Constable.

Skynner, A. C. R. (1975) 'The large group in training', in L. Kreeger (ed.) *The Large Group: Dynamics and Therapy*, London: Constable.

Skynner, A. C. R. (1976) 'Group analysis and family therapy', in M. Pines (ed.) *The Evolution of Group Analysis*, London: Routledge & Kegan Paul.

Skynner, A. C. R. (1976) *One Flesh, Separate Persons: Principles of Family and Marital Psychotherapy*, London: Constable.

Skynner, A. C. R., Bennett, D., Fox, C. and Jowell, T. (1976) 'Towards a family approach in a psychiatric day hospital', *British Journal of Psychiatry*, Vol 129: pp. 73–81.

Skynner, A. C. R. (1978) 'The physician as family therapist', in G. Usdin and J. Lewis (eds) *Psychiatry in General Medical Practice*, New York: McGraw-Hill.

Skynner, A. C. R. (1979) 'Reflections on the family therapist as family scapegoat', *Journal of Family Therapy*, Vol 1, No 7.

Skynner, A. C. R. (1981) *An Open System. Group-Analytic Approach to Family Therapy*, A. Gurman and D. Kniskern (eds) New York: Brunner/Mazel.

Skynner, A. C. R. and Brown, D. G. (1981) 'Referral for psychotherapy', *British Medical Journal*, Vol 282, June.

Skynner, A. C. R. (1982) 'Frameworks for viewing the family as a system', *Family Therapy: Contemporary Frameworks of Theory and Practice*, A. Cooklin and J. Gorrell Barnes (eds) London and New York: Academic Press/Grune & Stratton.

Skynner, A. C. R. and Cleese, J. (1983) *Families and How to Survive Them*, London: Methuen.

Skynner, A. C. R. (1984) 'Institutes and how to survive them', *Group Analysis*, Vol 15: pp. 11–12.

Skynner, A. C. R. (1986) 'What is effective in group (and family) therapy?', *Group Analysis*, Vol 19: pp. 5–24.

Skynner, A. C. R. (1987) *Explorations with Families: Group Analysis and Family Therapy*, London: Methuen.

Skynner, A. C. R. (1989) *Institutes and How to Survive Them: Mental Health Training and Consultation*, London: Methuen.

Dr E. G. Wooster: *Selected Bibliography.*

Wooster, E. G. (1983) 'Resistance in groups as a developmental difficulty in triangulation', *Group Analysis*, Vol 16, No 1: pp. 30–41.

Wooster, E. G. (1986) 'Working psychotherapeutically in a student health setting', *Psychoanalytic Psychotherapy*, Vol 2, No 2: pp. 99–110.

Wooster, E. G. and Rayner, E. (1990) 'Bi-logic in psychoanalysis and other disciplines', *International Review of Psychoanalysis*, Vol 17, No 4: pp. 425–33.

Wooster, E. G., Hutchinson, D. and Evans, C. (1990) 'Two examples of supervised weekly psychotherapy illustrating bi-logic in relation to birth', *International Review of Psychoanalysis*, Vol 17, No 4: pp. 445–55.

Dr Louis Zinkin: *Selected Bibliography.*

Zinkin, L. (1984) 'Three models are better than one', *Group Analysis*, Vol 18: pp. 17–27.

Zinkin, L. (1987) 'The hologram as a model for analytical psychology', *Journal of Analytical Psychology*, Vol 32, No 1.

Zinkin, L. (1989) 'A Gnostic view of the therapy group', *Group Analysis*, Vol 22, No 2.

Zinkin, L. (1989) 'The Grail quest and the analytic setting', *Free Associations*, Vol 17.

Zinkin, L. (1989) 'The group as container and contained', *Group Analysis*, Vol 22, No 3.

Zinkin, L. (1989) 'The group's search for wholeness: a Jungian perspective', *Group*, Vol 13, Nos 3 and 4.

Name index

Subject index

Subject index

psychotic disorders 43, 57, 60, 67, 98, 123–4

referrals 13–15, 20, 55–6, 71
registrar in outpatient unit 30–1
regression 70, 101, 102
relaxation techniques 64
repression 90
resonance 76

St Bartholomew's Hospital 19, 39, 51, 83
satellite: group 142–6; therapists 146–7
schizoid character 98, 110, 120–3
schizophrenic illness 60, 67, 98, 120, 123, 124–7, 156
selection of group members 28–9, 67–8, 157–8, *see also* matching
sexual feelings, discussion of 82
sexual problems 67, 104–6
silence 90, 121–2, 161
'slow-open' groups 19, 66, 67, 86, 108, 160, 161
social skills training 121
somatic symptoms 117–20, 159
splitting 99, 134, 145–6
sub-grouping 144

suicide, risk of 57, 124, 126
supervision of groups 20–1
supervisory conference 29–30

Tavistock Clinic 36
therapeutic: aims 21; factors 79–80; work 88–93
trainee group analysts 13–14, 148–54, 160
training groups 19, 149
transference 21, 25, 57, 76, 79–80; combined group 147; group (capital 'T') 75; levels of 78–9; neurosis 77, 90; split 146; to group 162
translation 75
transposition 75
treatment: duration 64, 74, 86, 93, 112–14, 117; outcome 23–4, 93; termination 22, 86, 93–4, 112
twice-weekly groups 42, 73–82, 89–92, 181–2, 183

waiting lists 15, 25, 68–9, 156, 157–8
'working through' 77–8, 90

'young damaged group' 125, 156–7
younger patients 64, 109–12